# Internet Ethics

# Internet Ethics

edited by

## Duncan Langford

St. Martin's Press
New York

St. Martin's Press, Scholarly and Reference Division, 175 Fifth Avenue, New York, N.Y. 10010

First published in the United States of America in 2000

This book is printed on paper suitable for recycling and made from fully managed and sustained forest sources.

Printed in Great Britain

ISBN 0–312–23279–9

Library of Congress Cataloging-in-Publication Data

Internet ethics / edited by Duncan Langford.
p. cm.
Includes bibliographical references and index.
ISBN 0–312–23279–9
1. Internet (Computer network)—Moral and ethical
aspects. 2. Computers and civilization. 3. Law and ethics.
I. Langford, Duncan, 1944–

TK5105.875.I57 I547 2000
175—dc21                                          99-059607

*For*

*George Richard Theodore and Margaret Ann Langford-Allen*

*with love and remembrance*

# Contents

# Contributing authors

DAVID BECKETT has worked for the Advanced Development Unit at the Computing Laboratory, University of Kent at Canterbury, UK since 1990. He researches into Internet technology issues such as searching the Web, and description using metadata. David currently works on the UK National Mirror Service project, a large Internet archive of free software and materials.

DON GOTTERBARN is the Director of the Software Engineering Ethics Research Institute at East Tennessee State University. He teaches several graduate courses in the software engineering program. He also teaches computer ethics and has developed ethics materials for the Software Engineering Institute. His research has appeared in more than a dozen professional journals and he has written several encyclopedia articles. He has done funded research on performance prediction for a distributed Ada closure, object-oriented testing, and software engineering education. He also worked as computer consultant developing systems for industry, the Saudi and US navies.

DEBORAH G. JOHNSON is Professor and Director of the Program in Philosophy, Science, and Technology in the School of Public Policy of Georgia Institute of Technology. She is the author or editor of four books, including *Computer Ethics* (1994) and *Computers, Ethics, and Social Values* (co-edited with Helen Nissenbaum, 1995). Professor Johnson co-edits the new, international journal, *Ethics and Information Technology* published by Kluwer, and she currently serves as President-elect of the Society for Philosophy and Technology.

JOHN MAWHOOD is a partner in the London law firm Tarlo Lyons (www.tarlo-lyons.com). For more than 10 years he has advised clients with businesses in, or who are customers of, the IT and telecommunications sector. He has provided advice globally and nationally on, for example, internet and electronic banking and commerce, Year 2000 exposure, systems purchasing and ERP, software patenting and licensing, and EC competition law. John was the architect of the UK government's Action 2000 Pledge 2000 initiative.

DR CHRIS POUNDER has worked in the field of data protection since the early 1980s. In 1984 he was appointed by the then Greater London Council to lead a team which applied the 1984 Act to its processing; there he developed a number of data protection training courses and began providing consultancies and helpline advice on privacy and security matters. In 1990 he launched *Data*

*Protection News*, and from 1988 until 1999 provided these services from within a large IT company. He now works in the London offices of Masons, a leading international law firm.

DR RICHARD A. SPINELLO is an Associate Research Professor in the Carroll School of Management at Boston College, USA. He has written two books on computer ethics, *Ethical Aspects of Information Technology* and *Case Studies in Information and Computer Ethics*, along with a book on knowledge management entitled *Corporate Instinct*. He has also written numerous articles and scholarly papers on business ethics and the ethical issues associated with information technology.

HERMAN TAVANI is Chair of the Philosophy Department and Director of the Liberal Studies Program at Rivier College, USA. The author of several publications in computer ethics, including a comprehensive bibliographic work in the field, he is currently Associate Editor of *Computers and Society* and Book Review Editor of *Ethics and Information Technology*. He has also worked in the computer industry as software technical writer and software publications supervisor.

DAN TYSVER is a partner with the Beck and Tysver, P.L.L.P., an intellectual property law firm in Hopkins, Minnesota. A graduate of Carleton College and Harvard Law School, Mr Tysver serves as an adjunct professor of law at the University of Minnesota Law School. He is a frequent lecturer and author on legal issues relating to the Internet and to computer technologies. Mr Tysver is also the author of the BitLaw Web site (www.bitlaw.com), an Internet resource on technology law.

JEROEN VAN DEN HOVEN is Professor of Philosophy and Information Technology at the Department of Philosophy of Erasmus University, Rotterdam, The Netherlands. He is founding chair of the international conference on moral philosophy and information technology Computer Ethics Philosophical Enquiry (CEPE) and editor of *Ethics and Information Technology* (Kluwer Academic Publishers).

JOHN WECKERT has qualifications and wide teaching experience in both information technology and philosophy. He is a senior lecturer in Information Technology at Charles Sturt University, co-Director of the Australian Institute of Computer Ethics, and Chair of the Ethics Task Force of the Australian Computer Society. His recent research and publications are in computer ethics and in knowledge-based systems. He is co-author of *Computer and Information Ethics* published by Greenwood Press in 1997.

# Commenting authors

## Australia

Melissa de Zwart BA (Hons), LLB (Hons), LLM (Melb) is a lecturer in the Law Faculty, Monash University. Melissa teaches and researches in the area of Internet law, including an online course on the Law of the Internet. She has published numerous articles on Internet-related issues, including copyright, trademarks, privacy, pornography and electronic commerce. She has recently acted as an adviser to the Victorian Parliament on the Y2K issue. Prior to joining the academic staff at Monash, Melissa was the Legal Manager at the Commonwealth Scientific and Industry Research Organisation, where she practised in intellectual property, licensing and technology law.

## Botswana

Dr Sunday O. Ojo holds degrees from the University of Ibadan and Glasgow University. His areas of speciality include database systems, object-oriented systems, information systems, social informatics, computer science and information systems education, internet use in business and education, and IT in socio-economic developments of developing countries. He has published extensively in these areas. He has published a book on computer science and also co-edited proceedings of a conference on IT in developing countries. Dr Ojo is currently Head of the Department of Computer Science, University of Botswana.

## Brazil

Alberto Levy Macedo was born in Rio de Janeiro, Brazil, and is a professional computing engineer with interests that include the internet, computer graphics, virtual reality and human interactions and relations. An academic and consultant, he has being working with the Internet since 1994, developing university courses and producing virtual worlds for the Web. Alberto is currently working at the Brazilian national TV Network, Globo, in the R&D Laboratory.

## Germany

Professor Dr Herbert Kubicek is Professor for Applied Computer Science and Head of the Information Management and Telecommunications Research Group at the University of Bremen, Germany. He has been editor/co-editor of *Jahrbuch Telekommunikation und Gesellschaft* (*Telecommunications and Society Yearbook*) since 1995, and was a member of the Enquete Commission of Deutsche Bundestag 'The Future of Media in Economy and Society, Germany's Way into the Information Society' in 1997–1998. He is also a member of the Management Committee COST A1, 'Government and Democracy in the Information Age'.

## Hong Kong

Robert Davison is Assistant Professor of Information Systems at the City University of Hong Kong. His research interests range from IT/IS in developing countries, through the application of group support systems in organisational contexts, to ethical and professional issues in IS. His work has been published in CACM, DSS and Information and Management, as well as at HICSS. He is also active in Web-enabling course materials at City University. Further details of his current work can be found at: http://www.cityu.edu.hk/is/staff/rd1.htm

## Japan

Shinji Yamane is currently researching Internet security as a PhD candidate in the Graduate School of Information Science, Tohoku University, Japan. Born in Brazil and educated in Japan, he graduated in 1992 from the International Christian University in Tokyo. His special interests include the hacker ethic and Internet culture. A member of the ACM, Shinji was also a foundation member of CPSR (Computer Professionals for Social Responsibility), Japan Chapter.

## Russia

Irina Alexeyeva is a senior researcher at the Institute of Philosophy, Russian Academy of Sciences, where she has worked since graduating from Lomonosovîs Moscow State University in 1983. She also teaches philosophy courses at several Moscow universities, including the Moscow Aviation Institute. Her book *Human Knowledge and its Computer Image* (in Russian) was published in 1993. Her research work is concentrated in two areas, the epistemological content of the computer revolution and the ethical dimension of technology.

## Singapore

Lim Kin Chew works in Singapore, as Manager of Temasek Polytechnic's Centre for IT in Education and Learning. He leads a team of instructional designers, programmers and computer graphic designers who help him put up IT-based educational courseware on the Internet. He uses the Internet very widely and has been involved with the Internet set-up facilities in his present workplace. He also helps disabled people to use the Internet.

## Sweden

Dr Viiveke Fåk is an associate professor at Linköping University, Linköping, Sweden. She received her PhD from that university in 1978 on a thesis treating cryptography as a mechanism for computer and network security. She has since then been a teacher, lecturer, consultant and researcher in computer security and cryptography. She has served as chairman for IFIP WG 11:4 on crypto management 1985–1989, and has taken part in other international scientific work, primarily as referee and as a member of the programme committee for conferences. She has also served as an expert on Government committees. Her general interests are in the effects of and possibilities created by modern information technology, with scientific interest concentrated on authentication of computer users and of data.

## United States

Terrell Ward Bynum is Director of the Research Center on Computing and Society at Southern Connecticut State University in the USA. He is Professor of Philosophy there and also Visiting Professor at the Centre for Computing and Social Responsibility at De Montfort University in the UK. Professor Bynum is Past Chair of the Committee on Professional Ethics of the Association for Computing Machinery, Past Chair of the Committee on Philosophy and Computing of the American Philosophical Association, and a lifetime member of Computer Professionals for Social Responsibility.

# Preface

Much of the vast quantity of material written about the Internet is concerned with 'how' – what buttons to press, which software to use, what Web sites to access. This Internet book is very different, because it is concerned with 'why'.

An international team of specialist authorities has brought together an up-to-the-minute analysis of the global Internet, looking beyond the surface to what is really happening. While this comprehensive analysis provides a substantial text in itself, there is a further unique development. Each chapter has been read and assessed by additional carefully selected international experts, who not only provide comments on the text from specialist perspectives – philosophy, law, computer science – but also from their *national* perspectives. The Internet is a global entity, so these views, from Russia, Sweden, Germany, Australia, Brazil, Tokyo, Botswana – and elsewhere – provide a fresh and very valuable contribution to Internet debate.

If you are concerned with values, whether you are using or expecting to use the Internet personally or professionally, *Internet Ethics* is for you.

# Acknowledgments

To my editor at Macmillan Press, Jackie Harbor, for her encouragement and enormous enthusiasm – surely an editor in a thousand! – not forgetting, of course, her assistant, Trisha Fielding, for help beyond the call of duty; to the very patient contributing authors and commenting authors of *Internet Ethics*, not only for their survival under a continual barrage of e-mail, but for the sheer quality of their work. While all authors deserve thanks, I must single out Deborah Johnson, now of the Georgia Institute of Technology, with whom this book was first conceived and without whom it could not have been written, and Robert Davison, of the City University of Hong Kong, whose unfailing help and rapid responses made my task much easier. Most of all, though, thanks to Gina, my unflagging supporter and partner throughout this very stressful period, and for over thirty years of marriage.

Thank you all.

DUNCAN LANGFORD

# 1 Introduction and Overview

**DUNCAN LANGFORD**

This opening chapter explains the conception, composition and organisation of this book. Should Internet technical phraseology be unfamiliar to you, specialist Internet terms are defined in the next chapter.

The premise on which the text is founded is the undeniable fact that the Internet is having and will continue to have a profound impact on the shape of the world. Essentially, wherever we live on Earth, the Internet is affecting and will increasingly continue to affect almost every aspect of our lives, including entertainment, work, sociality, the global economy, and even global politics.

The chapters in this book therefore focus in particular on the ethical and social value issues that surround the Internet. These issues are not likely to be resolved in the short term. Indeed, the Internet seems to present a continuing hazard to many aspects of human existence, including privacy, equity, personal responsibility, and indeed individual identity.

Such issues are in themselves of major significance. Additionally, although, while the establishment of an electronic international information infrastructure potentially may facilitate life on a global scale, this global scale alone challenges traditional conceptions, conceptions which are naturally based upon long-founded experience of face-to-face human interaction. Even when electronically transmitted data is accurate – and it may well not be – what happens, and what should happen, when information is instantaneously distributed and shared between very different cultures?

Although we provide a necessary technical underpinning to this debate, the emphasis in *Internet Ethics* is on ethical and social value issues. The text is emphatically not just another book on computer ethics; the focus is totally on the Internet, and Internet use. It is also deliberately global in its nature. While all contributing authors are expert in their field, they also represent many countries and nationalities.

## How the idea for the book developed

As we enter the twenty-first century, it may seem that the case for the responsible use of computers is now self-evident, and largely accepted. Today most people probably consider that the human effects of computer or computer network use are as relevant as the technical aspects of computing, but for many years the use of computers was considered purely in practical terms – 'what can be done', rather than 'what should be done'. However, principally following the work in America of philosophers such as Deborah Johnson (1994) and others, there was a growth of interest in 'computer ethics', rapidly spreading from philosophers to computer science professionals. This development inevitably led to a wider appreciation of the need to consider appropriate uses of computers and computer systems, and, in particular, to ensure the private, corporate and governmental use of computers is carried out responsibly. Recognition of the importance of computer ethics continued to increase, and appreciation of its importance quickly spread far beyond the USA. The first European computer ethics conference was held in 1995, and wider formal recognition has followed; for example, throughout the developed world most concerned professional associations now urge at least some consideration of ethical issues. A growing global expectation of ethical computer use continues to develop; in many countries the necessity for responsible computer use has probably been largely accepted by the general public, as well as by specialist academics and practitioners.

It is certainly true that much material is now available to support those who deal with human issues in technology. In recent years many books have been written both on the appropriate use of computers, and on the general problems involved in computer ethics and professional issues in computing. Attention is being given in university computer science teaching to many of the social aspects involved in the commercial and private use of computers, and computer networks. However, ethical consideration of the Internet, the largest network of them all, has typically formed only a small and fragmented part of this analysis. While the ethical back-ground to general computer use clearly remains of considerable importance, ethical analysis of the global information infrastructure we call the Internet is potentially of far greater significance; after all, the Internet is increasingly moving to influence many aspects of human life in every developed country in the world.

Given the obvious and central importance of the Internet to modern life, a detailed and comprehensive ethical study specifically aimed at the Internet, its background, operations, and in particular its human influences was clearly overdue. While there are many aspects of the Internet that may mirror more conventional human activities, there are others where the development of new behaviour has proved essential to handle the new medium appropriately. Even more importantly, the pace of technical development can be so rapid that there may well be aspects of Internet use where there is no general understanding of or agreement on what makes up appropriate behaviour, leaving even experienced users in trouble. For example, to what extent is it permissible to broadcast live WebCam images of an unsuspecting person over the Internet? Visitors to World Wide Web sites are encouraged, but what details of their visits might it be appropriate to record and store electronically? What is acceptable behaviour in these and many other instances involving the Internet lacks any general consensus.

If the driving force of developing technology means that even basic guidelines may still be in a state of flux, what guidance might there be on how such matters may be handled? To date there has been little assistance available. Much of the writing on Internet-related matters has been pragmatic, dealing with individual issues and problems on a empirical basis, rather than drawing upon a more substantial background of philosophical consideration. While there might be no shortage of intimidatingly thick Internet books explaining which button to press or what software to use, there is clearly a need for a much more broadly based text that would approach Internet use from a different perspective. Rather than becoming yet another technical how-to-do-it manual, such a book would contain a much deeper but more general approach, examining in human terms what was involved in using the Internet. It would analyse how use of the Internet might be interpreted, and understood.

However, when thinking seriously about how such a text could be produced, a major potential problem becomes apparent – an individual author would inevitably be approaching an enormous and complex subject from a single standpoint. This standpoint might be that of a computer scientist, or a philosopher, or perhaps of another relevant discipline, but, whatever the perspective, the analysis would inevitably be individual. While such an specific approach is not without value, to produce a comprehensive analysis of the interaction of human society with an entity possessing the size and complexity of the Internet is undoubtedly a very substantial undertaking. Further, any individual analysis would inevitably be rendered even more difficult, because the Internet is dynamic, constantly changing and evolving, rather than a static object to be cautiously observed and monitored over a lengthy period of time. Finally, as the Internet is by definition a global entity, any comprehensive analysis would need to consider different geographical perspectives, rather than assuming that a particular national view of the Internet could automatically be extended to cover the whole planet.

Consideration of such a varied and dynamic international creation would therefore have to involve the study of important issues from several different specialist and geographical perspectives within a compressed timescale, to ensure topicality and relevance. It was consequently apparent that to create a substantive and authoritative text providing expert commentary and analysis, a book must draw contributions from a range of professional disciplines, working together over a limited period. Any more restricted viewpoint, or extended timescale, would inevitably compromise the effectiveness of an analysis.

While philosophers are naturally well placed to discuss the substantial issues of Internet values, privacy and morals, given the technical background of the Internet such discussion should certainly be built upon a solid and relevant technical base. Also, in seriously considering use of the Internet, it is necessary to take account of statute law – but which laws might apply to an international entity, and how might they be implemented? The involvement of specialist Internet lawyers would unquestionably be relevant here. It became clear that to do adequate justice to the subject, a variety of differing approaches from several disciplines would be needed – essentially, a specialist team of appropriate experts.

The principal advantage of a carefully selected expert team would obviously be the potential it provided, specifically for combining the work of specialists from different disciplines into an integrated approach to a complex subject. Such a 'combination' approach encourages the amalgamation of comment and analysis from those best placed to debate the diverse aspects of the global Internet, while still allowing the prospective book to be presented as a cohesive whole. The solution to the original dilemma was consequently unambiguous; for an effective analysis of the ethical implications of the Internet, a variety of specialist perspectives are essential.

## Areas for discussion

Once that decision was made, the prospective contents of an edited book were carefully considered. Deciding upon a suitable approach was exceptionally difficult, as the possible range of contents of a book concerned with the Internet and its use is extraordinarily large. To simplify matters, it was eventually decided to seek a variety of expert authors able to focus upon specific questions and issues which, as well as being of the greatest potential interest to a wide audience, had clear practical implications for all those using or managing access to the Internet.

In order to give a comprehensive picture there were of course many important issues concerning the Internet that needed to be tackled. These included a history of the development of the Internet – where did it come from, and what might the *technical* constraints on its use and abuse be? Placing the Internet as a global communications medium in the context of earlier human communication is illuminating; after all, however impressive the Internet may appear, it can be argued that it is really just the latest of many aids that have evolved, over millennia, to aid human interaction. When applied to the Internet, what lessons can be learned from earlier experiences?

Innumerable ethical and social value issues surround the Internet. Many of these issues are of course unlikely to be resolved in the near term, and indeed, in many ways the Internet seems to present an accelerating challenge. For example, in some cases individual involvement with the Internet may threaten deeply held values, such as those concerning privacy, property, national identity, and responsibility. The issue of personal privacy on the Internet, together with the security of electronically held information, is particularly contentious. What, too, of the *reliability* of electronic data? For instance, what happens when false or even libellous statements can be spread across the globe in a matter of minutes? What of the behaviour of individuals, freed from the constraints of familiar face-to-face social interaction to communicate electronically, in an entirely new way? The moral evaluation of individual online behaviour would be well worth examination.

Analysis of individual behaviour would naturally be enhanced by larger scale analyses, examining how familiar verities might be overtaken by the move from clearly defined national boundaries and cultures to the electronically amorphous 'global' community of the Internet. As an example, what might happen to perceptions of a geographical national identity when enormous numbers of people are spending a major portion of their waking hours interacting with individuals who live on other continents? What might happen to democratic (and other) values in such circumstances?

Underpinning the human Internet is a technical Internet, and those who provide and maintain this huge network have moral as well as professional responsibilities. How might both be defined? Where do computer professionals involved with the Internet find their professional standards, and how might these standards be shaped?

## Contributors

After the overall form of the book had been defined, it was necessary to fix the broad outline and potential contents of individual chapters. Each chapter in this wide-ranging text would be original, and would be written by a proficient and knowledgeable authority. The demand for fresh original material of high quality inevitably meant a wide search, but a further decision made selection of authors even more difficult. As the book concerned the Internet, which is by definition global, it was logical that the search for authors should be global, too. The authors needed for *Internet Ethics* should not only be authorities in their respective fields, but should also be as geographically diverse as possible. Unfortunately, of course, such people are hard for an editor to find, and, once located, are inevitably already heavily committed. Nevertheless, an extensive search led to a considerable volume of electronic interchanges with a range of international experts. Specific interlocking 'briefs' were finally offered to a select team, all distinguished specialists, from the fields of philosophy, law, and computer science. Team members were located not only in North America, but also in Europe and Australia. *Internet Ethics* has become the creation of a team of specialists, with members from different disciplines, drawn – literally – from all over the world.

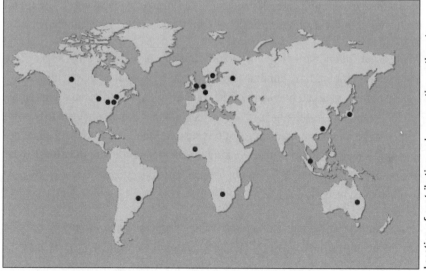

Location of contributing and commenting authors to Internet Ethics.

# The authors

As mentioned earlier, the overall text was designed as a unit, in a way perhaps unusual in an edited work. Of course, our book concerns the Internet, so it is probably important to emphasise an additional point – the indispensable role of the Internet itself in making this text possible. Most authors were recruited electronically, while both time zone differences and geographical distance meant e-mail was the only practicable method of communication between editor and contributing authors, and of course among the authors themselves. Electronic mail was exchanged very frequently among the writing team throughout the development of the book – almost as frequently as between writing team and editor! The World Wide Web was also used, particularly in providing technical definitions (from Chapter 2) which were made globally accessible at an early stage, and could therefore be considered and referenced by the writers of other chapters. Thanks to some impressive Open University software, the Web was even used to support collaborative work between our UK and USA lawyers. Many of our individual specialist authors have never have met but, thanks to the Internet, everyone was able to work closely together.

Frequent electronic communication meant that, despite comprehensive coverage, there is little overlap between chapters, while regular interaction between different contributing authors during the writing process generated many internal links, joining relevant material throughout the book. While the text has been designed to allow easy identification and location of material concerned with a specific area of interest, the book has been constructed as a comprehensive whole. Careful reading of each chapter in turn should therefore lead to a thorough understanding of the relevant issues concerning the ethical implications of the Internet, and its wider use and effects.

While chapters of the completed *Internet Ethics* were certainly impressive, at that point the book was still only *partially* a global text. Although our experts had produced a comprehensive analysis from a variety of different professional and geographical perspectives, with one exception each chapter was inevitably presented from a single viewpoint, however perceptive the author. (The exception was the legal chapter, co-written by two specialist Internet lawyers, one from the USA, one from Europe.)

What was needed for a truly global approach to the Internet was surely a further level of analysis, this time of the text itself. Perhaps an additional selection of international specialists, ideally from different cultures and nations, could view each chapter, and provide specific comment? The intention would be, first, to encourage a reader to appreciate the existence of a different, often radically different, professional perspective on the issues dealt with in a chapter. A familiar view is not necessarily the only one, and considering it in association with an alternative approach may sometimes lead to new insights. Second, and perhaps as importantly, viewing alternative opinions from different cultures should assist readers in obtaining a *global* view, one which more closely reflected the global nature of the Internet. The complications were obvious, but, despite considerable difficulties, this two-level approach was adapted.

Specialists were found. We were very fortunate in building up a truly international team, from Australia, Botswana, Brazil, Germany, Hong Kong, Japan, Russia, Singapore and Sweden. To avoid international bias, there was also a commenting author from the USA. These additional international experts – philosophers, computer scientists and lawyers – were asked to study carefully specific chapters of *Internet Ethics*, selected as relevant to their specialist interests. Their task was then to respond to particular aspects which they considered needed further discussion. Their responses were given both as those of an experienced professional in the relevant field, and as a national of their own country, able to look at specific issues from a national perspective.

## Identifying additional comment

Spread throughout the book are small, numbered tinted boxes with the name of a country or region alongside. These signify that at the end of that chapter there is a relevant comment on the current topic from one of our 'commenting' authors. While these markers are located at the relevant part of the main text, for space reasons the actual comments are always at the end of the chapter to which they refer, in number order. If, for example, during your reading you came across [JAPAN 2 ], this would indicate that comment 2 from our Japanese commenting author, Shinji Yamane, refers to that section of the current chapter. Sometimes, of course, especially when hotly debated issues are discussed, there may be two or even more comments from different national experts on the same section of text.

As was only fair, in case chapter authors felt they might have been misunderstood, or perhaps that original points may have been developed inappropriately by commenting authors, chapter authors were given space to 'comment upon comments'. When this occurs, an author's responses to comments on their chapter are written immediately below those of the commenting author. However, to avoid infinite recursion, such referral was only carried out once!

*Internet Ethics* was designed as a complete text, in which the views of established international experts in the consideration of Internet use were combined into a definitive whole. While specialists in several disciplines contributed, no single view is paramount; philosophers, computer scientists and lawyers have worked together to present an appropriate global overview of the Internet.

## Who the book is for

While the title of this book was carefully chosen, it is important to make clear that *Internet Ethics* is not intended solely for a specialist audience of philosophers. Our authors, by no means all of whom are philosophers themselves, were specifically asked to consider a very much wider readership. As many people in the developed world, and of course beyond it, either have or are likely to have experience of the Internet, it was very important to ensure an appropriately focused text. Our anticipated readers are therefore not only students on those courses that draw upon the resources of the Internet, or are specifically Internet-related, but also include anyone who uses or expects to use the Internet. Such anticipated Internet use may be commercial, as a broadcast medium, or personally, as a source of information, but it may indeed be almost anything. Internet use is hard to restrict.

## Some questions addressed in this book

While much may have been written about the technical operation of the Internet, in any serious discussion of *Internet ethics* possession of relevant technical knowledge should not be assumed. Appropriate technical information is particularly important when discussions and analyses, such as those in this book, may be read by non-technical specialists. Without some technical appreciation of the Internet, for example, it is disastrously easy to overlook the wider implications of practical issues, or to be unaware of the practical limitations of otherwise plausible ideas. Following the assumption that some understanding of the technical background to the Internet forms a necessary foundation for the proper consideration of its non-technical issues, the following chapter consequently provides a summary of the essential technical material relating to the Internet, presented in an accessible and concise form. This chapter provides definitions of most of the technical terms so freely used today in Internet discussions, and considers the general and specific background to today's Internet – for instance, where did it come from, and what actually *is* it? This chapter provides the essential ground-work material for later discussions, and it is strongly recommended that a reader is familiar with its contents before moving on to later chapters.

When faced with consideration of the philosophy underlying Internet behaviour, we should not, of course, assume that to evaluate philosophical issues concerning the Internet we must inevitably scrap all previous analysis, and start from a clean sheet. If there is 'nothing new under the sun', what is so special about the Internet? How might previous developments assist us in understanding it? Chapter 3 looks closely at these issues, and compares development of the global information infra-structure with the development of other powerful technology and systems. It iden-tifies activities which may be compared with previous experience, and distinguishes those which really are new or unique to the Internet medium. Such consideration is of importance because when faced with new experiences we tend automatically to apply cumulative knowledge; so when learning how to employ new communication tools, it is normally appropriate to apply previous experience.

Especially when dealing with international communications and other global topics, it is important not to overlook the rights and responsibilities of the indi-vidual. Experience has demonstrated that the relationship between an individual and a large organisation may often lead to the loss of personal rights and free-doms and, of course, as an organisation the Internet is larger than any other. Chapter 4 therefore deals with privacy and security, and their relationship to global Internet use. For example, what is privacy, and why is it important? What aspects of the Internet might there be which make for particular insecurities, and what might realistically be done about them?

Considering actions to preserve rights brings us to consideration of the legal aspects of Internet use, and to an examination of how application of the law might affect electronic commerce and behaviour. Chapter 5, written jointly by US and UK lawyers, examines Internet-related legal issues, and considers the implications of both American and European law. It discusses how business use of the Internet must be affected by statute law, and details the various pitfalls lying in wait for the unwary individual and business.

Of course, the actions of an individual are not only governed by legalities. Chapter 6 consequently addresses some of the wider philosophical issues involved in the moral evaluation of individual online behaviour. It is of course axiomatic that what may be classified as strictly legal behaviour in one part of the world may nevertheless cause considerable offence in another, regardless of formal legalities. Whether or not international law may be applicable, application of strict ethical approaches to individual behaviour online can allow insight into such problems. This chapter considers use of the Internet in relation to moral theory, and produces some interesting conclusions.

Much of the data flowing over the Internet may be viewed as information, so the Internet may appear to contain data in the same way that an envelope that contains a paper letter can be seen as containing information. However, it may be unwise to presume that assumptions based on experiences with earlier forms of communication can always be successfully transferred to use of the Internet. In particular, the integrity of electronically transmitted information should not be assumed. As is described in Chapter 2, the Internet is basically a sophisticated method of moving and exchanging data globally; all such data must necessarily be capable of representation in an electronic form. While the Internet, therefore, does force us to rely on electronic communication through exchange of data, there are ways such interactions may be more clearly understood. Chapter 7 looks in some detail at potential pitfalls and problems associated with the inevitable reliance of the Internet on electronic data, and concludes with a discussion on data security.

Any method of global communication potentially may be used for the free exchange of ideas; this exchange may of course be viewed, from different perspectives, as either subversive or liberating. Chapter 8 considers the association of the Internet with democracy, specifically through a study of the relationship between democratic values and the Internet. It also addresses the central issue of the governance of the Internet itself, through consideration of such questions as recognition of the autonomy of nation states, contrasted with the potential undermining of public interests by the mass of private interests currently shaping the Internet. Given the complexities and technical limitations of the continually developing Internet, we can by no means be certain that global freedom of expression will remain unquestioned, or whether electronic democracy can and should prevail.

Any ethical analysis of the Internet would be incomplete without consideration of the behaviour of those normally unseen technical specialists who make our use of the Internet possible. They ultimately control all interaction with the Internet, but what criteria are viewed by such people as forming appropriate professional standards? When their professional behaviour has the power to either reinforce or significantly undermine what may be widely considered as appropriate conduct, the answers are highly relevant to a discussion of Internet ethics. Chapter 9 consequently examines the responsibilities of computer professionals in relation to the Internet, and draws some conclusions about the technical governance of an international network.

Finally, Chapter 10 draws together recurrent themes from the selections, and makes some suggestions, predictions, and recommendations for future consideration .

Electronic commerce, already significant on the Internet, is of growing importance, and there has been much political debate on the use and abuse of computers and networked computer systems. Within the European Union (EU), such debate has led to specific legislation concerned with data protection. Given the European genesis of this book, Appendix 2 considers in detail the implications of European data protection legislation and its relationship with commercial and private Internet use. Written from a UK perspective, it presents a focused picture of current UK legislation, with particular reference to the 1998 Data Protection Act and its implementation.

The global Internet is already of considerable significance in the modern world, and this importance is set to increase dramatically. An understanding of the ethical background to this hugely significant international entity is clearly of considerable interest and importance to anyone concerned with using the Internet. The following chapters provide a carefully balanced introduction to the non-technical consideration of the Internet, and should provide a solid background for evaluative study.

# 2 Internet Technology

**DAVID BECKETT**

## Introduction

This chapter, a mainly technical description of the development and background of the Internet, initially may seem less relevant to the theme of the book; but appropriate technical knowledge is actually directly relevant to an examination of Internet ethics. Providing a necessary understanding of the physical Internet gives a solid foundation for later detailed discussion on Internet use. There are two further aspects of this chapter that should also be explained. The first is that computer scientists are notoriously prone to use acronyms, which are inevitably included here in some quantity; the second is that there are additional references in this chapter to World Wide Web locations, or URLs (defined below). These additional references are given as superscript numbers and are listed at the end of the chapter.

The Internet is not a superhighway and was not designed to survive a nuclear war (Hafner, 1996, p. 10). This chapter provides a background to Internet technology, from the cables in the ground through to describing a portal. Along the way some of the history of the Internet and the Web (World Wide Web, or WWW) will be outlined and how it was built from free software.

## The ARPANET and early networking

In 1966, the Advanced Research Projects Agency (ARPA) of the US Department of Defense was funding several research laboratories around the country with expensive computing machinery for researchers. The ARPA managers were concerned that these facilities were not being used cost effectively, since they were only available to people working locally. It was thought that there should be some way of providing access nationally to the ARPA scientists. There were two main applications that they wanted to be able to perform between the computers – to copy files and to operate the computers remotely (remote access). These needs were communicated to the managers who started to consider how to create such a network.

At this time, the phone system had been used to connect remote computers via dedicated trunk lines leased from AT&T.[1] Special devices called modems connected the phone cables and the computer terminals. These remote terminals were operated the same as local terminals; there were no computer to computer links. Since phone lines were expensive to lease, they could not be used to fully connect every site with every other site, but lines could be connected between near sites, with a few long distance lines. This network shape, or topology, demanded a special kind of communications network that knew how to direct messages along the correct lines to their destinations.

It was decided that a new computer networking technique called *packet switching* would be used for the network. A packet is a short message, usually part of a larger message. On this network, where the typical use was for terminal access, most messages were small containing key presses and thus made good use of the network.

Packets contain:

- source and destination addresses
- some control information
- data, usually in varying amounts.

Packets are transmitted from their source to destination via intermediate computers called *routers*. At each one, a decision is made where to send (or route) each incoming packet. With simple packets, this is quite rapid, and the packet can be sent on the best outgoing link towards the final destination. This made good use of expensive trunk lines, and hence was appropriate for this network.

In 1968, ARPA put out the Request for Quotation for the new network – the ARPANET to

> improve and increase computer research productivity through resource sharing. Technical needs in scientific and military environments were cited as a justification. (Heart, 1978, III: 34)

that is, not explicitly for surviving a nuclear attack. Bolt Beranek and Newman (BBN)[2] won the bid to manufacture the equipment to build the network interface devices, called interface message processors (IMPs). Bolt Beranek and Newman also designed the way that IMPs connected to the computers, and the host-to-host protocol that they used to communicate. *Host* is another term used for a computer on a network.

ARPANET sites were mostly at universities, where they were run day-to-day by graduate students. These students, to their great surprise, were left to determine the applications for the ARPANET and how they worked. They ended up designing and operating the network services but most of them 'expected that a professional crew would show up eventually to take over the problems we were dealing with' (Reynolds, 1987). This uncertainty led to the various documents being labelled rather cautiously Request for Comments (RFC) (Braden, 1999), since it was not clear if these were official documents. This informal tradition inspired an open discussion model for creating common standards by consensus, with no barriers, secret or proprietary content.

The conventions that computers use when networking are called protocols, which can be thought of 'in terms of diplomats exchanging handshakes and information' (Salus, 1995, p. 42). Protocols are operated by networking software to provide the network services that applications use. Most of the applications use the client/server model, in which there are two participants. A request is made for a particular service from the client (usually the user) to an entity that can perform it – the server. The server then usually responds with the result, or the conversation continues between the client and server until one of the participants ends it. This model is widely used in computer networking at various levels.

The two applications that were needed for the ARPANET on top of the basic Bolt Beranek and Newman host-to-host protocol were:

1. remote login – remote access to a computer on the network via the telecommunication network protocol, telnet.

2. file transfer – copying of files from host to host via the File Transfer Protocol (FTP).

These applications were also used as a basis for other services, which is a very common technique used throughout networking software called layering. This is often done by creating a hierarchy of protocols, with protocols for application 'above' ones for bare networking, or 'low level' protocols.

The major application not originally thought of was that of passing messages between people. The ARPANET was not intended as a message system but for resource sharing. However, as the network grew the designers and users found ways to communicate electronically and wanted better ways. Messaging systems already existed between users on one computer, but not over networks. The first

There was another e-mail syntax in use for many years that involved UUCP 'bang paths'; examining the path header of Usenet articles will show what this looks like. UUCP and Usenet are described later.

personal message sent over the ARPANET was by Lenny Kleinrock in 1973; however, Ray Tomlinson at Bolt Beranek and Newman wrote the first true e-mail programs, and introduced the @ sign as the punctuation for e-mail addresses, separating the user on the left from the site or computer on the right (Hafner, 1996, p. 192). Mail was originally called network mail, or netmail, and later electronic mail, e-mail or email.

## The Internet and the Internet protocols

The ARPANET host-to-host protocol design evolved several times, but by the mid 1970s it was showing its age, and a better protocol was needed. Developments had continued, and by this stage there were several other packet-switched research networks in use. However, these were using different formats, so some way to inter-network between these was required. A larger 'network of networks' is generally called an internet, so the new network was called the Internet. It was to be based on a foundation of a new Internet Protocol (IP), with other layered protocols above that. (Today, an *internet* implies a network that uses IP, as well as connecting multiple networks). To help in understanding how the Internet protocols operate, two examples may be used to illustrate different areas. The first example you may already have heard of.

### An information superhighway

Online, use of the phrase Information Superhighway is taken to be evidence that the writer using it is pretty unskilled.

This concept is that the Internet was funded federally by the Government (the US government) and that main electronic communication routes, like America's interstate highways, were built without commercial support. In this sense, the metaphor is true, but it provides no help in explaining the later development of the Internet, after the government withdrew its funding (discussed later in this chapter) and has no relevance to how the network actually works. In other words, the concept of an information superhighway is actually very little use in explaining the current global electronic network. [SINGAPORE **1**, BRAZIL **1**, AFRICA **1**, BRAZIL **2**]

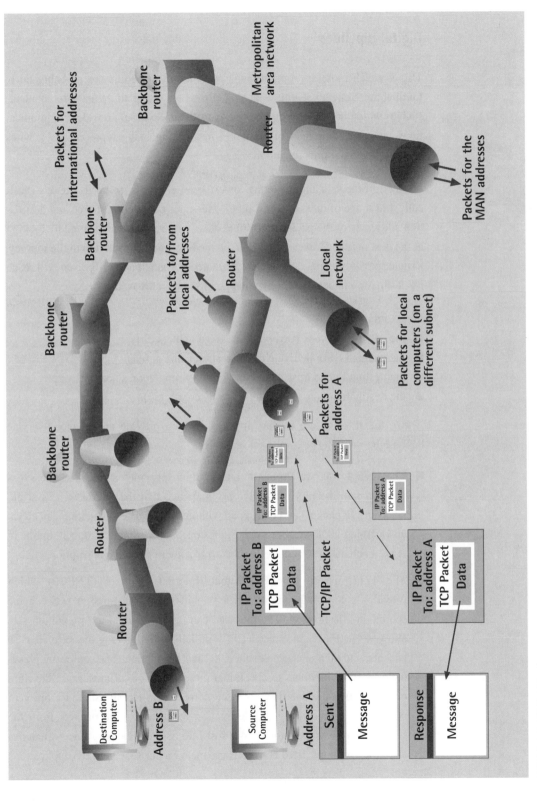

FIGURE 2.1: Digital Pipelines

## Digital pipelines

This is much more appropriate analogy, since most people are probably fairly familiar at a basic level with what a pipeline is – a 'thing' that transports 'content' such as water, natural gas, or gasoline/petroleum. So let us consider communications between computers or computer networking being represented by wires (digital pipelines) transferring messages.

Internet protocols standardise the lowest level elements in the IP packets (basically, the shape of messages in a pipe). Messages contain the source and destination addresses of the packet, and some data. These packets are routed by looking at the destination address written on the message; and at each hop in the journey, a router passes the message on. No guarantee is given that an IP packet will reach its destination intact; failure may happen for several reasons.

For example:
■ the packet becomes corrupted (message gathers dirt)
■ the packet is dropped, due to congestion (pipe is full)
■ the destination address cannot be found (wrong address on message)
■ the destination is not listening (pipe disconnected).

Above the IP layer are further protocols, which provide an enhanced service beyond the raw IP. The important ones are:

■ The User Datagram Protocol (UDP) which provides single-shot messages (thrown into the pipe) that give no guarantee that the packet arrives at all, since any IP packet can be dropped without notice. The destination can check any arriving UDP packet to see if it has become corrupted in transit, but there is no mechanism for correcting the error if there has been corruption.

■ The Transmission Control Protocol/Internet Protocol (TCP/IP) which provides guaranteed reliable, error free message transmission between the source and destination. The message can be longer than the maximum size allowed for IP packets, since TCP/IP initially splits up long messages into IP packets, and then reassembles them at their destination. The source and destination also collaborate, to check that the packets are all present, in the right order and that the data has not been corrupted in transit. Should a problem occur, it is corrected by the destination requesting more packets from the source. TCP/IP is used today for most Internet applications, since it handles all of the problems listed above. Its use means a message between applications is guaranteed to arrive either 100 per cent correct, or not at all. TCP/IP is, however, rather slow compared to UDP because of the extra work involved.

IP is concerned with the contents of the pipes. The diameter or width of the pipe represents the capacity for messages that can flow down the pipe; for data communication this is called bandwidth. [AFRICA 2] Different sized pipes can also be connected to each other via a device called a switch. Normally this is done because it is more efficient to use large pipes for liquids (or data) travelling long distances rather than to use many small pipes. This is directly analogous to the use of large fresh or waste water pipes between cities.

Devices also exist devices that switch traffic, and can also convert messages to and from different formats. These devices are sometimes known as *gateways*, and they may be used to connect IP networks to non-IP networks.

## Early Internet systems and applications

While the computer systems being used by the ARPA laboratories were made by different companies, their networking software obviously needed to be compatible. For efficiency, the software was developed by the users of the network collaboratively, and then distributed to users as *source code*. Source code is the form in which a computer program is written before it is compiled into a machine-specific version running only on a particular computer. This method of distribution meant that the software could be modified easily, improved and tested by many people at once. Such a development method had several advantages, including getting problems (or bugs) fixed quicker, fostering research into improving the network, and of course keeping a sense of community.

Many of the computers used in the ARPANET labs ran an operating system called Unix originally developed by AT&T Labs (formerly Bell Labs,[3] later part of Lucent[4]). Unix was written in the C programming language, like much of the networking software, and from early on was available with full source code. These combinations meant that Unix ran the majority of Internet networking software from very early in the 1970s. BSD Unix, from the University of Berkeley, California, was one of the most popular Unix versions. Its 4.x series of Unix operating systems (or systems based on it) were the main systems running the Internet throughout most of the 1970s and 1980s.

## File transfer

The *file transfer protocol* (FTP) was the main protocol for transfering files regularly used in the early years of the net. A protocol called UUCP was also used, since it was designed for dial-up, phone-based access, and particularly in the early years some sites used this to connect to the net. UUCP works by automatically making phone calls at regular intervals, then picking up or dropping files (or in this case, e-mails). The UUCP facility is still in use nearly 30 years later in situations where there is no Internet access available, or when making connections within networks built from dial-up phone connections, such as FidoNet.[5] [AFRICA 3]

## Remote access

The *telnet* protocol allows people to access remote computers as if they were actually sitting at directly connected terminals. This protocol has been enhanced over the years, but its functionality has basically remained the same, providing terminal-like access to computers, such as those running Unix, designed to handle multiple users.

A related application, called *talk*, was developed later. Talk allows a small number of people to contribute to a typed conversation over a network, sharing a split terminal window in order that all the participants may see each side of the conversation. This application is generally known as *chat* and has developed into more advanced systems such as Internet Relay Chat (IRC).[6] IRC takes place via a server and allows real-time chat between multiple participants. Each user picks a nickname, and selects subject-based channels. On each channel there are topics in current conversations that can be joined by an interested user.

## E-mail and mailing lists

E-mail was, as mentioned above, an unexpectedly important application that the original pioneers did not include in the original Internet design. However, it rapidly became the most popular application, and has remained so for many years. The early mail protocols worked on top of FTP, and were quite simple, but the protocols and software have since improved. E-mail headers are an important evolved feature of e-mail. They contain information about the message lying outside the body of the message. Header contents usually include the sender

(From), the recipient (To), the subject (Subject), and so on. They can be seen in some form in most e-mail software, although the full headers may only be available via a special menu option. The original FTP-based mail protocol was replaced by Simple Mail Transfer Protocol (SMTP) which was designed specifically for e-mail. SMTP was especially designed to be simple, and to allow e-mail to be sent and received easily over a TCP/IP channel. At the present time, the majority of global e-mail is sent using this protocol (or its direct successor, Extended Simple Mail Transfer Protocol, ESMTP).

One of the main original e-mail transfer agents (MTAs) was based on UUCP. A later MTA, called Sendmail[7] was developed by Eric Allman[8] to manage e-mail interactions – essentially, sending, receiving and forwarding messages between the various types of systems. The program Sendmail was made freely available, since e-mail was a key application and people were relying on it. This program is still free today, and is used by many large organisations.

E-mail was used for person-to-person messages, but several other systems evolved for communicating between many people. Ordinary e-mails can of course be sent to many people by listing them on the 'destination' or 'To' header, but this method becomes unmanageable for larger mailings. Software was therefore written to handle *mailing lists* or *listservs* (from 'list servers'), allowing people to broadcast messages to all the list members by sending a single message to the list e-mail address. Joining and leaving lists is done by sending a message to the relevant mail listserv address, usually listserv@somewhere. This is still used on mailing lists today.

Mailing lists were run and maintained on computers scattered around the network, but, for popular lists, this was a slow way to transmit the messages – particularly if there were thousands of participating users. A more efficient way was consequently developed to distribute messages for large audiences. An additional pressure for this development came as, at the time, the network was only available to connected Internet users, while people outside the network dialling in via UUCP wanted to participate in the shared information space.

## Usenet

The new system that evolved was called *network news* but is generally known now as *Usenet*. Usenet is based on messages in the e-mail format, with headers and a body. The messages are published or *posted* to one or more particular

If you look at the headers of a news posting, you can see via the Path header, the route that message took to get to you.

subject-specific *newsgroup*. The messages are then copied around the network, from one computer on to its neighbours. Each participating computer looks at the new message, and decides if it had already seen it, taking a copy if it has not.

Some newsgroups are moderated, meaning that each message or article is e-mailed to a human moderator for approval before being published. Most news-groups, however, are open access. The newsgroups were originally named in a similar manner to the early mailing lists. Later, although, they were reorganised into a hierarchy, with the top level categories based on eight main areas, with others for countries (for example, '.fr', France) and local sites. Below the top level were sub-groups for more specific topics, with more sub-groups added as the demand for them was seen.

Usenet has grown immensely since the original system design. Though there have been several predictions of its imminent collapse, this has yet to happen.

The software to read, post and serve new articles was made freely available, like the Internet software already discussed. The early news articles were copied by UUCP, but, later, since the number of newsgroups and articles had increased vastly, a dedicated news protocol was needed. This was called Network News Transport Protocol (NNTP) and was developed specifically to pass round the news articles more efficiently.

## The Internet culture and free software

The Internet was founded on what could be called the open philosophy – systems, and especially software, were developed openly; no proprietary protocols were used in the network, and there were no big restrictions on copying or modifying software. This approach was encouraged as many users based at universities, where there is generally an ethos of collaboration in order to advance common knowledge. The outcome of this original open philosophy included a willingness to share and help others, and to collaborate in advancing the technology.

The openness of the Internet standards process (RFCs) emerged from the people who formed it. Jon Postel[9] (1943–98) who was the RFC editor from 1969 till his death, established and ran the Internet Assigned Numbers Authority (IANA)[10] which maintains the lists of terms and protocol elements needed to keep the network communicating; he was the first individual member of the Internet Society (ISOC)[11] in 1992. Jon and others kept the spirit of fun going by publishing humorous RFCs on 1st April each year (All Fools Day). The main technical devel-opment body for RFCs and other Internet standards is the Internet Engineering

Task Force (IETF)[12] which developed from the ad hoc process of the early ARPANET people. The IETF operates through working groups on mailing lists, meeting three times each year; this arrangement derived from the initial ARPANET working group schedule. There is no formal membership – anyone may attend – but the ethos is on good, demonstrable technical work, or in the IETF's own words, to attain 'rough consensus… and on running code' (Carpenter, 1996).

Several new words emerged from the vibrant communications media that ran over the Internet. Usenet users created the rather clumsy term *netiquette*, the (suggested) way to behave in e-mail and newsgroup articles, *flaming* – being deliberately abusive or argumentative and *trolling* – writing outrageous articles to provoke a response just for fun! For more of this kind of thing, see Raymond (1996). The most infamous term that came from Usenet is *spamming* (Python, 1973) which was originally the posting of the same message to multiple news-groups (also called *cross-posting*) usually to try to sell something through an advertisement. The term spamming was later applied to e-mail messages sent to thousands of victims, most having been selected by copying e-mail addresses from posted news articles.

As the commercial exploitation of the Internet grew, most of the software that was actually running the network still remained non-commercial. (Some examples have been given above – BSD Unix, sendmail.) Established users began to be concerned that, with the new rush of commercialism, the open spirit of sharing would be lost. They wanted to foster the continued development and free distribution of software source code. In 1984, Richard Stallman[13] started the GNU's Not Unix (GNU)[14] project to create a free software version of the Unix operating system, including all its supporting software. To do this, and to protect its freedom, he wrote a new licence called the GNU General Public License (GPL)[15] which protects the freedom for people to copy software, and prevents the creation of derived works that change this state. The GPL was applied to many useful programs, such as the GNU C compiler, that were in use at the time.

In 1985, Stallman founded an organisation, the Free Software Foundation (FSF)[16] to protect and foster the idea of Free Software.[17] Their definition of free software:

> Free software is that which comes with permission for anyone to use, copy, and distribute, either verbatim or with modifications, either gratis or for a fee. In particular, this means that source code must be available. 'If it's not source, it's not software.' (Tower, 1998)

> 'Free software' is a matter of liberty, not price. To understand the concept, you should think of 'free speech', not 'free beer'. (Stallman, 1999)

The FSF is opposed to software patents, but not to people making money selling software.

Much other software already mentioned is free software, such as BSD Unix from Berkeley, although available under a slightly different licence – the BSD licence.[18] This allows commercial binary versions (and in Stallman's terms, is not as free as GPL'ed software). Kirk McKusick,[19] one of the leaders of the Berkeley UNIX project in its heyday, puts it something like this:

> Copyright is designed to protect the intellectual property rights of the people who create something. Copyleft is designed to protect the rights of the users. The Berkeley license is copy central: Take this stuff down to the copier and make as many copies as you want, for whatever you want.

The X Window System (X)[20] is a portable and flexible graphics technology developed from a project at MIT. It can be used to create graphical user interfaces and works well with Unix. This allowed better and quicker software development and made work with graphics more economic. X was released under the MIT licence[21] which was also pretty generous in its terms. Later on the terms were changed to be less free but a major free software version of X, Xfree86[22] forced the change to be reversed by planning to work from the older free versions.

In October 1991, Linus Torvalds[23] a student at the University of Helsinki in Finland released a new operating system he had been developing for fun under the GPL which he called Linux.[24] Linux was the first working implementation of an operating system based entirely on free (GPL'ed) software. It was delivered with the full source code of the system available for people to download by FTP, and then experiment. In a surprisingly short time, Linux attracted many developers, who in turn added improvements to the basic system created by Linus. Free software versions of BSD – FreeBSD[25] and OpenBSD[26] were also developed in the early 1990s, but Linux proved far more successful.

# The Internet expands

The ARPANET evolved into two distinct entities – the Csnet, a largely academic computer science network, and a separate military network for the US Department of Defense. These networks were constructed around several original long distance networks that formed the main network architecture of the ARPANet; this is commonly called the *network backbone*. Later, the civilian network became the National Science Foundation Network (NSFnet), funded by that US organisation. However, all such bodies normally forbid the use of their funding for commercial or business purposes. With the intensifying commercial nature of the Internet this was increasingly seen as a problem, eventually leading to the US government's withdrawal from operating the Internet backbone. This left participants to purchase connections from telecoms companies, and new commercial operators. IP also began to be used extensively within organisations over their own Local Area Networks (LANs); many such local networks were running on a cheap and relatively easy to install hardware technology called *Ethernet*. This was designed in 1973 by Bob Metcalfe,[27] one of the original Internet pioneers, when he was working for Xerox.[28] Metcalfe later founded the major network company 3Com,[29] and is now a prominent Internet columnist for InfoWorld[30] magazine. [AFRICA 4 ]

Computers use numbers for everything, including the addresses of machines, but humans prefer to use readable names. To accommodate these two preferences on a network, a map giving the relationship between names and the numbers is needed. Originally this was accomplished with one huge file that contained the names and addresses of all the Internet hosts in existence. As the number of machines on the Internet grew, this file was changing so frequently that it became impossible to keep it up to date. A more flexible solution was therefore developed, using hierarchical names for the networked computers with '.'s separating the elements of the names, such as parrot.example.com. These are called *domain names* and the system that makes them available is the Domain Name System (DNS). The DNS distributes the mappings from names to numbers around the network so that organisations are responsible for maintaining their own names – this is known as a *distributed database*. The distribution of responsibility for updating names means that there is no longer a single huge file of information, and details may therefore be kept more up to date. The most popular and complete implementation of the DNS was the freely available BIND[31] which remains the major implementation in use today.

Domain names are structured at the root (or top) into two types – *country* domains (.uk for the United Kingdom, .jp for Japan, for example) taken from the standard ISO two-letter country codes, and *top level* domains which include:

- .com for commercial sites
- .org for non-profit sites
- .net for networks
- .int for international sites
- .gov for US government sites
- .edu for US education sites.

Originally the first three suffixes were intended solely for sites in the USA, but com, org and net gradually began to be used for any type of site, anywhere in the world. If one of the listed top level suffixes is not employed, country suffixes must normally be used for addresses in every country – except the USA. (There is a .us domain for the United States, but it is at present mostly used for state schools and government.) [BRAZIL **3**]

Expansion of the use of global e-mail led to further developments in the protocols used. The Post Office Protocol (POP) allows people to use e-mail via a server – essentially to pick up and send mail items. This is particularly useful when the computer used varies from day-to-day , or if a user is working off-site and dialling in to read or send mail. A new form of e-mail encoding called the Multipurpose Internet Mail Extensions (MIME) was also introduced; this allowed e-mail to contain messages that were not just plain text. For example, MIME e-mail may be an internationalised message (not in the usual limited character set), multiple versions of the message in different encodings or even an attached binary file (such as a digital photograph) protected from being changed in transit by a special encoding. Attached binary files are now known as *mail attachments*.

BSD Unix was very popular in computer education and research. This popularity led in 1982 to a new company being formed to develop products for this market. Sun Microsystems[32] was founded by Stanford graduates including Scott McNealy[33] and Bill Joy[34] (who also designed some key technologies, such as BSD Unix, NFS, Java and JINI). Sun picked up and used X and developed new hardware specially to exploit it. This hardware sold widely to the Internet community, due to high performance and out-of-the-box Internet functionality. Today Sun Microsystems still provide a large proportion of the hardware behind many major Internet sites.

# The World Wide Web (WWW)

In the late 1980s and early 1990s, most of the file transferring on the Internet was done by means of ftp, postings to Usenet, or e-mail. In 1993, researchers at the University of Minnesota created a menu-based interactive system and protocol called *gopher*, which allowed users to find information and files on the Internet. It allowed browsing menus to be created by users, and searches to be submitted using them. For the first time, there was something more sophisticated than a raw list of ftp files. Gopher was used by a client program that displayed menus on a text terminal, and allowed navigation around them. This interface was much more consistent and easy to use across multiple sites than using ftp, because ftp works by entering and exiting each site, which is difficult for beginners to use. (Following the explosive growth of the WWW, gopher was turned off at the University of Minnesota in 1996, and today seems to have disappeared from the net entirely.)

O'Reilly and Associates[35] founded by Tim O'Reilly[36] began publishing Unix, X and related books in 1988, but also covered many free software programs. They commissioned a gentle introductory book about the Internet for novices from Ed Krol.[37] His book was called *The Whole Internet Users Guide and Catalog*[38] (Krol, 1994) and was originally published in 1992. The text covered e-mail, mailing lists, ftp, gopher (and its search system, veronica) although even with this help the net was still rather difficult for a beginner to use. Finally, the book covered a new system called the World Wide Web (WWW)[39] created by a British physicist Tim Berners-Lee[40] who worked for the high energy physics research laboratory CERN[41] in Switzerland.

In 1991 CERN and other labs around the world were communicating electronically, using the network to pass around research papers, images and other materials via e-mail and ftp sites. At CERN there was also a variety of other older information systems, but each of them needed to be accessed by a different program. Berners-Lee thought that it would be better if access to these systems could be made both much easier and essentially seamless. The information space he created to do this was the WWW, or the Web; and the program allowing access was called a *browser*, or a *Web browser*. Browsers used a new protocol called HTTP (HyperText Transfer Protocol)[42] – and delivered documents in a format called HTML (HyperText Markup Language).[43]

HTTP operates over a TCP/IP connection to a server; it is designed to transfer HTML, plain text or any other type of documents. The protocol allows the fetching of one document per connection to an HTTP server (at least initially; later versions allow more). The simplicity of the protocol, which was written using text-based commands, like SMTP and earlier protocols, ensured that HTTP was easy to understand and, importantly, it was easy to write client and server applications. For obvious reasons, HTTP servers are usually called *Web servers*. Unfortunately, the *computers* that run HTTP servers are also sometimes called Web servers!

An HTTP request and reply sequence is also known as *fetching* or *getting* a Web page or a Web request.

HTML is a format that describes hypertext – text that contains links to other documents. Hypertext systems had been used in the research community for several years but had not generally been integrated with networking. HTML is based on an another much more complex electronic document format called SGML (Standard Generalised Markup Language), in which the body of the document contains text surrounded by tags. Tags are description, formatting or other instructions to interpret the document, and are written as '<' followed by a tag name, and ending with '>'. Tags may mark the start or end of parts of the document, as in this example:

```
...some text....
<TITLE>This is the title</TITLE>
...some more text...
```

The first, or *opening* tag indicates the start of the title in the document and the second, or *closing*, tag marks the end of the title. Closing tags have a '/' before the tag name. Tags are not always used in pairs – an example is <P>, which can be used alone to separate paragraphs.

To understand a document, the browser must understand the tags; however in HTML, Berners-Lee added a new rule – that if the browser did not understand a tag, it should ignore it. The impact of this rule became more significant as further tags were added to HTML.

It is of particular importance that Web browsers understand special <A> (or *anchor*) tags in HTML. Such tags point to other HTML documents, and are the links that create the Web of documents, or hypertext. Other documents are identified by using a specific and unique address, called a Uniform Resource Locator or *URL*[44] (Berners-Lee, 1994). URLs can point to HTTP, ftp, gopher and news servers directly, indicate telnet access to resources, and other services. A URL has many parts, but all URLs start with the protocol, before a colon :, for example 'http:' or 'ftp:' as in

```
http://www.w3.org/Addressing/
```

Berners-Lee realised that the seamless unified access he wanted could be provided across many types of servers by the use of HTTP gateways that translated the Web requests into the language understood by other services. In this way, the web of hypertext documents could extend well beyond just those documents written in HTML. See Figure 2.2.

The original browser program spawned other versions that ran on almost all computers – mainframes, PCs, Unix systems, Macintoshes and many others. Each of these systems now had equal access to resources previously only available to a select few. The physics community understandably took up this new system rapidly, and began to create Web document trees around the world, using the clients and servers developed by CERN.

## New Web browsers, servers and sites

One early adopter of the Web technologies was the National Center for Supercomputing Applications (NCSA)[45] at the University of Illinois. The NCSA group developed software for the physicists and others using the supercomputers around the USA. Naturally they wanted to both use the materials at CERN and to share their own work. This led them to work on a new kind of browser for their applications, one involving the display of graphics across the network. The NCSA software development group developed a graphical server, the NCSA httpd,[46] and, in 1993, a graphical client called Mosaic[47] that ran on Unix, Microsoft Windows/Intel and Macintosh systems. The major innovation in the browser was a new <IMG> HTML tag that allowed authors to add pictures to HTML documents. As mentioned above, existing browsers that did not understand this new tag would automatically ignore it. Addition of the tag to a Web page therefore meant old browsers could still read the page, albeit without the benefit of the image. This was the start of backwards compatibility problems and access issues for Web pages.

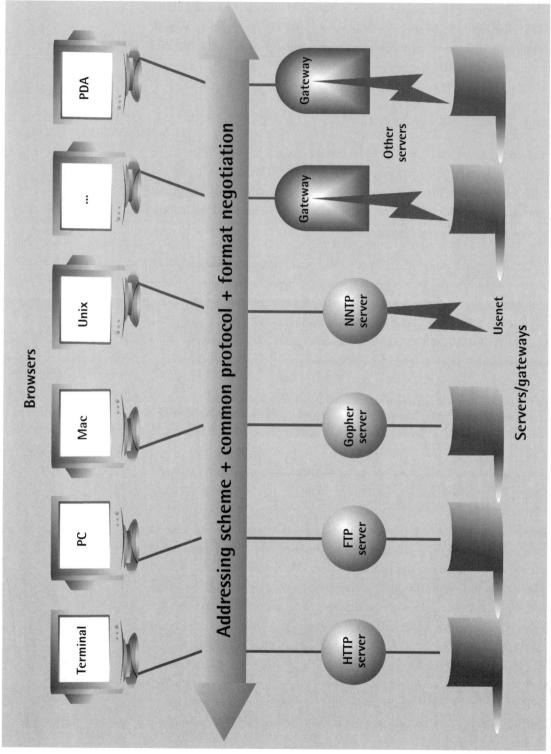

FIGURE 2.2: The Web client/server model

NCSA Mosaic was publicly released and was very quickly picked up by people all over the network, who could now not only use ftp, gopher and the Web in a much friendlier way but view images too – a big change from the terminal-based text Web and systems that were current at the time. Within a year Mosaic had an estimated 2 million users globally. The most popular Web servers at this time were from CERN and NCSA, although there were many others, since writing a server was relatively easy.

NCSA later added a facility to connect their Web server and external programs; called the Common Gateway Interface (CGI),[48] this was used by requesting a special URL. The URL called an external program which actually created an (HTML) page, allowing the generation of *dynamic* Web spaces, rather than the *static* ones which are formed from plain HTML files. Dynamic pages are particularly useful in creating gateways to legacy systems, databases and programs by converting their output to HTML, and thus making them world accessible via the Web. The CGI interface was rapidly added to all servers, and remains the standard today.

The best way to create CGI programs is by using what are called *scripting languages,* computer languages designed to allow programs to be written quickly and, usually, to work with text. The most popular of these is Perl[49] created by Larry Wall,[50] (which is available as free software). Perl is so often used for CGI and other Web tasks that it has been said that 'Perl built the Web'. Perl was designed in the Unix culture, and took lots of its syntax and ideas from other Unix tools; it was thus familiar and useful to many people. Since most CGI programs are written using scripting languages, they are most commonly known as *CGI scripts*.

In the period 1993–95 the Web grew rapidly and many people started to create their own personal Web areas. Berners-Lee created the idea of a person's Web home page – the starting point for people using the Web, containing links to their own documents as well as links to interesting or useful places on the Web. The basic concept evolved into two separate ideas:

- the *home page*, which tended to be a person's public home on the Web
- the browser *bookmarks* (later also called *favorites*) which were more structured Web links, containing the link, the title of the link, the date the bookmark was made, and usually the date it was last visited.

Browsers also stored all the links that were taken during a Web session in a browser *history*. A history usually contained records of several days' activity, to allow people to return to locations they had seen recently. There was also another sort of record, in the form of the 'go back' and 'go forward' buttons which allowed the user to travel back and forwards along the current route they were taking through the Web. The Web document trees, areas or sites that were constructed began to be known as *Web sites* and many innovative Web sites began being created. In April 1994, the Web was becoming so large that two graduates at Stanford University created a directory, classifying their favourite Web sites, which they called Yahoo![51] This directory was the foundation of a multi-billion dollar company. Incidentally, Yahoo! was built, managed and is still run using Perl and BSD Unix.

Coincidentally, it was also in April, 1994, that the core of the National Center for Supercomputing staff who wrote Mosaic (including the key designer Marc Andreessen[52]) left to form a new private company called Netscape.[53] Netscape soon began to design and build a new browser and server, and there was considerable interest in what the products would be like. On 13 October 1994, Netscape released a beta version of their new browser on the Net, free for personal use, and there was an immediate positive reaction. Millions of copies were downloaded. The browser had new and, then, unique features, such as displaying a document as it loaded, the ability to fetch multiple images simultaneously, and support of the JPEG image format. Netscape invented some new HTML tags to change and improve the look of Web pages, including <CENTER> to centre lines on the page; this was to be the first of many changes. Its impressive abilities made the new browser, Netscape Navigator, look very fast and slick compared to Mosaic. The next week, *Wired*[54] magazine created one of the very first commercial Web sites called HotWired,[55] and displayed the first advertising banner on the Web. The HotWired site was designed to be very graphical, and it worked very well with the new browser.

Some sites still use IP addresses as unique identifiers for people and I recommend you avoid them since it can expose your personal information to any person who shares the computer with the same address.

In December 1994 Netscape shipped its server products, targeted at commercial use of the Net, or e-commerce. For shopping sites, people need to be able to browse, add items to some form of 'shopping basket', and perhaps return several times before purchasing. This means that a commercial server needed to be able to identify individual customers. Some sites use IP addresses to do this, but such identification is of no use if several people come from the same machine or appear to. (This can happen when using caches, see later.) An alternative was needed. To resolve this problem, Netscape added a new feature to their browser, a feature they called *cookies*. These are small text files that sit on the user's computer, and are sent to Web sites when the user visits. For example, the netscape.com site may register a cookie called *user*, with some value. Whenever you visit any Web page below a netscape.com address, the *user* cookie and the value are sent as part of the HTTP request for every page. In this way, the content of the returned page can be customised for an individual visitor. The issue of cookies does have several privacy and other implications, discussed in other chapters.

Netscape was a major e-commerce user itself, selling its browser and server products online. Customers generally wanted to use their credit cards, and this meant card numbers had to be sent to Netscape on a normal TCP/IP connection. IP packets passing across the Internet can be read by any intermediate computer and, potentially, this meant credit card numbers and personal information could be intercepted. Netscape needed a way to encrypt data used for sending such sensitive information. Encryption is done by complex mathematical transformations of data called cryptography. [SWEDEN **1**] Netscape created a protocol called SSL (Secure sockets layer), which formed a secure wrapper protocol on top of HTTP; this appears in URLs as the protocol https:.

In February 1995 the popular NCSA Web server was not being maintained (the main author had left to join Netscape) so a group of Webmasters gathered their extensions and bug fixes as *software patches*, – which are text files describing the differences between the old and new versions of files. The group created a new server called Apache[56] (think 'A patch-y') and made their 1.0 release in December 1995. Within a year Apache was the most popular server on the Net; it has remained so ever since, and now runs the majority of Web sites.

## The Internet commercialises

In 1993, the US government removed the federal funding for the Internet backbone, and let it be operated by new commercial organisations. These specialist telecommunications companies run high-speed fibre optic cables over long distances, and provide connectivity by various switching centres. These networks are generally known as Metropolitan Area Networks (MANs) when they span cities, or Wide Area Networks (WANs) if the network is over a longer distance. Individual users dial into the Internet from home using their modems to connect to Internet Service Providers (ISPs), who then connect to the main Internet, sometimes via larger ISPs, and out to the whole of the worldwide network.

There were several organisations running large private online services with their own content and using their own protocols, such as AOL[57] and CompuServe,[58] but these organisations did not connect to the Internet directly until around 1995, and then only through select gateways. It was several years before they provided full Internet accessibility providing Web, e-mail, ftp, telnet and so on, but today they have turned almost completely into major ISPs with the 'extra' of additional Web content. Microsoft[59] also completely ignored the Internet for several years, and instead tried to build its own proprietary online service called MSN.[60] It eventually gave up when Bill Gates[61] re-targeted the company in 1995 to be Internet orientated. Microsoft then licensed the Mosaic browser source code from NCSA to build its own Web browser – Internet Explorer[62] – to compete with Netscape, who had over 80 per cent of the market share at the time.

The US government also gave the operation of the DNS, by open tender, to a private company called Network Solutions Inc.[63] Network Solutions was then solely responsible for the .com and other domains, providing the central database and handling the billing for them. The .com domain, intended for US companies, was used for most sites wherever they were located and hence was the 'place' to be if you were creating a Web site. In 1998 this situation needed reforming, since Network Solutions was in effect running a government-sanctioned monopoly, and there was additionally a need for more top level domains. Many discussions around the world took place on appropriate changes, with the help of bodies such as the Internet Society and IANA. In early 1999, IANA was reformed as The Internet Corporation for Assigned Names and Numbers (ICANN)[64] to oversee the new DNS arrangements. The first five new registrars, responsible for allocation of domain names, were announced in April 1999.

Some pioneer e-commerce companies starting up in this vibrant period included:

- Amazon,[65] who started selling books online in July 1995, using encryption to protect user data, and giving substantial discounts on the store prices
- Geocities,[66] which in May 1995 was one of the first sites offering free Web home pages (supported by advertising)
- Dell[67] who opened an Internet computer store in 1996, selling PCs online directly to the end user and consequently saving money in intermediate costs

- Hotmail,[68] who provide free Web-based e-mail, supported by advertising on their Web pages. Unfortunately HotMail accounts (and later, other free e-mail services) have been taken up enthusiastically by e-mail spammers, since such e-mail accounts can be created easily and without any responsibility
- CNN,[69] who in 1995 created the first major topical news Web site, with continuous updates from correspondents around the world, together with pictures, audio and video clips.

A new kind of service that allowed you to search the Web appeared in the mid 1990s, based on software that 'crawled' the links that made up the Web, or for short, a *Webcrawler*. These software agents (or robots) take the words from Web pages, store them, and create indexes that can be searched. One of the first commercial sites to do this was Lycos,[70] which was founded in June 1995. Later AltaVista[71] created a much larger search database that could be searched much faster. Several other large search companies also formed to do similar work, using advertising on their pages to support the services. These types of systems are now generally known as *search engines*.

## Security, privacy and ratings

By now there were malicious people online who took pleasure in cracking computers – breaking in to them. The term hacking, which is discussed in several chapters of this book, is a different thing; a very good programmer is a hacker, a cracker is a thief or vandal. To protect against such electronic attacks, there are various techniques including the *firewall* – a special computer sitting between the Internet and the organisation, with the task of checking access in both directions to try to prevent illegal operations.

Any computer on the Net can read IP packets that are transmitted through it, which are hence not private. This lack of privacy is even worse for packets on a LAN, such as Ethernet, where every computer connected to the cable can see every packet sent. Applications above IP thus need encryption for privacy (like SSL for Web traffic) and the most important application of these is for e-mail. A US programmer called Phil Zimmerman created a program called Pretty Good Privacy (PGP)[72] that allowed individuals to securely encode their e-mail such that even the most powerful military computers could not read the contents. PGP has become the de facto worldwide e-mail encryption standard, despite the US government trying and failing to prevent people using it outside the USA. The issue of encryption is discussed in more detail in Chapters 4 and 7. [BRAZIL **4** ]

E-mail and other Internet applications are generally built on top of TCP/IP, with no particular knowledge of who may be the person actually requesting the service. This means that e-mail or news can be faked easily, by installing a mail program, and setting it to use any outgoing e-mail address. However, experts can use the route the forged mail takes across the network to work out the likely source machine of the e-mail. This is how most spammers are found.

Some of these problems may be resolved, to provide service such as e-mail that cannot be traced, and e-mail that has a guaranteed known sender. For example, anonymous e-mail can be provided over the Internet, through the use of anonymous e-mail forwarders. These accept e-mail, rewrite the headers to remove the identification of the sender, and then forward the message to the intended recipient; this may also happen in reverse, so both people may communicate anonymously. PGP allows e-mail to be marked with a digital signature – a guarantee that the message was sent by the person with the PGP certificate. The recipient can check this if they already have information about the senders' PGP certificate.

## Advanced Web and Internet technology

The Internet Society, founded in 1992, oversaw the IETF and related bodies as well as encouraging development of the Internet around the world. The IETF concentrates mostly on protocols and lower level standards development. The Web, however, had no such body, and by the mid-1990s there were growing problems. Netscape and Microsoft (mostly) were adding features to HTML. Each browser version produced without consensus caused major problems for Web site authors. In 1994, the World Wide Web Consortium[73] (W3C) was founded at MIT in the US and CERN (later replaced by INRIA, France) to promote common specifications and cooperation. The W3C is an industry consortium, and the founder companies included both Microsoft and Netscape, as well as many other large computer companies. (In 1999 the membership was well over 100 organisations.) The W3C soon set to standardising HTML and related standards, as well as developing new ones, so Web authors could begin to rely on tags remaining at least mostly consistent. This consensus led to the many new standards, including HTML 2, 3.2 and 4. More recently the W3C has designed style sheets, which allow the look of Web pages to be separated from the content, and Extensible Markup Language (XML)[74] which will be the basis for future HTML and Web markup, in which there will be no HTMLs.

Netscape as well as extending HTML added *active content* to Web pages by licensing the Java language[75] from Sun in May 1994, and adding it to their browser. Java allows interactive Web pages to be created where the reader can run and use the Java programs running on the page. These programs are called *applets*. Java programs can run on any computer since they run in their own 'virtual computer' and are not compiled for any particular processor.

Netscape also developed a scripting language called JavaScript for use within Web pages in December 1995. This allowed HTML authors to add actions when the user interacted with the Web page by, for example, moving the mouse over an image. Microsoft introduced their own proprietary technologies to perform similar things – ActiveX and Visual Basic Script – which, however, only work on MS Windows systems. These are not used widely in Web pages on the Internet, since they requires browser users to modify their software which is at best inconvenient. Understandably, these technologies are used much more extensively inside Microsoft's Web server, although that is a minority of all Web servers.

The vast increase in users and traffic on the Internet meant that eventually the HTTP protocol dominated bandwidth and use. This led to the development of Web *proxies* or *caches* which fetch Web pages on the user's behalf, and then store copies of popular files so that they are not fetched repeatedly. Such storage can save considerable traffic and money. The most popular proxy is the free software Squid,[76] although there are several large commercial systems. All HTTP accesses are recorded or logged by the proxies. There are clear privacy issues here, which are discussed in detail in Chapter 4. Logging may also be carried out at the remote sites, and for some Web sites this is a problem, since caches hide or anonymise their customers, and ignorance of a caller's identity may have a real financial penalty.

By the late 1990s schools and children were using the Web significantly. Some caregivers demanded content ratings of Web pages (by the authors or by third parties) so they could select categories of Web page content types suitable for children in their community. The W3C created a format called the Platform for Internet Content Selection (PICS) for these descriptions, but the software that applies these rules, generally called *censorware*, has also to filter Web pages for particular words since PICS is used on very few Web sites. Censorware software has considerable pitfalls, such as tending to censor innocent terms that happen to be close to a forbidden word, such as might occur in descriptions of travels around Essex or to Scunthorpe, real places in the UK. [SWEDEN 2 ]

Large organisations now use the open Internet and Web technologies internally, rather than older proprietary systems. An internal IP-based network is called an *intranet*, but is generally closed to the outside world. It may be found useful to make some part of the private network visible outside the organisation, and this is generally known as an *extranet*. An extranet may link parts of one organisation or multiple organisations; this will usually need some security since the connections are running over the public Internet. This is done by use of a Virtual Private Network (VPN) in which an encrypted 'tunnel' is formed over a TCP/IP connection; all traffic between the organisations then passes through them, via gateways or proxies.

Broadcasters have begun to use the Web to transmit video and audio as well as Web pages with static pictures. They mostly have used RealAudio[77] for sound, but a variety of video standards are used including RealVideo. A camera pointing at the action and putting the images directly on a Web page is also popular. Such a camera is called a *Webcam*. Musicians (and, later, publishers) started experimenting with digital online music published directly to fans, usually in RealAudio or a new format called MP3[78] which made the data containing songs small enough in size to transmit online. Multimedia content could also be added to Web pages by using technology such as Java or ShockWave, which allows the creation of multimedia 'shows' or performances running inside a Web page.

The free software community expanded with companies like RedHat[79] selling millions of copies of Linux in shrink wrap form, the creation of Web sites such as freshmeat[80] and slashdot[81] keeping the community together, and the new idea of Open Source.[82] This was invented by Eric Raymond[83] (Raymond, 1997) and is free software, but presented in a way that could be understood more easily by the commercial software world. This influenced Netscape, who made their new browser into free software in 1998, codenamed Mozilla.[84]

Several early applications evolved or spawned newer versions. The POP protocol was joined by variants and by a new one, Internet Message Access Protocol (IMAP), that was more useful for dialling in and manipulating e-mail stored on a server. IRC attracted a new commercial competitor ICQ,[85] a chat system that allows a user to log into a server and be signalled when friends arrive and depart.

Finally, all the big companies such as Yahoo!, the search engines, and the commercial sites realised that they were really providing entrances to the Net – most people started at one specific site when they looked for things online. Large Web operations had become entrances, or portals to the Web. Yahoo! developed a 'my' customisation concept for its portal, adding many services, and it has remained a very popular Web site. The browser manufacturers realised that adding searching systems to the software could direct people to their own portals, and expanded accordingly. Most of the portals today offer some additional content such as news, a Web search service, and customisation.

## Future Internet technology

These technologies will continue to grow in use in the next few years. The next version of IP, Internet Protocol version 6 (IPv6), is designed for a much larger Internet, including bigger IP addresses, more data and encryption in the packets. More applications of metadata on the Web are likely, including Dublin Core[86] format written in the Resource Description Framework (RDF)[87] format, an application of XML for better Web searching, digital libraries, e-commerce and multimedia applications. Dynamic HTML (DHTML), HTML together with JavaScript and style sheets, offer authors ways to rewrite Web pages on a browser when the user interacts with them. There are more advanced search engines in development, including those such as AltaVista that support language translation, and AskJeeves[88] that allow users to narrow searches by answering questions.

It is quite impossible to keep up with these technologies, since major new applications can appear within weeks or a few months. There will undoubtedly be novel Web systems and expansions which have appeared since this chapter was written in June 1999.

# Comments

**SINGAPORE**

In Singapore, the Internet started with its introduction at the National University of Singapore some time in 1991. However, at that time, it was entirely for research and development use. By 1992, the Singapore government formed the TechNet Unit and promoted its use among R&D and educational organisations. In 1994, the first Internet Service Provider was set up by Singapore Telecommunications Ltd. This ISP is known as SingNet. By 1995, it became obvious that the Internet was really taking off in a big way. The Singapore government decided to sell off the TechNet Unit. This new entity became the second Internet Service Provider called Pacific Internet, or PacNet for short. Subsequently, a third Internet Service Provider, CyberWay, was set up. In 1996, the Singapore government announced the set-up of the high speed, broadband, multimedia network called Singapore ONE (One Network for Everyone). This high speed network is based on Internet and ATM (Asynchronous Transfer Mode) technologies. Its pilot project was officially launched by the Singapore Prime Minister on 9 June 1997.

In Singapore, it is the government that takes the lead in introducing and funding the information superhighway.

**BRAZIL**

In Brazil, in the mid 1980s, academic computer networks were linking big universities and research centres in the cities of Rio de Janeiro, Sao Paulo and Porto Alegre to the United States. But these networks were independent and were not working together. At the end of the decade, in 1989, all the efforts became coordinated by the foundation of RNP (Rede Nacional de Pesquisas – National Network of Research) and the creation of the national computer network backbone.

From 1991 to 1993, the work was focused in the development of the backbone and by the end of the third year had 11 of the 23 states connected in speeds from 9.6 to 64kbps. At the same time, the Internet services available were being explained to the academic community, through seminars and training showing their strategic value to the country, while the computer communication addicts started the big BBS boom in the country. The second part of the Internet development in Brazil happened from 1994 to 1996, concerning the need for increasing the backbone speed and reliability due to the great number of institutions connected to the Net. In addition a big change was being noticed: people used to Gopher and FTP started to use the new World Wide Web. In May 1995 the commercial Internet started to work in Brazil bringing new frontiers to be explored.

The current phase started in 1997 and brought infrastructure developments such as increasing the number international connections to five and promoting high speed metropolitan networks (MANs). The first tests with the Internet2 project have just happened (April 1999) and were successful.

**Author response**

Internet2 is, despite the rather arrogant name, a project to connect mostly American universities via newer, faster network technology. There is no 'second Internet' under construction.

The growth of the Internet on the planet was really amazing. From 213 Internet hosts in August of 1981 to 43.2 million in January of 1999 (source: Network Wizards). Meanwhile, what happened in Latin America? As we all know, big changes take time to arrive and settle in the developing and third world countries. Cultural, political and economical issues are responsible for that. But as the world is being changed and the 'Global Village' is more and more a reality, technology is coming faster and these countries already have an important role in cyberspace.

Take Brazil as an example. There were more than 215 000 Internet hosts as at January 1999 (ibid.) in the country, which makes Brazil the world's 17th largest country in number of hosts and the first in Latin America. The second place is Mexico showing around 112 000 Internet hosts. If we look at South America, Brazil has a big lead. The second place in number of hosts is Argentina, with about 66 000 hosts.

Countries in Latin America have a great Internet growing potential. Internet users in Brazil represent only 2.1 per cent (source: NUA Internet surveys) of the population and in Mexico 0.5 per cent (ibid.). Comparing to Canada (5th in number of hosts in the world) and Denmark (14th place), that have respectively 26 per cent and 22 per cent of Internet users among the population. The Latin American countries have a lot to show. As development countries become more developed and more technological, these numbers should increase. In the next 5 years we should see a Latino country in the world's top 10 countries in number of Internet hosts and users.

**BRAZIL**

**2**

---

When you are looking for a company on the Net, what is the first thing you do? Well, you guess the URL, like www.company.com. If you are looking for a company in a certain country, just after the TLD (Top Level Domain), you add the country domain, as in www.company.com.br.

But there is not an international standard for TLDs and it is becoming more and more difficult to guess. Some countries adopt different number of letters for TLDs acronyms, as in South Africa (co.za, gov.za, school.za) and also some countries adopt their own language to build the TLDs, as in Brazil (psi.br for Internet service providers, lel.br for auctioneers, esp.br for sports) and Mexico (gob.mx for government).

**BRAZIL**

**3**

---

The Internet is not American. The Internet doesn't belong to anybody or any country. Once PGP was released on the Internet it was already part of it – the Internet that knows no borders. How could it be possible to control something like that on the Internet?

**BRAZIL**

**4**

Maybe it should be mentioned here that a) credit card numbers are not secret, and knowledge of one is not sufficient proof that you have a right to bill the corresponding account and b) numbers can also be stolen by waiters, hotel receptionists and so on.

**SWEDEN**

---

There are other pitfalls of such screening. A friend of mine just got an e-mail censored because its subject was 'examination in quality criteria', which in Swedish contained 'kvalitetsexamen'.

**SWEDEN**

**2**

**AFRICA**

Unlike their counterparts in the Western world, the African academic community did not make any known contribution to the Internet development in its early stages. A major role they played within the African context is in the adoption of the Internet in their respective countries. For instance, in South Africa, an Internet user community was first established some years ago within the academic community, who were the only ones with local access to full Internet. The academic network was called UniNet. A number of store and forward dial-up services operated for the non-govermental organisation (NGO) community and computer enthusiasts, and some businesses used CompuServe (before it had full Internet). As more of these services sprung up, UniNet relaxed its membership policies a little, allowing the NGO e-mail service provider (SANHGONet) to become the first non-academic or government system on full Internet in South Africa (Jensen, 1996).

At the continental level of academic network, the AAU (Association of African Universities) has been playing a significant role. The AUU presently links 119 universities in 42 African countries.

For lack of adequate telecommunications infrastructure, less than 1 percent of the world's Internet traffic currently reaches Africa: the telephone network hardly exists. Compare Sweden (with 68 telephone connections per 100 inhabitants), the USA (with 57), and the Netherlands (49) on the one hand to Zimbabwe (with 1.22), Ghana (0.3), and Chad (0.07) on the other. Not all Internet traffic travels via the public telephone network. Very busy routes are served by lines with very large throughput capacity, which are dedicated to Internet traffic and usually leased from the public network. But these backbones of the Internet are found nowhere in Africa except South Africa. To obtain a fast Internet connection in Kenya or Cameron, you need a leased line to the UK, France, or South Africa. Hegener (1995) reported Donald Ekong, the AAU Executive Secretary, as observing that African scientists often hardly know what their colleagues at other universities are doing, and they lack the capability to disseminate their own research results throughout Africa. The extreme shortage of up-to-date academic publications at practically all African universities could be remedied with a robust Internet link, a powerful printer, and a plentiful supply of paper.

**AFRICA**

Bandwidth is measured in number of bits per second (bps). As the bandwidth capacity is commonly in thousands of bps, the standard units of measurements are in Kbps (Kilo bps), Mbps (Mega bps), Gbps (Giga bps), and so on. Bandwidth usage for Internet ranges from the 9.6Kbps, 14Kbps, 24Kbps, 64Kbps, 128Kbps, 256Kbps, ...2.8Mbps.

As the bandwidth capacity is directly proportional to its costs, in most African counties, bandwidth capacity usage for Internet purposes is often limited to the lower range.

**AFRICA**

The dial-up (also called store and forward) Internet connection is the common starting point for Internet development in African countries. In fact, it remains so up till present time. Fidonet, Healthnet, Esanet, and other similar NGOs do effectively use the dial-up Internet connections for institutional electronic networking purposes.

**AFRICA**

The fact that Ethernet is a relatively cheap and easy to install network technology has made it one of the popularly used network protocols in African countries.

# Further African Comments

Further comments on this chapter from the African commenting author, Sunday Ojo, were much longer than most other comments in this book. Like those following Chapter 6, from Terrell Ward Bynum, they form an entire essay. However, the issue of Africa and the Internet is relevant not only to discussions on Africa itself, but is equally applicable to consideration of other Third World countries and the Internet. Dr Ojo's commentary is therefore included here in full.

# African Commentary

### Sunday Ojo on Chapter 2

It is a well-known fact that the utility of the Internet depends to a great extend on the quality of the underlying telecommunication infrastructure. Unlike the economically advanced world, the poor quality of the network still remains a basic impediment to rapid development of the Internet in Africa.

Generally, African countries, except for a few, are experiencing rather slow extension and modernisation of their telecommunication networks, Sub-Saharan Africa's (excluding South Africa) teledensity has continued to remain at less than 1 per 200 inhabitants, most of the telecommunication network is analogue and many sections are highly unreliable, especially during the rainy season. Despite the poor telecommunication infrastructure, in recent times, 94.5% of the 54 African countries presently have some level of Internet development.

As at June 1999, 51 out of 54 African countries have Internet access in the capital cities, 3 have no local Internet access, 7 have only one public access ISP, while 13 have local ISPs or points of presence (POPs) in some secondary towns. Dial-up Internet access remains the commonest in most African countries. As at March 1999, for the whole of Africa, dial-up Internet accounts stood at 428 075, international bandwidth at 114 454 Kbps, public access ISPs at 319. South Africa is counted among the top 20 countries worldwide for the number of Internet hosts. If South Africa is excluded from the African Internet statistics, the rest of Africa put together is still behind in Internet developments. For example, of these figures, South Africa alone accounts for 46%, 30%, and 78% of the Internet accounts, international bandwidth, and public access ISPs, respectively. The Internet density (population/user) for Africa as a whole is 1819, while that of South Africa alone is 4123 (AIC 1999a, 1999b).

The costs of Internet access vary widely from one African country to another. Monthly subscriptions for dial-up Internet access with ISPs average US$53.49 and range between minimum US$13.97 in South Africa to maximum US$197.74 in Djibouti (AIC, 1999b). This means that in some countries, even if a computer is available, the service is beyond the reach of all but the top elite. Also, because telephone call charges to the service provider are usually the major cost, the absence of a national service effectively cuts off the majority of the population from the Internet. Reflecting the high cost of full Internet-based services, and also because of the overriding importance of electronic mail, the small e-mail-only store and forward systems with dial-up connections to the Internet are generally continuing to attract subscribers.

In recent times, some African public telecommunications operators, PTTs, have started to establish Internet services. For example, PTTs in Benin, Central African Republic, Djibouti, Mauritius, Madagascar, Senegal, Botswana and South Africa have recently brought full Internet services on stream.

The majority of international connections to the rest of the Internet operate on analogue circuits rated at 9.6Kbps, but often pushed to 14Kbps and sometimes to 24Kbps or even 64Kbps. None of the countries outside South Africa had international circuits larger than 64Kbps until very recently when Tunisia and Egypt upgraded to 128Kbps. By contrast, South Africa has a half dozen international links, most of which are over 256Kbps and some are up to 2.8Mbps. While some Internet circuits in Africa connect to the United Kingdom and France, (as well as one to Italy), the majority connect to the USA where suppliers include AT&T, Global One, UUNET/AlterNet, MCI, NSN, Sprint and BBN. Nevertheless, France Telecom/FCR has more Internet connections into Africa than any other single supplier, largely because of its close ties with Francophone PTTs.

Aside from the marine optical fibre link in South Africa and Djibouti, which has access to the SEA-ME-WEA cable, most of the other international connections are carried via satellite, except for the countries having borders shared with South Africa. For these countries, the lower-cost terrestrial links and historical ties have resulted in all of the ISPs there connecting to the South African infrastructure.

Because of the high cost and low international bandwidth available in many African countries, increasing attention has recently been drawn to the possibility of using satellites for Internet services using VSAT. It offers reasonably high bandwidth (64K–2Mbps) and substantially lower costs than most PTT-supplied international leased circuits. Existence of regulatory barriers has stymied most attempts to use this technology so far, except in a number of countries including Botswana, Ghana, Uganda and Zambia, where the telecoms market has been substantially relaxed. As a result there are a number of countries with VSAT-based Internet Service Providers, for example InfoMail and Starcom in Uganda, and one each in Ghana (NCS) and Zambia (ZamNet).

The recent availability of the higher-powered KU-band satellite footprint in southern Africa, and the prospect of other KU bands being directed at Africa shortly, further improves the potential for VSAT. There are other satellite-based communication systems being planned that are expected to radically improve access from the most remote areas of the continent. However, the costs are unlikely to be within the reach of the average African citizen.

Most countries in Africa have some form of local or internationally-hosted Web server with varying degrees of comprehensiveness, but the quantity of information is generally very limited.

Of particular importance for Internet developments in Africa has been the establishment of national cross-sectoral Internet working groups comprising actual or potential Internet access providers, users, telecommunications operators and government. These groups have been formed in Angola, Ethipia, Gabon, Gambia, Namibia, Sierra Leone, South Africa and Tanzania. On a related note, in East Africa, the East African Internet Association (EAIA) has formally been registered. It is the first regional grouping of Internet Service Providers, collaborating to improve their service, share resources and ultimately to set up an international hub to share leased line costs.

Donor agencies including NGOs and multilateral organisations are playing major roles in Internet development in Africa. For example, in Zimbabwe in 1990, a co-operative of local and international NGOs established MANGO, the first store-and-forward e-mail gateway to the Internet in sub-Saharan Africa outside South Africa. Used as a model for many of the other store-and-forward systems in Africa, the non-profit service grew quickly to the point where there are now over 250 users accessing the service through a single phone line using the highly efficient FIDO protocol. Despite the recent emergence of full Internet services, MANGO continues to operate successfully as a low-cost alternative for those whose primary requirement is e-mail. In November 1995 a collaboration between BellaNet, UNESCO, IDRC, UNECA and ITU, called the African Network Initiative (ANI), made a study on future information-infrastructure building activities in Africa. It identified a substantial number of ICT-related development projects being planned or in process in Africa. These and over 100 other finalised projects were identified during the study, with others added subsequently in preparation for this report, indicating an unexpectedly high level of activity in this area from the international community (Jensen, 1996).

# URLs

1. http://www.att.com/
2. http://www.bbn.com/
3. http://www.bell-labs.com/
4. http://www.lucent.com/
5. http://www.fidonet.org/
6. http://www.irc.net/
7. http://www.sendmail.org/
8. http://www.sendmail.com/company/manage.html#CTO
9. http://www.iana.org/postel/
10. http://www.iana.org/
11. http://www.isoc.org/
12. http://www.ietf.org/
13. http://www.gnu.org/people/rms.html
14. http://www.gnu.org/
15. http://www.gnu.org/copyleft/copyleft.html
16. http://www.gnu.org/fsf/
17. http://www.gnu.org/philosophy/free-sw.html
18. http://www.opensource.org/bsd-license.html
19. http://www.mckusick.com/
20. http://www.x.org/
21. http://www.opensource.org/bsd-license.html
22. http://www.xfree86.org/
23. http://www.ssc.com/linux/linus.html
24. http://www.linux.org/
25. http://www.freebsd.org/
26. http://www.openbsd.org/
27. http://www.idg.net/metcalfe/
28. http://www.xerox.com/
29. http://www.3com.com/
30. http://www.infoworld.com/
31. http://www.isc.org/bind.html
32. http://www.sun.com/
33. http://www.sun.com/corporateoverview/ceo/mgt-mcnealy.html
34. http://www.sun.com/corporateoverview/ceo/mgt-joy.html
35. http://www.oreilly.com/
36. http://www.oreilly.com/oreilly/tim_bio.html
37. http://www.uiuc.edu/ph/www/krol
38. http://www.oreilly.com/catalog/twi2/
39. http://www.w3.org/
40. http://www.w3.org/People/Berners-Lee/
41. http://www.cern.ch/
42. http://www.w3.org/Protocols/
43. http://www.w3.org/MarkUp/

44. http://www.w3.org/Addressing/
45. http://www.ncsa.uiuc.edu/
46. http://hoohoo.ncsa.uiuc.edu/
47. http://www.ncsa.uiuc.edu/SDG/Software/Mosaic/
48. http://hoohoo.ncsa.uiuc.edu/cgi/
49. http://www.perl.com/
50. http://www.wall.org/~larry
51. http://www.yahoo.com/
52. http://home.netscape.com/company/about/backgrounder.html#execteam
53. http://www.netscape.com/
54. http://www.wired.com/wired/
55. http://www.hotwired.com/
56. http://www.apache.org/
57. http://www.aol.com/
58. http://www.compuserve.com/
59. http://www.microsoft.com/
60. http://www.msn.com/
61. http://www.microsoft.com/BillGates/
62. http://www.microsoft.com/ie/
63. http://www.networksolutions.com/
64. http://www.icann.org/
65. http://www.amazon.com/
66. http://www.geocities.com/
67. http://www.dell.com/
68. http://www.hotmail.com/
69. http://www.cnn.com/
70. http://www.lycos.com/
71. http://www.altavista.com/
72. http://www.pgp.com/
73. http://www.w3.org/
74. http://www.w3.org/XML/
75. http://java.sun.com/
76. http://squid.nlanr.net/
77. http://www.realaudio.com/
78. http://www.mp3.com/
79. http://www.redhat.com/
80. http://www.freshmeat.net/
81. http://www.slashdot.org/
82. http://www.opensource.org/
83. http://www.tuxedo.org/~esr/
84. http://www.mozilla.org/
85. http://www.icq.com/
86. http://purl.org/dc/
87. http://www.w3.org/RDF/
88. http://www.askjeeves.com/

# 3 What is New or Unique about Internet Activities?

**JOHN WECKERT**

*The thing that hath been, it is that which shall be; and that which is done is that which shall be done: and there is no new thing under the sun.* (Ecclesiastes, Chapter 1, Verse 9).

Whether this statement of King Solomon's is true or not with respect to the subject of this chapter depends on how one looks at it. The way that many activities are conducted on the Internet are, or seem to be, new or unique, but in many cases they could be considered merely as variations on what has been done for years, or even millennia. For quite some time, people have been talking to each other, sometimes face to face, sometimes using the telephone, and sometimes by letter. Now e-mail, chat groups and other Internet facilities may be used as well; but it is still talking! People have been reading printed material in various guises, and sometimes copying what they read, for several thousand years. Now of course we read material that has been transmitted and stored in electronic form on the Internet; but the process is still one of gaining information from the written word.

There is a sense, of course, in which these and many other activities are new or unique in their Internet incarnation, where the Internet is defined, as in Chapter 2, as a large network of networks with various connection protocols. Many common human activities have never been conducted in quite this way before. What is of more interest here is whether the way in which these activities are conducted raises new or unique ethical questions. It can be argued that the problems might not be new, but the context is, and so it is important to examine the issues in their new context, to see if new answers are required. A number of features of the Internet do seem to be sufficiently different from anything that has gone before to allow it to be said that ethical questions are raised in new or unique ways. Those features to be considered in this chapter are the global scale of the Internet, the increased scope for anonymity, the possibilities for interactivity and repro-ducibility, and the uncontrollability of the Internet. Other people, of course, might include different features.

These features for discussion have not been chosen arbitrarily. A number of ethical controversies have flared up in recent years as a result of this medium, especially in the areas of intellectual property, privacy and censorship. None of the issues themselves are unique, but they have become more urgent than before because of the Internet's global scale and certain of its features, for example, the ease of duplication and distribution of material, and the facilitation of recording activity.

## Global scale

The Internet is a global medium, allowing easy personal international communication. It is not the first medium with this capacity, of course; the telephone also allows for easy international communication. The telephone, however, on its own does not allow the same *level* of communication, particularly with respect to an individual's ability to send messages to large numbers of people. On the Internet this may be done using, for example, list servers, mailing lists or news groups. In addition, the recipients of such messages can respond, which makes the medium very different from, say, satellite television, which also give the ability to distribute messages worldwide (although not, in general, to separate individuals).

Thus the Internet is notably different from other media. However, to what extent can the Internet be described as global? From a world population of some 6 billion, there are approximately 150 million Internet users, that is about 2.5 per cent of the world's population. When we examine usage statistics, it appears that the 15 countries (actually *domains* since China and Hong Kong have different domains, .cn and .hk respectively, while China would argue that Taiwan, .tw, and Macau, .mo, are Chinese territories that are temporarily under other jurisdictions) that make most use of the Internet have a combined population of about 2 billion, with about 130 million Internet users, that is a user rate of about 6.5 per cent. The remaining 200 or so countries have a total population of some 4 billion, but only about 20 million Internet users, that is a user rate of about 0.5 per cent.

| Table 3.1 | Population and Internet users | | |
|---|---|---|---|
| | *Population* | *Internet users* | *Percentage of population* |
| *World* | 6 billion | 150 million | 2.5 |
| *Top 15 countries in Internet use, including P.R. China* | 2 billion | 130 million | 6.5 |
| *Top 15 countries in Internet use, excluding P.R. China* | 0.8 billion | 127 million | 16 |
| *Rest of world Internet use, including P.R. China* | 5.2 billion | 23 million | 0.4 |

Furthermore, when we examine volume of traffic, the top 15 countries account for about 89 per cent. It is interesting to note that although China is one of these 15 countries, the number of actual users in China is rather low – about 3 million out of a total population of 1.25 billion. Considering the 15 countries in terms of users, all are Western apart from China, Japan and Taiwan, and just over half of the total number of users are in the USA (Computer Industry Almanac Inc., 1998; World Population Profile: 1998). Given this Internet user distribution pattern, is it appropriate to consider the Internet a global medium? Certainly it is global to the extent that it appears to have a presence in most countries, but not to the extent that most of the worlds' inhabitants use it or even have the opportunity to use it. Thus, while a global medium exists that permits personal international communication of a type not available previously, this facility is not yet widely used or even widely available on a global scale. Furthermore, given the extent of poverty in the world, it is unlikely that availability will increase in the foreseeable future.

We now consider a couple of uncontroversial benefits of the Internet's global nature, such as it is, before examining some of the more controversial ones.

For the first time it is easy and relatively inexpensive for ordinary people to communicate with others around the world. This enables individuals to gain a greater understanding of other cultures, other lifestyles and other points of view. This increased understanding between peoples and greater knowledge of other places has a number of obvious benefits. Greater understanding can lead to increased tolerance, and this in turn could enhance the chances for a more peaceful world. Unfortunately however, communication does not necessarily increase understanding in a way that leads to tolerance, as recent events in many countries illustrate. [RUSSIA **1**] Another benefit is that exposure to other cultures, places and peoples increases the richness of the human experience, which has the potential to make our lives more satisfying and rewarding. Such experience also shows that there are alternative ways of conducting our lives, which can help individuals to break out of what Mill calls the 'despotism of custom' (Spitz, 1975, p. 66). Certainly these benefits are also possible, and to some extent have been realised, with the telephone and satellite television. However, the Internet facilitates broader communication than is possible with the telephone, as well as the transfer of files containing information, music and images. Satellite television transmits images all over the world, but it does not enable the average person in the street to broadcast their own messages or pictures, or to receive responses if they could.

*benefits*

These benefits make it appear that the global nature of the Internet is something which morally ought to be fostered. Of course it is moral to work for world peace, with fuller and richer lives for all. It would appear that this leads to a moral responsibility to make the Internet available to all. Perhaps this is right, but there is much more to be said about the global aspects of the Internet before we come to any firm conclusions.

We look next at electronic commerce because of its perceived importance on the Internet. The importance of the Internet here is largely a result of its unique features, compared with other media, especially the telephone and satellite television. Ordinary people can sell their wares worldwide in a manner not easily possible before.

We are regularly told what a great thing electronic commerce is. A recent joint statement by the Australian and United States governments on electronic commerce says:

> The growing information economy is a truly global phenomenon, which has the potential to improve the lives of all citizens, whether they live in our cities, or rural and regional Australia. Harnessed effectively, the information economy will continue to provide more and more opportunities to businesses large and small, and employment growth.

> Co-operation will take place in a range of areas designed to accelerate the growth of the information economy and electronic commerce, to promote better standards of living for all in our emerging networked economies (Australia-US, 1998).

It is true that electronic commerce has the potential to open up new markets, give greater choice to consumers and make shopping more convenient so to this extent it could promote better living standards [HONG KONG 1] if also leading to less exercise, and perhaps fatty degeneration of the heart in consequence, and to a regrettable reduction in face-to-face personal interaction. However there is an underlying ethical issue which must be considered with respect to equity – that is, will the existence of the Internet help reduce or increase the distribution of wealth?

Electronic commerce is more than just buying and selling goods via the Internet, but we will concentrate on that aspect, briefly exploring the issue of freedom, and make a few comments on cultural imperialism. Of course other ethical problems have frequently been raised in connection with the Internet, particularly those concerning privacy and intellectual property. Important as those are, they will not concern us for the moment. Privacy is discussed in detail in Chapter 4, and we will consider intellectual property in a later section.

A number of freedoms underlie current thought on electronic commerce, principally free trade, freedom of choice, and to some extent, freedom of expression. While the first of these may be seen largely as a political and legal matter, the issue does nevertheless contain moral aspects. It is difficult to control Internet activity, so trade in that medium, by its very nature, is free. National boundaries are largely irrelevant to electronic communication, and it is consequently difficult to stop products which can be transported electronically entering a country, or to place tariffs on such goods. Does this matter, many may ask? We live in a world where the virtues of free trade are extolled, even if more in the rhetoric than in the practice. But is free trade really so good, and just how free is Internet trade in reality?

The first of these questions has relevance here because there is a sense in which trade conducted over the Internet is difficult to control, therefore if free trade is not so good, perhaps we should seriously reconsider this form of trade. The second question calls into doubt common claims made about electronic commerce on the Internet. Trade can really only be free among more or less equal trading partners, but this is not the case on the Internet, any more than elsewhere. The situation is not one in which all Internet users have more or less equal resources and abilities. The situation is rather one of great inequality. Where this is the case, stronger groups will have more material available, it will be of higher quality and more sophisticated, at least in appearance, it will be promoted more effectively, and so on. Despite what is often said, there is no level playing field, even on the Internet: the Internet does not provide the environment for truly free trade, as its proponents often claim. The richer and more knowledgeable have a large advantage over others.

An implication of freedom of choice is that, while pleasant in the short term, it can easily limit choice in the longer term. For example, if too many people in Australia buy their books through Internet vendors, eventually all will be forced to buy that way, as local bookshops will go out of business. Another aspect of free trade and freedom of choice concerns trade in so-called 'cultural products': movies, television programmes, music, and the like. There has been some debate about this in recent years, and it is not obvious that limiting free trade in such products is not justified. Questions of respect for others, and of self respect, as well as rights are involved. Do groups have a right to protect their culture, or should freedom reign supreme? It can be argued plausibly that they do. [HONG KONG **2**]

This leads on to a consideration of cultural imperialism, a topic which has long been discussed with regard to satellite television. According to Bullock and Stallybrass (1977, p. 303)

> *Cultural imperialism* may be defined as the use of political and economic power to exalt and spread the values and habits of a foreign culture at the expense of a native culture.

Electronic commerce (EC) does seem to contribute to cultural imperialism. Consider the following example. For EC to be successful, there must be certain uniform global regulations, or at least practices. In the West, we are rather wedded to the notion of intellectual property, but this is not the case worldwide. However, to facilitate the kind of commerce practised in the West, pressure has been put on those with different traditions to conform with Western practices. Given that the idea and practice of intellectual property is very much a cultural thing, this is a clear case where electronic commerce does encourage cultural imperialism. [RUSSIA **2**] This case is a clear example of an old problem appearing in a new guise largely because of the Internet. The problem of intellectual property did not arise because of the Internet and is not limited to it. However, with the advent of the ease of copying and transmission using that medium, it has become more important that this form of property is recognised and protected by law, worldwide.

Another area where the global nature of the Internet impinges on the ethical is 'giving offence'. On the Internet, people of various religions, customs and moralities come into contact, and in such situations, offending those we do not understand well is a constant danger. In the Internet context, one can be offensive (intentionally or unintentionally) by how one behaves, for example by insulting others or being aggressive, or by the design and content of Web pages. Designing one's own Web pages shares features with paintings, drawings and other art work, as well as with the design of book covers, posters, television images and so on, but it allows people to be on the world stage, as it were, much more easily. Few people get to design book covers that will go on display to the world, but many design and create Web pages that are accessible worldwide.

There are various reasons why someone might consider a Web page offensive, potentially relating to language, images, layout or colours. Mullet and Sano (1995, p. 198) give a few examples of icons that might offend. These include images depicting death or violence, and the thumbs up or down signs, which have different meanings in different cultures. How much this should be taken seriously into account by Web users, whether individuals or corporations, is debatable. After all, almost anything might offend someone. However, because certain language, images and so on are undoubtedly potentially offensive to many, it is worth looking more carefully at the risks of giving and taking offence.

Two questions emerge: (1) What, if anything, is wrong with giving offence; and (2) Why do people take offence? In answer to (1) one may be inclined to say that there is nothing really wrong with giving offence. After all, if people are so silly or sensitive that they become hurt at something said or seen, so much the worse for them. While this contains some truth, it is a little severe, but we will return to this after a brief look at (2).

Obviously offence is taken for different reasons by different people and over a wide range of areas, religion, sex, cultural practices and beliefs, and so on. A reasonable explanation of why I am hurt is that I identify closely with beliefs that this sort of behaviour is wrong, and in a way I feel violated. If you expose me to these things that you know I do not like, then you are not showing me the respect that I deserve as a person. Even if the offence-causing incident was not directed at me in particular, I may feel that it indicates people like me are not sufficiently respected. In both cases I may feel devalued as a person.

Giving offence, of course, is sometimes serious, and therefore should be taken into consideration in Web page design. Clearly, however, there cannot be a sensible law against giving offence in general. Almost anything might offend some sensitive soul; we would be reduced to virtual silence. On the other hand, some offences seem serious enough to warrant restriction. Various governments have attempted this, with mixed results. The Communications Decency Act in the USA had only a short life, although perhaps resurrection is possible; currently in Australia (May 1999), a bill to restrict Internet content is before Parliament.

Offence is a relevant consideration in Web page design. While it is almost certain that not all offence can be avoided, care should be taken to avoid giving offence to particular groups. Web page designers and owners have a moral obligation to know something of the culture and values of those likely to use their pages.

This section has considered various aspects of the global nature of the Internet. Other media are also global, particularly the telephone and satellite television, but there are relevant differences between these and the Internet, with respect, especially, to the capacity of ordinary people to transmit messages as well as files of information, pictures and so on, to large numbers of others worldwide. This raises some ethical questions, none of which are new in themselves, or raised only in this medium, but which have become more important or important in new contexts because of the medium.

## Anonymity

If the editor of this book, let's call him Duncan, received the material for this chapter unsolicited and without knowledge of its authorship, but published it anyway, its author would be anonymous. If Duncan received the material from me knowing that it was from me, but published it without revealing my name, it would still have an anonymous author, although in this case I would be fairly easily traceable. In both cases I would be anonymous to the readers of this book, and in the first, to Duncan as well. What is important here is that anonymity only makes sense in some context. Nobody is just anonymous, but rather he or she might be anonymous with respect to some group of people at some point in time. If Duncan publishes this chapter without my name or anything that could identify me, then I would be anonymous to the readers of this book, but not anonymous to my colleagues; and this would remain true even if these two sets of people overlapped, that is if some of my colleagues read the chapter without knowing its authorship. I could be an anonymous author and a non-anonymous colleague to the same person at the same time.

Anonymity has become an important issue on the Internet for several reasons. One is its relationship with privacy. Some degree of privacy on the Internet is desirable, so anonymity is often seen as useful, or perhaps even essential in some contexts. But anonymity has become an important issue for another reason, as well. An anonymous person cannot be held accountable for his or her actions, which clearly must make it easier for law breakers to avoid detection.

Anonymity is not new. Authors have been publishing anonymously for centuries; it is not difficult to send letters anonymously, or to make anonymous telephone calls. So there is no absolute difference here between the Internet and other media. But there are two significant differences. One is that on the Internet someone can, somewhat paradoxically, have a great degree of anonymity. I may telephone individuals, send letters and write books anonymously, but I can reach many more people anonymously on the Internet. A second difference is that on the Internet, because of the ease of recording activity, anonymity has taken on a new importance. In some circumstances it appears to be the only practical way to protect individual privacy, and perhaps peace of mind.

We will now consider three issues regarding anonymity on the Internet: first, given the technology, is there, or can there be real anonymity; second, for what purposes do people use or want to use anonymity; and, finally, what – if any – are the moral issues raised by anonymity?

First, there are various technical means available that enable one to achieve anonymity of varying degrees; these issues are discussed in detail in Chapter 2. Essentially, technology does provide various means that allow Internet users, for most practical purposes, to be anonymous on that medium. Of course, technology is usually a two-edged sword, and undoubtedly as new and more sophisticated methods are developed that enhance anonymity capabilities, parallel developments will provide ways of discovering the sources of messages. On the Internet, however, if one wants to remain anonymous, most of the time it is possible without too much trouble.

The second issue concerns the *uses* of anonymity. One use is communication in a chat group, without revelation of true identity. Another is sending e-mails, particularly, although not exclusively, for the purposes of spamming and flaming. A third, and perhaps the most important use, is to protect privacy. For example, visits to Web sites can be easily recorded, and the records used for a variety of purposes, not all of them necessarily in the best interests of the user. Visiting sites anonymously, while cumbersome, grants a degree of protection. Visiting Web sites anonymously is a way of protecting personal privacy, and privacy is commonly thought to be a good thing. (For a detailed discussion of Internet privacy, see Chapter 4.)

There are also concerns about *cookies* (defined in Chapter 2) and other ways in which personal information on a visitor to a Web site is collected and stored. If the site cannot identify the origin of a particular visit, no information can be collected with respect to the person who visited. It might be objected that this is not a good way of protecting privacy; it would perhaps be better if the information was not collected in the first place. This is probably true, but in the Internet world it must be remembered that information is easy to collect and store, and may well be very useful to those collecting it. Lack of anonymity also has some benefits for those visiting Web sites, in that presented information may be tailored to their particular needs. Given these facts, it is unrealistic to assume recording of information will cease. In order to protect personal privacy, there may therefore be no real alternative to anonymity. Anonymity then can be seen as an aid to something, personal privacy, which is desirable.

The final, and for us the most important, issue is the moral questions raised by Internet anonymity. There is a sense in which the desire for anonymity seems morally dubious. If you have nothing to hide, why act anonymously? If you are not ashamed of your actions, why are you not willing for others to know about them? But clearly the situation is not necessarily like this. Consider chat groups. Many people, it seems, like to chat anonymously for a variety of reasons, most of which are not morally objectionable. People feel freer to express their opinions, some of which it might be dangerous to express any other way. Some like to explore different personae in a safe and non-threatening way. Others simply like to 'make believe' (see examples in Dyson, 1998, and Turkle, 1997).

This may be fairly innocuous morally, but things become more interesting when there is intentional deception involved. Consider the case of the male who posed as a disabled female psychiatrist on a chat group. It is in general wrong to intentionally deceive, although this can be overridden if the deception is necessary for bringing about a greater good, and it might be argued that the fake psychiatrist did good where, without the deception, this would not have been possible (discussed in Stone, 1995, pp. 71ff.). The situations mentioned in this paragraph would be very difficult to create in any current environment apart from the Internet. It is not easy to find environments in which one can talk with groups of people in ways that make identification impossible. So anonymity is not necessarily morally objectionable, but can in fact be an important good. Indeed, at times it may be the only practical way to protect personal privacy.

There is, however, a downside to anonymity. As was noted earlier, it is easier to annoy and insult others when anonymous, and it is much better to be anonymous when committing a crime. Crime *is* committed on the Internet, and it would be much better for all, except obviously the criminals, if there were no anonymity in those cases. Money is laundered, terrorist activities organised, confidential information acquired, and it may be difficult to discover the perpetrators. If everything on the Internet were transparent, Internet related crime would be much more difficult.

Two further issues which reveal a negative side to anonymity are accountability and trust. While individuals ought to be able to be held accountable for their actions, this cannot happen where they are anonymous. To have a well functioning society in which most people can be happy, there must also be a high level of trust. However, it is difficult to build up such trust if we cannot be sure with whom we are dealing. If anonymity is vital for privacy, we may have to pay the price of loss of accountability and trust. It is true that much in this paragraph also applies in the non-Internet world, but it is worth remembering why anonymity looms so large an issue on the Internet. Recording, and therefore monitoring and surveillance of activity in this medium, is extremely easy, and hence there is great potential for concern about personal privacy. Anonymity takes on an importance that it does not normally possess in other contexts. The debate about caller IDs on telephones concerned the same issue, but the degree of loss of privacy is much less. Anonymity on the Internet is more akin to anonymity with respect to telephone calls, library borrowing, shopping, recreational activities, and so on. We might not care about anonymity in all of these activities all of the time, but neither do we want all that we do recorded. Indeed, if the actions of all people were recorded, wouldn't that be an Orwellian state of affairs, and unacceptable to most of us? This emphasises the special nature of the anonymity debate with regard to the Internet.

## Interactivity

The Internet is a medium that enables easy and rapid communication between people who are geographically remote from each other. The telephone also allows this, but in addition to one-to-one communication, the Internet permits one-to-many, group-to-group, and many-to-many interaction, through News Groups, MOOs, Listservers, Web sites and so on. (See Chapter 2 for technical discussions of these.) In addition, the Internet allows the transfer of digitally stored material, for example, articles, pictures and music. This interactivity allows electronic, or virtual, 'communities' to develop in a way not previously possible. Such communities are not restricted by geography, and being a member of one is voluntary in a way that membership of a local geographical community is not. We briefly consider what might be the good and not so good points of these communities.

There are many good points. We can communicate with others from many parts of the world much more easily than previously, and can be part of communities composed of people from various cultures and countries. Housebound people can be part of communities in ways not possible before, and can therefore overcome much of their isolation. Indeed, anyone can, as (Rheingold, 1991) mentions, have a sense of security in having a community available twenty-four hours a day to which one can go for advice. The housebound can even be part of work communities by telecommuting (Khalifa and Davison, forthcoming). Telecommuting enables the housebound to be productive members of the workforce. It can also reduce the need for office and other workspace, thereby reducing costs to employers, and can lessen the number of people regularly travelling to work, which in turn is beneficial for reducing traffic problems, including pollution, in cities. Although teleworking is not limited to the Internet it has increased the scope and flexibility of these alternative work arrangements.

However, as usual, there is another side to consider. While we all like to communicate and socialise with those with similar interests and views, in our geographical communities we are forced to mix with many different sorts of people, not all of whom we particularly like or with whom we agree. On the Internet it is easy to just mix with those with whom we agree, thereby reinforcing our beliefs and attitudes.

The interactivity created by the Internet, could, somewhat paradoxically, lead to greater bigotry. Telecommuting is not an unqualified good for all either. For many people, work is where they have much of their social activity. Working at home can be lonely and isolating, and it can increase the risk of exploitation. It is much more difficult for workers working alone to unite to fight for acceptable working conditions.

## Reproducibility

Copying and distributing works of art, music, poems and other literature in itself is nothing new, but now we seem to have moved into another phase. Copying and distributing material that is stored electronically is easy, quick and inexpensive and, moreover, the copy is indistinguishable from the original. In consequence, such copying and distribution has caused problems for the software industry since its inception. Not only is there a vast amount of material to copy on the Internet, but this material normally can be distributed over a network with the greatest of ease, allowing a very much wider distribution than before. It may be directed, for example via a mailing list, or collected, for example through a home page.

This ease of reproducibility and distribution has a number of important consequences. One is that it is now possible to develop virtual libraries, which can give access to vast amounts of material in a way never before possible. It matters not where I live, because the total content of the virtual library is accessible to me anywhere that I can use my computer and where there is a telephone connection. Thus people living in remote areas are not so disadvantaged with respect to their city cousins in what they can read. The same is true, in a more restricted sense, with virtual art galleries. If the art is electronic, then everyone visiting can view what are in effect originals, regardless of where they are geographically located. More conventional art works, particularly paintings, can be scanned, and copies placed in the virtual gallery. While this has undoubted value, it is not quite the same as seeing the original. Another consequence of reproducibility and electronic distribution is online music. No longer is it necessary to go to town to buy a record, tape or CD. One can just download the music and play it. While it costs more connecting to the Internet from remote regions, that cost is usually still less than travelling hundreds of kilometres to the nearest library, art gallery or music shop, something not uncommon in some countries.

These are all good things, and, used appropriately, can improve our quality of life. However, there are a number of problems, especially related to the preservation, altering and copying of material. First, preservation. This may not seem at first sight to be a major problem. In principle electronically stored material can last as well as that on paper and, anyway, most things are not so valuable that it matters if they are destroyed or lost. Both of these points are true, but to some extent miss the point. A major problem with electronically stored material is that relatively elaborate equipment is required to read it. I cannot read a computer file in the way that I can read a book. So not only does the file need to be preserved, but so does the technology necessary to read it. On the Internet there is a further problem. The addresses, or URLs, of Web sites that contain information are frequently changed, thereby making it difficult to find locations that one had previously seen, while some sites disappear altogether. These problems are not, of course insurmountable, but more care is required in preservation than with more conventional media. While most written material has a very short useful life, this is not the case with all. The world would undoubtedly be a poorer place without ancient texts and significant literature from the last few centuries; the same is true with respect to works of art and music.

A related, but different issue is that of the ease of altering material. Electronic text can be altered without any trace of the change being easily detectable. This can clearly lead to problems in knowing whether what one is reading is actually what the original author really wrote. If the text was obtained from a suitably protected and trustworthy site, the problem is minimal, but not all sites are, and one does not always know if they are. The issue of trust on the Internet is currently one of the most important research and development fields, and rightly so (see Schneider, 1999). The case of altering images is even more interesting, and raises a number of ethical questions, for example, when is it legitimate to manipulate an image, who owns the altered version, and how can such images be used? (see Weckert and Adeney, 1996). The manipulation of images is not unique to the Internet, but with the plethora of material on Web sites, and much of it images that can readily be copied to one's own hard disk, the scope for doing both interesting and creative things as well as potentially damaging things has increased dramatically. It would not be difficult, for example, to publish on the Web a 'photograph' of a public figure in some compromising situation; indeed, the Web site www.whitehouse.com formerly had such a picture, involving the President of the USA and his wife in just such a compromising position.

While the issues of preservation and manipulation are important ones, the chief ethical concern raised by this ease of copying and distribution relates to the idea of intellectual property, an idea to which the capitalist West is very wedded. However, largely because of the impact of the Internet, it seems that some basic ideas may need to be rethought. Current copyright and patent laws do not suit software or any digitally stored information very well, and there are difficulties in enforcing restrictions on copying and distribution of material over the Internet. Current copyright laws in countries like Australia have been fairly successful in controlling the copying of paper documents, the medium for which the laws were established. Physical documents are published and these cannot be copied except for fairly clearly defined purposes and within narrow parameters. The widespread use of photocopiers raised some initial problems, but these seem to have been largely overcome. Whether solutions are possible on the Internet is still an open question. Technologies are available to block those without permission from visiting particular Web sites, so it is possible to allow only those who have paid to see the material that it contains. It is also possible to create files which are difficult to alter, and these can have various levels of password protection. But, it can plausibly be asked, is all this worth doing? It does, after all, limit the Internet as a place for the free exchange of ideas and free communication. Is it really a good idea to make the Internet little more than an electronic version of what we have already, just to protect intellectual property? Perhaps we should forget the whole idea of intellectual property on the Internet, and stop treating it as a variation of a paper-based medium.

## Uncontrollability

Although the anarchic nature of the Internet with its high levels of freedom of speech and expression are lauded by a vociferous few, many people are genuinely concerned about cultural invasion and the spread of undesirable material such as pornography.

However, can content and activity on the Internet be controlled? Certainly domain names can be, and the interconnection gateways between backbones can be cut, as can the content of individual servers. (These terms are defined in Chapter 2.) While it is commonly claimed that the Internet is difficult to control, perhaps a more accurate statement would be to say that it is difficult to control just certain content and activities of the Internet in a way that would leave the rest untouched. Internet Service Providers can be made responsible for content, as is the case in Singapore, but whether they can effectively filter out only unwanted material without degrading the service is another matter. Sites containing prohibited material can be shut down, but there is nothing to stop a new site containing identical material from being established. Limited and effective control is difficult because of the very nature of the network.

A second problem with control is its global nature. Who will make the rules, who will enforce them – and how? We now examine whether there are any good reasons to want to control Internet content, and issues of non-technical content control.

Although some may argue that the Internet should be completely unregulated, there do seem to be good reasons for some degree of regulation, assuming of course that regulation is technically possible. While freedom of speech and expression are seen as good by many in the West, few even in the West believe that anybody should be able to say anything at any time. Privacy laws, for example, protect what can be said publicly about someone's private life. Regulations protecting trade secrets restrict the publication of those secrets, and libel laws limit what can be said about other people. To this extent, the Internet is already regulated, at least in jurisdictions with those kinds of laws. This seems reasonable, and is accepted by most people.

Temperatures rise much more when regulation, real or proposed, concerns things such as pornography and hate language. This reaction is a little odd, given that in most countries the popular media are restricted in these areas. Perhaps the argument is that on the Internet these things must be sought out, they do not 'hit one in the face', as they would in the press. This is true, but such information is easily accessible, and it is difficult to stop access once it is available. If it is also justifiable for other media, some degree of Internet regulation does appear to be justifiable.

While it might be justifiable to control some aspects of Internet activity, problems arise with respect to how this might be done. Suppose that pornography (assuming a clear definition is available) is made illegal. Where will it be illegal? In all countries in which the Internet operates? Such international cooperation would be amazing. It is not even easy to get agreement within one country. Consider the case where a Californian couple placed pornographic material on a site in the California Bay Area:

> [A California couple] were indicted for transmitting pornographic material to a government agent in Tennessee. A jury in Memphis wasted little time ruling that the images – which included pictures of women having sex with animals – were obscene. But [this] case raised the tricky constitutional question of which locale's community standards should have been used to make the judgement: Tennessee's Bible Belt, California's Bay Area or the virtual community of cyberspace? (Cole, 1995, p. 53)

Suppose that the necessary cooperation did occur internationally, how would the law be policed? Given the nature of the Internet, large scale monitoring and surveillance would be required to keep track of the offending sites and to see who was visiting them. The Internet Service Providers (ISPs) potentially could be made responsible, but then they would have to monitor all Internet traffic. Even if it were technically possible, this would hardly make for an efficient Internet; privacy questions also emerge.

It is not only those who would like to censor pornographic material who can have problems with the content of the Internet. Finding reliable information among the vast amount available can be difficult. Articles in journals have passed peer review and editorial examination, and magazine and newspaper proprietors must take some responsibility for what is printed, but on the Internet there is not even minimal control. Anything can be placed on a Web site. This is not necessarily bad, but it does mean that more care is needed in giving credence to what is read or seen. This problem has led to various techniques, such as trust marks, being developed to ensure that certain Web sites do contain reliable information.

Several other moral problems follow from the abundance of uncontrolled content. One is plagiarism and cheating. This has always occurred, but it is much easier now for dishonest or fearful students, for example, to obtain assignment answers and so on from sources which are unlikely ever to be discovered by their assessors. Another, raised by (Nissenbaum, 1999), is how to establish priority for a discovery, invention or idea. There is a certain amount of prestige, and sometimes financial benefit, involved in being the first to write or make something. Once it was relatively easy to know who was first. Just see who published first in a reputable journal. It was never quite this simple – private correspondence in the form of letters could also be relevant – but now the problem is immense. In order to claim priority is one required to examine all the material on the Internet? That impossibility suggests that this is another area where some rethinking is in order.

## Conclusion

This chapter just scratches the surface of what might be new or unique about the Internet medium, new or unique in degree if not in kind. In particular, it does not go into depth on the ethical questions raised, but hopefully, it does at least hint at what some of the important questions may be.

## Comments

This makes assumptions about current patterns of shopping. Perhaps it is true in Australia and the USA, but it is not true in many other locations, least of all Hong Kong where, despite quite high penetration of the Internet, e-commerce has spectacularly failed to make a big mark. Why? Because of a) trust and b) the delight in hands-on purchasing, – a social activity, and c) convenience, 5 minutes walk, maximum, for 99 per cent of the 6.5 million population.

**HONG KONG**

**HONG KONG**

A cultural comment – Bhutan only legalised access to the Internet and ownership of a TV with effect from June 1st, 1999. The Kingdom of Thunder deliberately chose to protect its culture and people by banning all forms of access. While one of the poorest countries in Asia, it does not have the grinding, abject poverty so commonly seen elsewhere in the continent, notably in its neighbour India. Was lack of freedom to watch or participate a bad thing?

**RUSSIA**

I would agree with the contention that the chances for a more peaceful world are enhanced with increased tolerance. However it must be said that interconnection of such things as 'increased tolerance', 'greater understanding of other cultures' and 'communication with others around the world' is not of a simple type. It seems to be useful (for clarification of this interconnection) to pay attention to the verb 'can' in John Weckert's assertion: 'Greater understanding can lead to increased tolerance...' Yes, greater understanding can lead to increased tolerance. But can it lead to increased intolerance? Sometimes a person becomes less tolerant to a foreign country's inhabitants just after his or her visit to that country. Normally one knows more about people of neighbour nations and ethnic groups than about people of remote countries, but conflicts often emerge just between neighbours. Did a long history of German and Slav peoples' communication make for anti-Slavism as an important part of German Nazi ideology? It can be argued that there is rather misunderstanding than understanding in cases like that mentioned above. But without doubt communication does take place in all these cases. So communication and understanding are connected but in an involved way. Is war conditioned by lack of understanding? How can communication contribute to more peaceful world? The Internet seems to inherit these problems from 'old', 'non-electronic' ways of communication.

**RUSSIA**

I doubt if there is cultural imperialism in the Internet at all. Anyway the Internet looks a less appropriate medium for 'imperialistic cultural policy' in comparison with television. For example, groups pretending to promote Russian native cultural values tend to accuse Russian TV companies of serving the US interests. While there is practically no room for such groups on TV, they are rather active on the Internet. I believe one should be careful employing the notion of cultural imperialism. This notion can conceal contradictions within national self-reflection. How can one distinguish between 'native' and 'foreign' cultural values? What is 'native' and what is 'foreign' in present Russia: religiousness or scepticism towards religion? Collectivism or individualism? Respect or disrespect for property rights? Cultural imperialism is bound up with prevalence of foreign informational production. Now we have such a prevalence of American movies in Russia. But what 'foreign values' do the movies promote? If there is a lot of violence in the movies, should one conclude that violence is a value of the USA? If actors do not look overburdened with intelligence, should one conclude that low intellectual level is an American value? If computer games – including those available in Internet – are full of violence , does it follow that violence is a cultural value in the countries where the games are produced? All these conclusions would be too hasty. So reference to cultural imperialism can conceal a problem of informational production quality.

# 4 Privacy and Security

**HERMAN T. TAVANI**

In this chapter, a range of privacy and security issues associated with the Internet are examined. The first section considers some definitions and theories of privacy, and it concludes with a brief look at why privacy is considered an important human value. The next section contrasts privacy concerns currently associated with the Internet with privacy issues introduced by earlier information and communications technologies. Certain privacy issues introduced by pre-Internet technologies, but which are now exacerbated by activities on the Internet, are then examined, and privacy threats attributable to Internet-specific tools and techniques are considered. Finally, issues and concerns directly related to security on the Internet are examined and some current proposals – both legal and technological – for resolving security and privacy issues on the Internet are considered. The chapter concludes with the suggestion that in establishing privacy policies for the Internet era there are good reasons to proceed according to what DeCew (1997) and others describe as a 'presumption in favor of privacy'.

## What is personal privacy?

Some authors suggest that it is more useful to view privacy as either a presumed or stipulated *interest* that individuals have with respect to protecting personal information, personal property, or personal space than to think about privacy as a moral or legal right. For example, Clarke (1999) points out that privacy can be thought of as an 'interest individuals have in sustaining personal space free from interference by other people and organisations.' Others have suggested that personal privacy be viewed in terms of an economic interest, and that information about individuals can be thought of in terms of personal property that could be bought and sold in the commercial sphere. For practical considerations, it might seem fruitful to approach privacy issues simply from the vantage point of various stipulated interests. Many Western European nations have preferred to approach questions involving individual privacy as issues of *data protection* – that is, as an interest in protecting personal information – rather than in terms of a normative concept that needs philosophical analysis. In the US, on the other hand, discussions involving the concept of privacy as a legal right are rooted in extensive legal and philosophical argumentation.

A brief description of some of the philosophical and legal foundations of privacy will be useful in helping us to understand exactly what privacy is, why it is valued, and how it is currently threatened by certain activities on the Internet. It will also help us to differentiate between some subtle, yet significant, aspects of personal privacy. For example, it will enable us to distinguish between the *condition* of privacy (that is, what is required to have privacy) and a *right* to privacy, and between a *loss* of privacy and a *violation* of privacy. The purpose of our brief look at certain privacy theories is not so much to determine whether privacy is or ought to be a right – moral, legal, or otherwise – but rather to understand better how one's privacy is threatened by certain activities on the Internet. Privacy theories can, for purposes of this chapter, be organised into four broad types or categories: the 'non-intrusion,' 'seclusion,' 'limitation,' and 'control' theories (see Tavani, 1996). Let us briefly consider each theory.

## Theories of privacy

Expanding on a view of privacy introduced in an influential article by Warren and Brandeis (1890), some argue that personal privacy consists of 'being let alone' or 'being free from intrusion'. Certain proponents of this view, which we can call the *non-intrusion theory* of privacy, tend to confuse the condition (or content) of privacy with a right to privacy. Brennan (1972), for example, describes privacy in terms of a *right* to be free from intrusion. Another problem with the non-intrusion theory is that in equating privacy with being let alone, this theory seems to confuse privacy with liberty. Critics point out that it is possible for one not to be let alone (that is, to be denied liberty) but still have privacy, and for one to be let alone and yet not have privacy. So while privacy and liberty may be closely related, the two notions can and should be distinguished. Unfortunately, the non-intrusion theory of privacy fails to do this.

Another view of privacy, which we can call the *seclusion theory*, equates personal privacy with 'being alone'. Westin (1967), for example, describes privacy as the 'voluntary and temporary withdrawal of a person from the general society through physical [means] in a state of solitude'. A virtue of the seclusion theory is that, unlike the non-intrusion theory, it differentiates privacy from liberty. Its weakness, on the other hand, is that it tends to confuse privacy with solitude by tacitly assuming that the more alone one is, the more privacy one has. On this view, it would seem to follow that a person stranded on a deserted island would have maximum privacy. Critics point out, however, that it is possible for one to have privacy while not necessarily having complete solitude, and for one to have solitude and yet not have privacy. So the seclusion theory would not seem to be an adequate account of privacy.

A relatively recent theory that has received considerable attention is the *control theory* of privacy. On this theory, one has privacy if and only if one has control over information about oneself (see Fried, 1970; Rachels, 1975). One virtue of the control theory is that it separates privacy from both liberty and solitude. Another of its virtues, and perhaps its major insight and contribution to the literature on privacy, is that the control theory correctly recognises the aspect of choice that an individual who has privacy enjoys in being able to grant, as well as to deny, individuals access to information about oneself. However, critics note that the control theory has at least two major flaws: one that is practical in nature, and the other that is theoretical or conceptual. On a practical level, one is never able to have complete control over every piece of information about oneself. And a theoretical or conceptual difficulty arises for control theorists who seem to suggest that one could conceivably reveal every bit of personal information about oneself and yet also be said to retain personal privacy. The prospect of someone disclosing all of his or her personal information and still somehow retaining personal privacy, merely because he or she retains control over whether to reveal that information, is indeed counter to the way we ordinarily view privacy. Another weakness of the control theory is that in focusing almost exclusively on the aspect of control or choice, it tends to confuse privacy with autonomy.

Another relatively recent theory that has received much attention is one that can be described as the *limitation theory*. According to those who subscribe to this theory (see, for example, Allen, 1988; Gavison, 1980), privacy consists of the condition of having access to information about oneself limited or restricted in certain contexts. The limitation theory of privacy, unlike the control theory, correctly recognises the importance of setting up contexts or 'zones' of privacy. Another strength of this theory is that it avoids confusing privacy with autonomy as well as with liberty and solitude. One problem with the limitation theory, however, is that it tends to underestimate the role of control or choice that is also required in one's having privacy. That is, it ignores the fact that someone who has privacy can choose to grant, as well as to limit or deny, others access to information about oneself. Some variations of the limitation theory also suggest that to the extent that access to information about a person is limited, the more privacy that person has. On this view, privacy would seem to be confused with secrecy.

So it would seem that none of the four theories examined thus far is adequate. Each theory confuses privacy with one or more related notions: liberty, solitude, autonomy, or secrecy. Also, none of the theories clearly distinguishes between the condition of privacy and a right to privacy, and between a loss of privacy and a violation of privacy. However, each theory seems to offer some insight into what is essential for individuals to have privacy; and the control and limitation theories are particularly useful in helping us understand privacy issues involving personal information and access to that information (that is, what some now call 'informational privacy'). Can these various accounts of privacy somehow be successfully combined into one coherent theory?

Recently, Moor (1997) has advanced an account of privacy, called the *control/restricted access theory*, in which he argues that an individual has privacy in a 'situation' if in that particular situation the individual is 'protected from intrusion, interference, and information access by others'. Two points in this definition of privacy are worth noting. First, by including the notions of intrusion and interference as well as information access in his definition, Moor's theory provides a more comprehensive account of privacy than any of the four theories considered above. Second, Moor's definition of a *situation* is left deliberately vague so that it can apply to a range of contexts or 'zones' that we normally regard as private – for example, a situation can be an 'activity', a 'relationship', or the 'storage and access of information' in a computer or on the Internet.

Central to Moor's theory is his distinction between 'naturally private' and 'normatively private' situations, which enables us to differentiate between the condition of privacy and a right to privacy, and between the loss of privacy and a violation of privacy. In a naturally private situation, individuals are protected by 'natural' means – for example, physical boundaries in natural settings, such as when one is hiking alone in the woods – from access, interference, or intrusion by others. Here, privacy can be *lost* but not *violated* because there are no norms – conventional, legal, or ethical – according to which one has a *right* to be protected. In a normatively private situation, on the other hand, individuals are protected by conventional norms. Moor's account is similar to the limitation theory in that privacy is understood in terms of contexts, namely, situations, in which access to individuals is limited or restricted. And it is similar to the control theory in arguing that individuals affected by a certain situation must have some control or choice – albeit limited (not absolute) control – in determining whether that situation will be declared normatively private. To consider the control/restricted access theory in the detail that it deserves would, unfortunately, take us beyond the scope of this chapter. See Tavani (1997, 1998) for examples of how Moor's theory can be applied to two different kinds of privacy concerns on the Internet.

## Why is privacy important?

The privacy theories briefly considered in the preceding section provide a backdrop for our discussion of particular Internet-related privacy issues in this chapter. Before directly considering those specific issues, however, it is perhaps first worth considering whether and why privacy is considered an important human value. Also if we hope to arrive at meaningful Internet privacy policies, which would ideally have international application, it would be useful to understand some of the attitudes and beliefs that individuals and groups in various nations and cultures hold about the value of privacy. We can begin by inquiring into whether privacy is something that is valued only in Western industrialised societies, where much emphasis is placed on the importance of the individual, or whether it is universally valued.

It would appear that in some non-Western nations, such as Singapore where the government openly uses information technology to track the activities of its citizens, individual privacy is either relatively unimportant or is a value that is significantly less important than in Western industrialised countries. [SINGAPORE 1] It would also appear that individual privacy is generally valued less in non-democratic nations than it is in countries with strong democratic political institutions. Nations such as the People's Republic of China, which currently restrict their citizens' access to the Internet, seem to assign less importance to individual privacy and greater importance to the value of national security. [HONG KONG 1] Even in countries with strong democratic institutions, but where a priority for national security is paramount, as in the case of Israel, individual privacy does not appear to be viewed as important a value as it is in many democratic nations where there is no continuous threat to a nation's security or to its survival. However, even though privacy is not valued to the same degree in all nations and cultures, and although the degree to which it is valued differs significantly in Western and non-Western countries as well as in democratic and non-democratic nations, privacy does nonetheless seem to be universally valued. Its value in any given nation or culture is, of course, determined by various cultural influences, conditions, and circumstances. For more information on democratic values and the Internet, see Chapter 8.

It would also seem worthwhile to consider whether privacy is an *intrinsic* or an *instrumental* value. That is, does privacy have value in and of itself, or is it valued because it serves as a means to some end(s)? Although few claim that privacy is an intrinsic value, some have suggested that privacy is more than a mere instrumental value. Fried (1970), for example, argues that privacy is essential or necessary for human ends such as trust and friendship. So unlike most instrumental values which are merely a contingent means to various ends, privacy is arguably a necessary means to certain important human ends. Along lines somewhat similar to Fried's, Moor (1997) argues that although privacy is an instrumental value, it also expresses a 'core value' – namely *security* – which is essential or necessary in all cultures for human flourishing. [GERMANY 1] So, again it would seem that privacy can be viewed as more than simply an instrumental value. We return to the question of privacy as a human value in the concluding section of this chapter.

## How is privacy threatened by the Internet?

A number of recent US studies and surveys suggest that online users are very concerned about their privacy while engaged in activities on the Internet. According to a study conducted by the Boston Consulting Group in 1997 (see Wright and Kakalik, 1997), over 70 per cent of 9300 users responded in an online survey that they were 'more concerned about privacy on the Internet' than they were about privacy threats from any other medium. A recent survey conducted by Business Week/Harris survey (see Benassi, 1999) indicated that privacy is the 'number one consumer issue' – ahead of ease of use, spam, security, and cost – facing the Internet. Wang *et al.* (1998), who cite a recent survey undertaken by Equifax and Harris Associates that determined that over two-thirds of online consumers surveyed are very concerned about their privacy on the Internet, believe that the most crucial issue currently facing the emerging e-commerce market is the 'fear and distrust regarding loss of personal privacy'.

Some authors now use the expression 'Internet privacy' to refer to privacy concerns associated with the Internet (see, for example, Cranor, 1999). The use of such an expression might cause us to ask whether we need a separate category of privacy called 'Internet privacy'. To answer this question, we should determine whether any – and if so, which – privacy threats currently associated with the Internet are uniquely attributable to the Internet. However, even if it is determined that some privacy issues are indeed unique or even special to the Internet, we can still consider whether such privacy issues might be adequately handled under certain existing categories of privacy. A brief look at some of those categories would perhaps be useful.

## Two categories of privacy

Some authors draw a distinction between *information privacy* and *communications privacy* (see, for example, Johnson and Nissenbaum, 1995; Regan, 1995). Johnson and Nissenbaum differentiate information- or database-privacy issues from issues in communications privacy by placing in the latter category the set of privacy concerns related to technologies such as electronic surveillance, encryption, e-mail, and digital telephony. Information privacy issues, on the other hand, include those associated with personal information contained in large databases. On this two-fold distinction, it might seem that privacy issues related to the Internet would fall under communications privacy. After all, the Internet is among other things a communications medium.

Certain activities on the Internet have raised privacy concerns that would seem to fall under the heading of communication privacy. Other Internet activities, however, have raised privacy concerns that seem more closely related to information privacy. For example, concerns regarding Internet access to personal information that resides in databases have also been raised. So it would seem that Johnson and Nissenbaum's distinction, which generally works very well in parcelling out pre-Internet privacy issues into two useful categories, will not help us to sort out Internet-related privacy issues from those privacy issues associated with earlier technologies. It might also seem that because there is no easy way to differentiate these privacy issues, a separate 'Internet privacy' category is needed. Of course, we have not yet determined whether any privacy issues currently associated with the Internet are qualitatively or even significantly different from pre-Internet privacy concerns. In deciding whether a separate privacy category is warranted, then, it would be useful to contrast certain Internet and pre-Internet privacy concerns. We begin by briefly examining privacy concerns raised by relevant pre-Internet technologies.

## Privacy threats involving pre-Internet information and communications technologies

First, it is worth noting that concerns about personal privacy existed long before the era of the Internet. For that matter, they existed long before the advent of either modern information or communications technologies. Prior to the information era, for example, certain uses of technologies such as the camera and the telephone raised concerns about personal privacy. Earlier forms of record keeping also raised privacy concerns. The advent of information technology, however, has enabled the collection of information about individuals on a scale that would not have been possible in the pre-computer era. Consider, for example, the amount of personal information that can be gathered and stored electronically in computer databases. Also consider the speed at which such information can be transferred across databases. Contrast these factors with record-keeping practices used before the information technology era, where data had to be manually recorded and stored in folders, which in turn had to be stored in physical repositories.

Since privacy controversies regarding the use of technology to collect and communicate personal data predate the Internet era, it might seem that there is nothing at all new with respect to the privacy issues currently associated with the Internet. For example, it might appear that Internet technologies have merely intensified the debate over concerns already introduced by earlier information and communications technologies. However, merely because certain privacy concerns currently identified with the Internet may have originated with pre-Internet technologies, we should not underestimate the magnitude of the impact that the Internet has had for personal privacy. And more importantly, we should not infer, based on what we have seen thus far, that no new or special privacy threats have been introduced by Internet technologies.

Activities on the Internet have contributed to the ongoing privacy-and-computers debate in at least two ways. First, the Internet has made it possible for certain existing privacy threats to occur on a scale that would not have been possible, in a practical sense, with pre-Internet technologies. This set of privacy concerns, while not original to the Internet, can be said to be *enhanced* by the Internet. Second, it has made possible, by virtue of certain tools and techniques unique to the Internet itself, specific privacy threats that were not possible with earlier information and communications technologies. These latter privacy concerns could be said to be *specific* to the Internet. We next consider both kinds of concerns, which we shall henceforth refer to as *Internet-specific* and *Internet-enhanced* privacy concerns, beginning with an analysis of the latter.

## Internet-enhanced privacy concerns

Privacy concerns that may have arisen because of certain uses of earlier information and communications technologies, but which are now also inextricably associated with and exacerbated by the Internet, can be analysed under two general headings: (i) dataveillance and data gathering, and (ii) data exchange and data mining.

### Dataveillance and data-gathering activities on the Internet

Some authors suggest that the Internet can be viewed as a new 'surveillance medium'. Clarke (1988) uses the term *dataveillance* to refer to the systematic use of systems, which would include the Internet, in the 'monitoring of people's actions or communications'. It has also been suggested that the Internet, because of its surveillance (data monitoring and data recording) mechanisms, poses a threat to privacy on a scale that could not have been realised in the pre-Internet era. In considering such a claim we should first note the obvious, but relevant, point that privacy threats associated with surveillance are by no means unique to the Internet. Long before the era of information technology, private investigators and stalkers engaged in surveillance activities. Some governments have used various means, including both electronic and non-electronic devices, to conduct surveillance of individuals and groups. Private telephone conversations have been subjected to surveillance in the form of wire-tapping. Employees in certain corporations have been frequently placed under surveillance through an employer's use of video cameras and computers. Consumers who shop at certain department stores, or who engage in telephone conversations with businesses have often been subjected to surveillance – for example, video cameras monitoring an individual's physical movements, or telephone-related recording equipment capturing conversations – by those businesses. So surveillance is by no means a recent concern or, for that matter, one that is associated solely or even mainly with the Internet. Nonetheless, concerns over surveillance have, in more recent times, been aggravated by certain activities on the Internet.

In the early days of computing, when computers were owned and operated mostly by large public agencies, it was feared that strong centralised governments would be able to monitor the day-to-day activities of their citizens. Today, however, the threat of surveillance comes not so much from governments and their agencies, at least not in Western democratic societies, as it does from surveillance by online businesses and corporations in the private sector who can now monitor the activities of persons who visit their Web sites, determine how frequently these persons visit those sites, and draw conclusions about which preferences those visitors have when accessing their sites. Even the number of 'click-streams' – key strokes and mouse clicks – entered by a Web-site visitor can be monitored and recorded.

Nissenbaum (1997) points out that very few online users realise that their activities may be 'placed under surveillance'. Data about Internet users can be gathered either directly or indirectly from their online activities. One *direct* method of information gathering involves the use of *Web forms*, a data-gathering mechanism into which Web users enter information online. Forms technology, often used to collect information about Web visitors (such as a user's name and address) can, as Kotz (1998) notes, also be used to track the sequence of pages one visits within a given Web site. For the most part, the use of Web forms would seem to be uncontroversial since online users voluntarily submit the requested information. However, information gained from forms can be combined with other directly gathered information, such as information about the items a user purchases online, and can then be combined with online information about individuals that is gathered indirectly. One *indirect* method for gathering personal information involves the use of *Internet server log files*. Kotz points out that because Web browsers transmit certain kinds of data to a Web server, such as the Internet address of the user's computer system as well as the brand name and version number of the user's Web browser and operating system software, Internet server logs can be used to gather personal data in an indirect manner. [GERMANY 2] Information gathered indirectly from server logs can also be combined with information gained directly from Web forms, which can then eventually be used by advertising agencies to target specific individuals.

Although Web forms and Internet server logs can be used in ways that pose significant threats to the privacy of Internet users, it is worth noting that neither of these two technologies is unique to the Internet since the development and use of both technologies predates the Internet era. However, the scale on which dataveillance and data gathering can be now be carried out has increased dramatically because of the use of forms- and server-log technologies on the Internet.

## Data-exchanging and data-mining activities on the Internet

Whereas the dataveillance and data-gathering tools described in the preceding section are used mainly to monitor and record activities of online users, other tools are used to exchange that data on the Internet. This exchange of online personal information often involves the sale of such data to third parties, which has resulted in commercial profits for certain online entrepreneurs, often without the knowledge and consent of individuals about whom the data is exchanged.

Techniques for exchanging personal data online are hardly new to the Internet. Data-exchange techniques such as the merging and matching of electronic records stored in databases occurred before the Internet era (see, Johnson, 1994; Tavani, 1996). However, Internet technology has facilitated the exchange of online personal information at a rate that was not possible in the pre-Internet era. In response to earlier data-exchange practices involving computer networks, certain privacy laws and data-protection guidelines, such as the 1980 Organization of Economic Cooperation and Development (OECD) principles, have been enacted and implemented. These laws and principles, which specifically address the exchange of personal information between databases in computer networks, would also seem by extension to apply to the exchange of personal data on the Internet as well. More will be said about existing privacy laws and data-protection guidelines later.

Although earlier privacy issues involving the exchange of personal information in databases have centred mainly on the transfer of such information between databases in computer networks, some recent privacy concerns have emerged because of the kind of personal information that can now be extracted or 'mined' from *within* a single database. These concerns arise from certain uses of a technique commonly referred to as *data mining*. Data-mining technology, which combines research in artificial intelligence (AI) and pattern recognition, is defined by Cavoukian (1998) as a 'set of automated techniques used to extract buried or previously unknown pieces of information from large databases'. Using data-mining techniques, it is possible to unearth patterns and relationships, which were previously unknown, and to use this 'new' information – that is, new 'facts' and relationships in the data – to make decisions and forecasts.

Through the use of data-mining algorithms, individual pieces of data about an online user's activities, which in themselves might seem innocuous, can be recorded, combined, and recombined in ways to construct profiles of individuals. As a result of data-mining applications, an individual might eventually discover that he or she belongs to some consumer category or some risk group, the existence of which he or she had been previously unaware. Furthermore, decisions can be made about an individual based merely on his or her identification with a certain consumer group. For example, an individual with an impeccable credit history could be denied a loan on the basis of that individual's identification with some 'new' consumer risk group or category that was 'discovered' via data mining (see Tavani, 1999).

The mining of personal data in the pre-Internet era, which depended on the use of large commercial databases called *data warehouses* to store the data, focused mainly on transactional information. Personal data mined from the Internet, however, need not be (and frequently is not) transactional. For example, information typically included in and mined from personal Web pages, as well as non-commercial Web sites, is non-transactional. Because of Internet commerce, however, much transactional information can now also be gained from the Web as well. When an individual orders a book from Amazon.com (an online book store), for instance, transactional information is recorded about the purchase, and information about that particular transaction can be (and frequently is) used for future business decisions. What distinguishes the Internet as a mining resource from the large databases or data warehouses used in data mining, however, is the vast amount of non-transactional, personal information currently available for mining on the Internet.

Cavoukian (1998), who points out that one of the purposes of data mining is to 'map the unexplored terrain of the Internet', notes that the Internet is becoming an 'emerging frontier for data mining'. She also notes that with access to an Internet server, it is possible to FTP (file transfer protocol) the data from the client's server and then conduct various data mining activities. Fulda (1998) points out that because data-mining software employs certain AI techniques, it can 'learn' about the Web by coming to understand the content associated with common HTML tags. Eisenberg (1996) notes that *intelligent agents* can 'sift through' the potential wealth of data on the Internet, and Etzioni (1996) describes the use of 'learning techniques' or systems such as *softbots* (intelligent software robots or agents that use tools on a person's behalf) and metasearch engines (such as MetaCrawler and Ahoy) to uncover general patterns at individual Web sites and across multiple Web sites. So data-mining techniques that previously raised privacy concerns only at the database or data-warehouse level now raise concerns that impact Internet users as well.

Although data-mining techniques are currently used on the Internet, we have also seen that the use of that technology predates the Internet era. So in this sense, privacy issues associated with data mining on the Internet are similar in kind to privacy concerns associated with Web forms and Internet server log files. Like the privacy concerns raised by the use of these latter tools or technologies, concerns raised by data-mining technology are not unique to the Internet. Instead, they are instances of what we have earlier identified as Internet-enhanced privacy concerns.

## Internet-specific privacy concerns

We next examine privacy issues that are specific to, rather than merely enhanced by, activities on the Internet. Privacy concerns that are attributable to tools and techniques provided by the Internet itself, which we described earlier as 'Internet-specific' concerns, arise mainly from the use of two new types of online tools and technique. One technique is used for gathering personal data, whereas the other tool can be used to locate personal information on the Internet.

### Internet cookies: a new technique for gathering personal data

Through the use of a data-gathering technique called *Internet cookies* (see Chapter 2 for a complete definition) online businesses and Web-site owners can store and retrieve information about a user who visits their Web sites, typically without that user's knowledge or consent. Cookies technology has generated considerable controversy, in large part, because of the novel way in which certain information about Internet users can be collected and stored. Information about an individual's online browsing preferences can be 'captured' while that user is visiting a Web site, and then stored on a file placed on the hard drive of the user's computer system. The information can then be retrieved from the user's computer system and resubmitted to a Web site the next time the user accesses that site. Cookies technology is the only data-gathering technique that actually stores the data it gathers about a user on the user's computer system.

The owners and operators of one Web site cannot access cookies-related information pertaining to a user's activities on another Web site. However, information about a user's activities on different Web sites can, under certain circumstances, be gathered and compiled by online advertising agencies. For example, online advertising agencies such as *DoubleClick.net*, who pay to place advertisements on Web sites, include a link from a host site's Web page to the advertising agency's URL. So when a user accesses a Web page that contains an advertisement from *DoubleClick.net*, a cookie is sent to the user's system not only from the requested Web site but also from that online advertising agency. The advertising agency can then retrieve the cookie from the user's system and use the information it acquires about that user in its marketing advertisements. The agency can also acquire information about that user from cookies retrieved from other Web sites the user has visited, assuming that the agency advertises on those sites as well. The information can then be combined and cross-referenced in ways that enable a marketing profile of that user's online activities to be constructed and used in more direct advertisements.

Several privacy advocates have argued that because cookies technology involves the monitoring and recording of a user's activities while visiting Web sites (without informing the user) as well as the subsequent downloading of that information onto a user's computer system, that technology violates the user's privacy. Defenders of cookies, who are usually owners of online businesses and Web sites, maintain that they are performing a service for repeat users of a Web site by customising a user's means of information retrieval and by providing the user with a list of preferences for future visits to that Web site. Despite any alleged advantages provided by cookies to users who frequently visit one or more Web sites, most users surveyed indicated that they are more concerned about not losing their privacy while visiting Web sites than they are with gaining customised retrieval preferences for their favourite sites. According to a 1996 Equifax/Harris Internet Consumer Privacy Survey (cited in Wright and Kakalik, 1997), 64 per cent of respondents believed that providers of online services and Web sites should not be able to track users' activities on the Internet, including the Web sites they visit, regardless of whether that information is eventually used by online advertisers.

To assist Internet users in their concerns about cookies, a number of privacy-enhancing tools (see below) have recently been made available. One such product from Pretty Good Privacy (PGP) is *pgpcookie.cutter*, which enables users to identify and block cookies on a selective basis. In the newer versions of most Web browsers, users have an option to 'disable' cookies. As such, users can either opt in or opt out of cookies, assuming that they are aware of cookies technology and assuming that they know how to enable and disable that technology on their Web browsers. The reason that privacy threats associated with cookies can be categorised as an Internet-specific privacy concern, of course, is that the privacy threats posed by that particular data-gathering technique are unique to the Internet.

## Internet search engines: a new tool for retrieving personal information

Internet technology has also provided tools that support new techniques for retrieving information about persons. Wright and Kakalik (1997) note that a certain kind of information about individuals, which was once difficult to find and even more difficult to cross-reference, is now readily accessible and collectible through the use of automated search facilities on the Internet. These facilities are called *Internet search engines*. Included in the list of potential topics on which search-engine users can inquire is information about individual persons. By entering the name of an individual in the search-engine program's entry box, search engine users can potentially retrieve information about that individual. However, because an individual may be unaware that his or her name is among those included in a database accessible to a search-engine, or because he or she might be altogether unfamiliar with search-engine programs and their ability to retrieve information about persons, questions concerning the implications of search engines for personal privacy have been raised (see Tavani, 1997).

A search for a person's name will often return the addresses of Web pages written by that person or the addresses of Web sites that include information about that person. Kotz (1998) points out that since many e-mail discussion lists are stored and archived on Web pages, it is possible for a search engine to locate information that users contribute to electronic mailing lists or *listservers* (defined in Chapter 3). Search engines can also search through archives of *newsgroups* (defined in Chapter 3), such as *Usenet*, on which online users also post and retrieve information. One such group, *DejaNews*, is set up to save permanent copies of new postings and thus provides search engines with a comprehensive searchable database. DejaNews also provides 'author profiles' which include links to all of the online articles posted by a particular person. Because the various newsgroups contain links to information posted by a person, they can provide search-engine users with considerable insight into that person's interests and activities.

It could be argued that information currently available on the Internet, including information about individual persons, is, by virtue of its residing on the Internet, public information. We can, of course, question whether all of the information currently available on the Internet *should* be viewed as public information. The following scenario (see Tavani, 1997) may cause us to question whether at least some information about individual persons that can be included on a Web server or in a database accessible to Internet users should be viewed as public information. Consider a case in which an individual contributes to a cause sponsored by a homosexual organisation. That individual's contribution is later acknowledged in the organisation's newsletter (a hardcopy publication that has a limited distribution). The organisation's publications, including its newsletter, are then converted to electronic format and included on the organisation's Internet Web site. The Web site is 'discovered' by a search-engine program and an entry about that site's address is recorded in the search engine's database. Suppose that you enter this individual's name in the entry box of a search-engine program and a 'hit' results, identifying that person with a certain homosexual organisation. Since the person identified may have no idea that such publicly available information about his or her activities exists, the use of search-engine technology in this case might indeed raise privacy concerns for the individual in question. [GERMANY **3** ] As in the case of privacy concerns associated with Internet cookies, privacy issues involving search engines did not exist prior to the Internet era.

## Security and the Internet

We now turn to issues directly involving security on the Internet. Many representatives from both the public and private sectors have argued for increased security measures on the Internet, claiming that current security mechanisms are either outdated or inadequate. Earlier we saw that many individuals and businesses have been reluctant to use the Internet because of concerns about privacy. Recent studies show that several individuals and businesses also have elected not to join the Internet because of concerns about security (see Oppliger, 1997).

Before identifying and discussing specific security issues on the Internet, it is useful to note that the concepts of security and privacy are closely related and that certain issues associated with these two notions frequently overlap. However, some important distinctions can and should be drawn. Internet-related privacy concerns often arise because online users are concerned about losing control over personal information about themselves to organisations (especially businesses and government agencies) who claim to have some legitimate need for that information in order to make important decisions affecting them as individuals or affecting the public good. Internet-related security concerns, on the other hand, typically arise because of fears that personal or proprietary information might be accessed and manipulated by individuals (and sometimes by organisations as well) who have no legitimate need for or right to such information.

## Two senses of 'security'

It is important to note that the term 'security' is often used ambiguously and sometimes equivocally in information and communications technology contexts. In one sense, 'security' refers to the set of concerns involving a computer system's vulnerability to viruses, worms, and other 'rogue' programs that can 'attack' a system and its resources. Here, the concern is that individual computer systems connected to the Internet, as well as the Internet itself as a system of computer networks, could be 'sabotaged' because of a lack of adequate security measures. 'Saboteurs' can, through the distribution and execution of rogue programs, severely disrupt activities on the Internet and potentially render the Internet itself inoperable. Internet users realised this possibility for the first time in 1988 when Robert Morris unleashed a program, later described as the 'Internet worm,' that brought activity on the Internet to a virtual standstill. (For a discussion of the morality of individual online behaviour, see Chapter 6.) There is also another sense of 'security' that is concerned not with vulnerability to attacks from rogue programs, but instead with protection from unauthorised access information that either (a) resides in databases accessible to the Internet or (b) is communicated over the Internet from one point to another. Our concern in this chapter is with security issues involving the protection of personal and proprietary information from unauthorised access, and not with security issues involving system sabotage.

To protect against security threats involving unauthorised access to proprietary and highly confidential information, many organisations have used access-control technologies such as *firewalls* (described in Chapter 2). Oppliger (1997) describes a firewall as a 'blockade' between an internal privately owned network that is believed to be secure and an external network, such as the Internet, which is not assumed to be secure. Firewalls help to secure systems not only from unauthorised access to information in databases, but also help prevent unwanted and unauthorised communication into or out of a privately owned network. Recent concerns over secure electronic communication, especially those communications having to do with e-commerce and e-mail, have resulted in a series of proposals involving encryption on the Internet. To appreciate these concerns as well as some of the finer points proposed in certain solutions they have generated, it is useful to understand some basic concepts in cryptography and data encryption.

## Cryptography and data encryption

*Data encryption* or *cryptography*, the art of encrypting and decrypting messages, is hardly new. The practice is commonly believed to date back to the Roman era, where Julius Caesar encrypted messages sent to his generals. Essentially, cryptography involves taking ordinary communication (or 'plain text') and encrypting that information into 'ciphertext'. The party receiving that communication then uses a 'key' to decrypt the ciphertext back into plain text. So long as both parties have the appropriate key, they can decode a message back into its original form or plain text. One challenge in ensuring the integrity of encrypted communications has been to make sure that the key, which must remain private, can be successfully communicated. Thus, an encrypted communication will be only as secure and private as its key.

The cryptographic technique described thus far is referred to as private-key encryption or 'weak encryption', where both parties use the same encryption algorithm and the same private key. A recent technology, called public cryptography or 'strong encryption', uses two keys: one public and the other private. If *A* wishes to communicate with *B*, *A* uses *B*'s public key to encode the message. That message can then only be decoded with *B*'s private key, which is secret. Similarly when *B* responds to *A*, *B* uses *A*'s public key to encrypt the message. That message can be decrypted only by using *A*'s private key. Here the strength is not so much in the encryption algorithm as it is in the system of keys used. Although information about an individual's public key is accessible to others, that individual's ability to communicate encrypted information is not compromised. (See Chapter 2 for more information on strong encryption and cryptography.)

Public-key or strong encryption is of particular interest to governmental agencies responsible for protecting national security and military intelligence, preventing terrorism, and enforcing laws. This type of encryption is also used by many individuals and organisations in the private sector as well in transmitting e-mail messages, where applications such as those provided by PGP (described earlier) are used to prevent unauthorised access to e-mail communications over the Internet. Perhaps no group has been more interested in the security features made possible by strong encryption than those involved in e-commerce. Because many online entrepreneurs believe that strong encryption is essential for realising the full potential of e-commerce, they have looked to encryption-based applications to solve some of their online commerce worries. One current solution has been to ensure authentication between online consumers and merchants through strong-encryption tools that use a system of *digital signatures* (defined in Chapter 2). VeriSign (www.verisign.com), for example, uses a public-key encryption technology to produce a 'digital certificate' which is checked for VeriSign's authentication by both online consumers and online merchants in e-commerce transactions. (For more information on the authentication and integrity of information, see Chapter 7.) VeriSign is also one example of a growing number of recently available *privacy-enhancing technologies*, designed to provide a greater sense of confidence for potential online consumers. We consider some of these technologies in the next section of this chapter, where we also examine some non-technological solutions aimed at resolving security and privacy issues on the Internet.

## Some proposals for an Internet privacy and security policy

A number of proposals that respond to privacy and security concerns on the Internet have recently been put forth. Some proposals call for stricter privacy laws on the part of governments and for the formation of privacy oversight commissions to enforce those laws. Others call for more serious self-regulatory measures by those in the commercial sector. Still other proposals call for technological solutions through the use of privacy-enhancing tools by Internet users. We begin with a look at proposals involving privacy-enhancing technologies.

### Privacy-enhancing technologies and industry self-regulation initiatives

In our discussion of encryption and security features involved in the use of VeriSign in the preceding section, we briefly considered one type of privacy-enhancing technology. Other tools and techniques for enhancing individual privacy are also available for Internet users. One type of application allows online users to be *anonymous* while they interact with the Internet. Certain 'anonymizing' programs provide online users with a considerable degree of anonymity in so far as they make it extremely difficult to identify individual users by linking the Internet activities of those users to a particular Internet (or IP) address. Although many privacy advocates have championed the use of anonymity programs because they allow for greater privacy for online users, it must be also be noted that these tools have raised concerns for security on the Internet. Since anonymity tools also make it difficult to identify and trace the activities of those individuals who engaged in unauthorised activities on the Internet, some government agencies and law enforcement organisations have been critical of these tools.

One of the best known anonymity tools is a program called the *Anonymizer* (www.anonomizer.com). It is important to note, however, that although Anonymizer users enjoy anonymity while visiting Web sites, they are not anony-mous to the Anonymizer itself or to their Internet Service Providers (ISPs). As we saw earlier, most users' activities on Web sites are recorded in server log files and thus, in certain cases, can be traced back to a specific ISP or IP. To enjoy complete anonymity on the Internet, online users need tools that do not require them to place their trust in a single third party. Two currently available anonymity programs that do not require such trust are *Crowds* and *Onion Routing*. Crowds is an anonymity tool based on the idea that people can be anonymous when they 'blend into a crowd'. When Crowds users submit an Internet request such as the URL of a certain Web site, the request is sent to a 'randomly selected member of their crowd'. So neither the server at the end of the destination (such as a partic-ular Web site) nor any member of the 'crowd' can determine where the request originated (see Reiter and Rubin, 1999). A slightly different solution to the problem of needing to trust in a third party is offered by the Onion Router program, through which users submit encrypted requests. An 'onion' – that is, a 'layered data structure' that specifies cryptographic algorithms and keys – is sent to the intended recipient. On this scheme, one 'layer of encryption' is removed according to the 'recipe' contained in the onion, as the data passes between each onion-router along the way. Only the IP address of the last onion-router on the path is revealed to the requested Web site (see Goldschlag *et al.*, 1999). For more information on anonymity on the Internet, see Chapter 3.

While anonymity programs are useful for Internet activities in which users have neither a need nor a desire to be identified, they are not useful for certain online activities which require identification of users. For example, when Internet users wish to make online purchases, they often need to provide some identi-fying information. To attract online consumers who might be inclined to avoid e-commerce activities because of privacy worries, many online entrepreneurs have supported the need for a set of Internet-wide privacy standards. The World Wide Web Consortium (W3C), an international industry consortium, was commissioned to provide these standards. In 1997, W3C announced its Platform for Privacy Preferences (P3P), a standard through which Internet users would be able to specify their own individualised Web privacy preferences. For example, users would be able to enter their privacy preferences into their Web browsers, choosing from a range of options. Users would also have the ability to change their privacy preferences each time they accessed a Web site. On the P3P standard, data exchange between a user and Web site would occur only when a user's indicated privacy preferences match that Web site's stated privacy policy. Although W3C was charged with establishing privacy standards on the Web, it was not set up to enforce the actual protection of personal data. Thus, additional measures are needed to assure users that any personal information that they release to a Web site will be used only in the ways they had specified. Various technologies, sometimes referred to as 'negotiation agents' and 'trust engines' have been developed to assist users in this process.

One industry-backed, privacy initiative, called TRUSTe (www.trustee.org), which is self-regulatory in nature, was designed to ensure that Web sites would indeed adhere to the privacy policies they advertise. TRUSTe uses a branded system of 'trustmarks' (graphic symbols) which represent a Web site's privacy policy regarding its use of personal information. Trustmarks provide consumers with the assurance that a Web site's privacy practices accurately reflect its stated policies, and online users are assured that there will be an audit of the Web site and a means of recourse for them if the Web site does not abide by its stated policies (see Benassi, 1999). Any Web site which bears the TRUSTe mark must satisfy several conditions regarding the disclosure of personal information about users who visit that site. For example, the Web site must clearly explain in advance its general information-collecting practices, including which personally identifiable data will be collected, what the information will be used for, and with whom the information will be shared. Also, the Web site must disclose whether the user will be able to correct and update personally identifiable information, and whether the user information will be removed from that Web site's database upon request (see Wright and Kakalik, 1997).

Critics point out that the practical application of TRUSTe and similar tools may prove difficult. For example, certain critics worry that the amount of information users are required to provide may discourage some users from carefully reading and thus adequately understanding what is expected from them. Other critics point out that the various 'warnings' these tools display may appear 'unfriendly' and thus work against the ideal of easy Web site access and use. They also note that, unfortunately, 'friendlier' trustmarks or graphic icons might result in online users being supplied with less direct information that is important to protecting their privacy. Despite the concerns raised by critics, advocates of tools such as TRUSTe argue that since online users will be better able to make informed choices regarding electronic purchasing and other types of online transactions, those users would clearly benefit from programs like TRUSTe. Certain critics, however, worry that such programs do not go far enough, and some argue that what is also needed is stronger privacy legislation and enforcement of privacy laws.

## Privacy legislation and data-protection principle

In response to recent concerns about privacy and security concerns on the Internet, some nations have recently passed or are currently in the process of seriously considering strong privacy legislation. **[SINGAPORE  2 ]** The US, however, has not been at the forefront of this movement. In 1974 the US Congress passed the Privacy Act, which has been frequently criticised for containing far too many loopholes and for lacking adequate provisions for enforcement. This Act is also restricted in its application to records in federal agencies and thus is not applicable in the private sector. Subsequent privacy legislation in the US has resulted in a patchwork of individual state and federal laws that are neither systematic nor coherent. Generally, the US government has resisted requests from the public for stronger privacy laws, siding instead with various business interests in the private sector whose concerns are based on a belief that such legislation would undermine economic efficiency and thus adversely impact the overall US economy. Critics point out, however, that many of those US businesses who also have subsidiary companies or separate business operations in countries with strong privacy laws and regulations, such as nations in Western Europe, have found little difficulty in complying with the privacy laws of the host countries, and that profits for those American-owned companies have not suffered because of their compliance. In any event, there is now increased pressure on the US government to enact stricter privacy laws and on American businesses to adopt stricter privacy polices and practices because of global e-commerce pressures, especially from Canada and the European Union. For more information on legal issues involving the Internet, see Chapter 5.

We also saw earlier that European nations have, through the implementation of strict data-protection principles, been far more aggressive than the US in addressing privacy concerns of individuals. In 1980, most Western European nations signed up to the Organization for Economic Cooperation and Development (OECD) Principles, and in the early 1990s the European Union began to consider proposals for synthesising the data-protection laws of the individual European nations. The European Union has recently instituted a series of directives, including EU Directive 95/46/EC of the European Parliament and of the Council of Europe of 24 October 1995, which protects the personal data of its citizens by prohibiting the transborder flow of such data to countries that lack 'adequate' protection of personal data. As in the case of Canada, which has also set up privacy oversight agencies with a Privacy Commissioner in each of its provinces, many European countries have their own data-protection agencies. More information on data-protection laws in Europe, including a discussion of the 1998 Data Protection Act as it relates to the Internet, is included in Appendix 1. For a discussion of privacy policies in some Asian nations, including Hong Kong, see Lee (1993). [HONG KONG **2**]

## Two comprehensive proposals

We have seen some of the strengths and limitations of privacy legislation and data-protection principles, industry self-regulation initiatives, and privacy-enhancing technologies as separate privacy proposals. Each type of proposal seems to be important, but at the same time each alone seems inadequate. Perhaps, then, some combination of these individual solutions can be integrated into a more comprehensive and robust privacy policy for the Internet. Clarke (1999) and Wang *et al.* (1998) have recently suggested some possible ways of combing the individual pieces. Arguing for a 'co-regulatory' model, Clarke believes that a successful online-privacy policy must include strong legislation, a privacy oversight commission, and industry self-regulation, and that these provisions must also be accompanied by privacy-enhancing technologies that individuals can use to ensure their privacy. He further believes that a 'privacy watchdog agency' and sanctions are also both needed for the overall privacy scheme to work. [GERMANY **4**]

Wang *et al.* also suggest that governments, businesses, and individuals each have a key role to play in any successful privacy policy. For example, the role of government would be to promote strong privacy laws in both the public and private sectors, to establish independent privacy commissions to oversee the implementation and enforcement of those laws, and to educate the public about privacy issues. Whereas businesses would be responsible for promoting self-regulation for fair information practices and for educating consumers about their online-privacy policies, individuals themselves would be responsible for using privacy-enhancing technologies and security tools. The authors admit, however, that developing an adequate privacy for the Internet is 'one of the most challenging public policy issues of the information age'.

From what we have seen thus far, it would seem that a comprehensive policy similar to the models proposed by Clarke and by Wang *et al.* are clearly needed to ensure adequate privacy protection in the Internet era. Yet some fear that we have gone too far in favor of privacy protection, and that as a result we are in danger of jeopardising the interests of the larger public good (see, for example, Etzioni, 1999). To appreciate this apparent tension, it would be useful to return to our earlier discussion regarding the importance of privacy as a human and social value. [JAPAN **1**]

## Conclusion

We conclude this chapter by briefly elaborating on some points made initially in the earlier section regarding the value of privacy. There we saw that, because privacy is essential for certain ends that are important to us as humans, privacy is considered by many to be more than merely an instrumental value. We later noted that we noted that new technologies often come into conflict with the privacy interests of individuals, and that the Internet is by no means the first technology to raise serious threats to personal privacy. A standard way of framing the debate over interests involving individual privacy and the implementation of a new technology has been in terms of a need to *balance* competing interests (see, for example, Johnson 1994). Because of recent activities on the Internet, some believe that there is an urgent need to balance the privacy interests of individuals against the economic interests of online businesses as well as against the interests of the greater public good – that is, to balance the interests of those groups (such as government agencies and corporations) who claim to have a legitimate need for information about individuals collected on the Internet against the needs or rights of those individuals about whom the information is collected. Others, however, believe that simply using a balancing scheme based on the tradeoff of interests involving the individual good versus the larger social good misses an important point because such a decision procedure fails to take into account the significance of privacy as a social (as well as an individual) value.

Regan (1995) and Blanchette and Johnson (1998) note that when we frame the debate simply in terms of how to balance privacy interests as an individual good against interests involving the larger social good, support for those interests believed to benefit the latter good will generally override concerns regarding individual privacy. For example, if evidence were put forth to show that the use of a certain Internet technology would increase the number of jobs in a community or would raise that community's standard of living, then a decision to use that technology would likely be perceived as yielding a greater overall good than to forgo that technology for the sake of protecting the privacy of individuals. If, however, privacy is understood not merely as a value involving the good of individuals but as one that also contributes to the broader social good – that is, a value that is essential for democracy and freedom – then concerns for individual privacy might have a greater chance of receiving the kind of consideration they deserve in those debates involving the balancing of competing interests. Keeping in mind this understanding of the importance of privacy for our social institutions and human values, it would seem that in future debates involving privacy and the Internet, especially in those nations where strong democratic institutions are valued, there are good reasons to proceed from a position that DeCew (1997) and others describe as a 'presumption in favor of privacy'. [GERMANY **5**]

Throughout this chapter, there has been a presumption on my part that privacy is a positive value which is worth protecting. Essentially, I agree with DeCew (1997) that we should presume in favour of privacy and then develop ways that would 'allow individuals to determine for themselves how and when that presumption should be overridden'. There are, of course, some who would take issue with such a presumption (see, for example, Etzioni, 1999). I agree with Fried (1970) and Moor (1997) that privacy is not an intrinsic value, but rather one that is instrumental in some sense. I also agree with Fried (1970), Johnson (1994), and others that while privacy is not an intrinsic value it is nonetheless essential – that is, a necessary condition – for certain ends such as democracy, autonomy, liberty, and so forth. Clearly, the points raised in the final section of this chapter deserve further development and they require supporting argumentation. To provide that development and support here, unfortunately, would take us beyond the scope of the present chapter. My principal aim in this chapter has been to show how personal privacy and security are currently impacted by certain activities that are either made possible through or exacerbated by the Internet.

# Comments

It is a fallacy to assume that individual privacy is valued less in some countries (for example non-democratic ones) than in others. It is also a misleading statement, since no subject is supplied – is it the individuals themselves who value their privacy less, or their governments, or some other entity? The distinction is important if we are to attempt to reach consensus on a global standard for Internet privacy.

In Hong Kong, the concept of privacy is perhaps not quite so well developed as in other countries, but this does not imply that it is less valued. To borrow from Moor's (1997) normative privacy, Hong Kong people generally have private spaces that, although small, are also considered inviolable. On the MTR (underground trains), people are often crammed together like sardines, yet the conventional norms still apply and so the space remains inviolate, even when one is literally in contact with many other people on all sides. In China, personal privacy has traditionally been 'compromised' by neighbourhood committees. However, the younger generation are much more sensitive about their privacy and much less willing to divulge any private details about themselves to others.

Where the Internet is concerned, Hong Kong people who use the Internet for electronic commerce applications are extremely sensitive about releasing their personal data, especially name, address, salary, contact numbers, credit card or bank details, and so on. In China the same is true, although the opportunities for e-commerce transactions in China are more limited. It must be remembered that a very small fraction of the Chinese population is Internet literate.

### Author response

I agree with the commentator that a distinction can and should be drawn between ways in which privacy might be valued by the individuals in a given nation and by that nation's ruling government. And I agree that such a distinction might be important in helping us to arrive at consensus on a 'global standard for Internet privacy'. I must, however, note one small point of clarification regarding a claim the commentator attributes to me. To be precise, I did not claim that privacy is valued less in some countries (such as non-democratic ones) than in others. Rather, I made the weaker claim or assertion that 'It *would... appear* that...' (italics added).

I am willing to accept that any claim based on the assumption attributed to me by the commentator – namely that privacy is generally less valued in non-Western and non-democratic countries than in Western democratic nations – can be construed as somewhat 'misleading'. I believe that the stronger claim based on such an assumption might even turn out to be empirically false. However, I do not accept the charge that my own claim involves a *fallacy*. Strictly speaking, a fallacy occurs only in argumentation (where a faulty reasoning process is used). An argument exists only where there is an inference involving two or more statements (claims). So even if the stronger claim (attributed to me) about the value of privacy in non-Western nations and cultures turns out to be false, I do not see how any fallacy has necessarily been committed.

Hong Kong currently has some of the strictest data protection legislation to be found anywhere in the world. The Personal Data (Privacy) Ordinance was brought into effect on December 20th, 1996 – see

http://www.pco.org.hk/ord/section_00.html for the full text. The Ordinance covers any data that relates directly or indirectly to a living person (data subject) from which it is 'practicable' to identify that individual and in a form that is readily processible or accessible. It applies to any person (data user) who is responsible for collecting, holding, processing or using the data.

Six data protection principles are specified: data should be collected in a fair and lawful manner; data should be accurate, current, and kept for no longer than necessary; data should be used for the purpose for which it was originally collected – unless the data subject gives specific consent otherwise; appropriate security measures should be applied to the data; data users should be open regarding the data that they hold and the main purposes for which they hold data; data subjects have the right to access and correct their personal data. Exemptions to the Ordinance are specified for data that is: held for domestic or recreational purposes; employment related personal data (access requirements restricted); data that relates to security, defence, international relations, prevention or detection of crime,

assessment and collection of tax, news activities and health.

The Ordinance does cover all data held privately, by public bodies or by government. The Ordinance is overseen by the Privacy Commissioner of Personal Data who, among other powers, has the authority to investigate suspected breaches of the Ordinance's requirements and issue enforcement notices to data users as appropriate. For more details, please see the home page of the Privacy Commissioner's Office: http://www.pco.org.hk/

**Author response**
The commentator correctly points out some of the details in the Hong Kong data-protection scheme described by Lee (1993) and alluded to in Wang, Lee, and Wang (1998). Unfortunately, because of space limitations, I was unable to cover these privacy and data-protection schemes in any detail in the present chapter.

From a Singaporean perspective (and I am not representing the Singapore Government when I make my comments here) I find that there is a lot of misconception that the Singapore Government is using information technology to track the activities of our citizens. In addition, I totally disagree with the author that individual privacy is either relatively unimportant or is a value that is significantly less important than in Western industrialised countries. These two statements are totally untrue.

Being a very small country, we have long recognised that we need to be efficient in order to compete with the Western industrialised countries. As such, our government has embraced the use of technology, especially information technology, for communication, scientific, engineering, business, financial, educational and research purposes. Singapore is perhaps one of the most wired nations in the world. We now have a nation-wide high speed, broadband network called Singapore ONE. All our government ministries and departments have Internet connections.

However, being a Singaporean myself, I must say that our government does not track our activities. On the contrary, our government has done a very good job of using the Internet for the benefits of our community. For example, we can file our income tax returns by submitting our income tax details via the Internet. We have information on child care centres and we can even make online purchases of concert tickets. In fact, the government welcomes feedback from our citizens and the Internet is one of the preferred communication channels. I personally have found that our government agencies have become very responsive to citizens' feedback and complaints about mundane things like dirty public toilets! With the fast Internet connections, our civil servants are always kept on their toes. They know that with the Internet, particularly e-mail messages, no one can escape any sort of criticism for bad or poor service.

I also do not accept the author's other point about individual privacy being relatively unimportant in Singapore. To us, we value social harmony, racial and religious tolerance

**SINGAPORE**

in Singapore. We have people of different races living and working in Singapore. Perhaps some of the things that our government have done might give other Western people the misconception that we do not value individual privacy. However, doing things differently in Singapore does not mean that we do not allow our people freedom of speech and movement. We welcome criticisms but with every criticism of our actions, we have the right to respond and rebut the criticisms with facts and figures. At the end of all these, it is the credibility of our nation that is at stake. We certainly do not encourage our people to engage in antisocial activities all in the name of individual freedom. Imagine what would happen to us if we have many of our students keeping pornographic materials, racial hatred e-mail messages, instructions on making bombs and Internet places to buy weapons. Although we do have the Singapore Broadcasting Authority to set some guidelines for Internet usage and requiring proxy servers to put up a list of 100 undesirable Web sites, there is no such thing as having the government reading our e-mail messages or vetting Web sites before they can be set up.

### Author response

In noting that I failed to differentiate privacy values held by the ruling government of Singapore from privacy values held by individual citizens of that nation, the commentator raises an important criticism. However, I refer the commentator to an interview with Singapore's Minister of Trade and Industry, Brigadier General Lee, in the early 1990s. When questioned about the controversial aspects of the 'People Data Hub' – a database being developed by the government of Singapore to contain detailed information on every Singapore citizen – Lee offered the following remark:

> We do quite a number of things that Western governments would hesitate to do, either because ideologically they feel they should not intrude on personal lives or sometimes because they just don't have the time to do it because the next election is too close around the corner. But [Singapore] is a different society and we have to govern the way the populations accepts being governed. (In Palfreman and Swade, 1991, p. 179)

Lee and other Singapore government officials interviewed during that period (see Palfreman and Swade, 1991, pp. 177–9) suggest that Singapore's citizens are willing to make certain trade-offs regarding individual privacy in order that Singapore as a nation could become a fully fledged information society by the end of the 1990s. Those interviewed Singaporean officials also point out that many of the privacy-related concessions granted by the citizens of Singapore would probably not be so willingly granted by citizens in most Western nations. Remarks such as these are at the basis of my suggestion that individual privacy as a value may be viewed as relatively less important in certain non-Western nations like Singapore than in many Western nations.

On the point of the *value given to individual privacy*, please see response to Hong Kong 1, above.

---

**SINGAPORE**

As far as I know it, we do not have any legislation on privacy and data protection. The only one which is close to it is our Computer Misuse Act of 1993. However, it appears that this Act is very comprehensive and the offences are framed so as to cover every conceivable misuse of computers. We have offences like unauthorised access to computer material, unauthorised access with intent to commit or facilitate commission of further offences, unauthorised modification of computer material, unauthorised use or interception of computer service and abetments and attempts punishable as offences.

Recently, we have an interesting situation in which one of our Internet Service Providers, SingNet, resorted to scanning the computers of their 200 000 customers. These scannings were done without the customers' knowledge and they were carried out to see if their systems 'are vulnerable to hacker attacks'. There is now a debate on whether this Internet Service Provider has done the 'right' thing in not informing the customers but acting in the best interests of their customers. This incident came about when a university student discovered that her computer account had been hacked into from an account with the Ministry of Home Affairs. She had used a protection programme called Jammer and this software detected the intrusion. She subsequently reported to the police and the Internet Service Provider admitted to doing the scanning.

The point about this is that we are still grappling with the issue of privacy. In this particular incident, the student was glad that her computer was not hacked into but she added: 'I strongly think that the subscribers should have been informed about it because anyone with a protection program would think that their systems had been hacked into. And that would have caused a panic.'

Singapore intends to be an electronic commerce hub. So, while we do not have legislation on privacy and data protection, we have started work to provide better infrastructural and promotional services for electronic commerce over the Internet. Recently our government have tabled the Electronic Transaction Bill (ETB) in our parliament. Some of the things that the government wants to do are to: (i) provide commercial code to support electronic commerce transaction, (ii) enable electronic applications and licences for the public sector, (iii) provide public key infrastructure, and (iv) provide limitations on liabilities of intermediaries. The Computer Misuse Act of 1993 will also be updated and there will be a review of the Copyright Act.

**Author response**

The SingNet controversy raises a number of interesting privacy issues, especially with respect to certain trade-offs involving privacy and security as related but competing values. Clearly, both values are important and each needs to be balanced against the other. As I have also pointed out, many cultures and nations – including Western democratic countries such as Israel – tend to place a higher value on national security than on individual privacy.

---

According to German legislation, privacy is a basic human right, not just a means but rather an aspect of the free personal development guaranteed by constitution. This has been clarified by the High Constitutional Court in 1983 within its Census Decision. The most frequently quoted sentence is that free personal development will be hindered if people no longer know what others know about them. The term informational self-determination was introduced into the political and legal debate and legislation was obliged to actively make provisions for protected (communication) and enable informational self-determination. Besides an amendment of the General Data Protection law, this resulted in several special regulations of privacy in telecommunications and information and communication services that will be dealt with below. In 1996, German Parliament set up a study commission on the Future of the Media in Economy and Society which devoted a special report on the subject of 'Security and Protection in the Net' (Enquete-Kommission 1998).

**Author response**

The fact that privacy is a basic human right guaranteed to every German citizen by Germany's Constitution is clearly worth noting. In the US, many citizens speak of their presumed *right* to privacy; yet there is, at present, no such explicit legal right guaranteed in the US Constitution or in its various Amendments. There has, in recent times, been legislation proposed in the US calling for a 'Privacy Bill of Rights' that would guarantee privacy protection to all US citizens. To date, however, US citizens, unlike German citizens, do not enjoy any explicit constitutional protection regarding individual privacy.

## GERMANY

**GERMANY**

**2**

To be technically precise, Web server log files log Internet accesses which are not necessarily related to individual persons. Most Internet service providers have a number of IP addresses, which are given to their users at random when they enter the Internet. If they visit a Web site, the Web server can only log this IP address which might have been used by some other user of this provider some time ago. Therefore the ISP serve as a kind of anonymiser as mentioned below. And therefore owners of commercial Web sites try to get personal information by other means, technical (such as cookies) and organisational (such as forms). As far as IT addresses contain the number or name of an individual computer, they might be anonymised automatically. I have run the city information system of the city of Bremen (www.bremen.de) for some time. We wanted to learn whether our visitors were coming from Bremen, from other areas of Germany or from abroad. We had no interest in knowing their

names. A student changed the log file program in such a way that the part of the IP address that might be related to a person automatically was exchanged by xxxx, like the German Telekom has been obliged by law to anonymise the last three digits of the telephone numbers dialled on their files and single item invoices. However, the standard servers used today no longer allow for this kind of adaptation. Companies like Oracle or Netscape, however, could offer such a privacy option.

**Author response**

Commentator's points accepted. Kotz (1998), however, suggests that through the use of server log files *in conjunction with* other direct and indirect data-gathering mechanisms, such as Web forms, the identities of many online users can eventually be discovered.

---

**GERMANY**

**3**

While I completely agree with the two categories of Internet-enhanced and Internet-specific privacy concerns, I would like to stress a third and perhaps even more severe concern: the decreasing effectiveness of existing privacy regulations with the risk of uncontrollability of any legal provisions by the bodies created during the last ten years. Many European countries have data registrars or data protection officers who are entitled to make inspections and even to decide on sanctions if data protection rules are violated by the owner or provider of computer systems. These institutions and the respective regulations originate from the late 1970s and early 1980s when there were large mainframe computers with well-defined data processing programs and databases, log files of usage and so on. In this well-defined and stable environment, rights and duties also could be well-defined. Access to personal data has to be controlled. These data may not be given away to a third party without notice. Most of these systems were technically isolated because the computer

systems were not integrated into a network at all or only in a proprietary network. The Internet allows for the first time for the transfer of and access to data regardless of hardware manufacturers, operating systems and telecommunication networks. Data can be transferred within seconds. Registrars and inspectors cannot follow so quickly. Data may be stored in the country with the most liberal privacy regulations.

**Author response**

I agree with the commentator's concerns with respect to both the 'decreasing effectiveness' of existing privacy regulations in the Internet era and the problems that Internet has posed for 'controlling access to personal data'. However, I believe that these problems are not so much ones that constitute a separate (or third) category of privacy concern, but rather are examples of privacy issues that cut across the Internet-specific versus Internet-enhanced distinctions described in the present chapter.

In 1997, the German Parliament passed – in addition to the General Data Protection law – two specific laws for information and communication services (see: http://www.iid.de/iukdg/dge.html for the English translation). The Teleservices Data Protection Act restricts the collection of personal data by providers to those cases where these data are necessary for providing the service or where the user has given his consent. Providers shall offer anonymous use and payment of teleservices or use and payment under a pseudonym. There are additional rules for accounting data. After two years it seems that most providers have not even started to adjust their systems to this law. Although their system is illegal, nobody intervenes. In addition, German Parliament has passed the Digital Signature Act creating a legal and organisational structure for the certification of digital signatures according to employing public key systems. But only a few institutions build up a Certification Authority

(CA) according to this law. As the law does not forbid CAs following a lower level of security provisions and checks, two levels of security are emerging. However, the law does not regulate the acceptance of digital signatures within public administration. Unless public administration accepts digitally signed forms, they will not be widely used. The city and state of Bremen, one of the 16 German Länder, recently passed an experimental law that allows for restricted procedures when the digital signature is accepted as equivalent to a personal handwritten signature.

**Author response**
The commentator raises some critical issues for legislation involving digital signatures and public administration. Unfortunately, this topic was not able to be addressed in the present chapter in the depth that it deserves.

**GERMANY**

**4**

---

While I completely agree with this conclusion, I would like to point out that the success will finally depend on the individual's ability to recognise privacy risks and to apply the appropriate privacy-enhancing technology. As the complex structure and extreme dynamics of the Internet limit what inspectors, registrars and commissioners can do for the individual user, he has to take his privacy in his own hands. We talk about computer literacy or media competence, but still have not integrated the privacy issues discussion into the respective programs and curricula. But with-

out meeting this educational challenge, there will be no presumption in favor of privacy.

**Author response**
The commentator correctly points out the need for consumer/user education with respect both to (a) the kinds of privacy threats that exist because of certain activities made possible by Internet tools and techniques, and (b) the existence of available privacy-enhancing technologies and how those technologies can be used to protect individual privacy.

**GERMANY**

**5**

---

As in the case of Canada, which has also set up privacy oversight agencies with a Privacy Commissioner in each of its provinces, many European countries have their own data-protection agencies. More information on data-protection laws in Europe, including a discussion of the 1998 Data Protection Act as it relates to the Internet, is included in Appendix 1. For a further general survey, see GILC (1998); for a discussion of privacy policies in some Asian nations, including Hong Kong, see Lee (1993).

**Author response**
Commentator's point acknowledged and appreciated. GILC (1998) contains a very useful URL that includes reports from more than 50 countries regarding their privacy laws and policies. It is also interesting to note that a tenet of this Global 'Campaign' is that privacy is a 'fundamental human right recognised in the UN Declaration of Human Rights...'

**JAPAN**

**1**

# 5 Law and the Internet*

JOHN MAWHOOD AND DANIEL TYSVER

## Introduction

Governments around the world are creating Internet law right now – a process that is both exciting and frightening to watch. Unlike other areas of commerce that can turn to historical traditions to help settle disputes and guide the development of the law, there is no Internet history on which the law can rely. 'Internet law' is instead being developed by judges, who must do their best to fit legal disputes about the Internet into pre-existing legal frameworks, and legislators, who struggle to understand the technology they govern.

Each generation since the Industrial Revolution has seen advances in technology that make it possible for people to do things that previously were impossible; changes that range from powered transport to the ability to choose the sex of a baby. Each new development may challenge the concepts of law that have existed before, but through court cases and new statutes, the law is adapted, extended and clarified.

The Internet is yet another technological advance. It offers an unprecedented ease and richness of communication to enable people to extend the reach of their actions. In the late 1970s it was only companies and business people who had access to technology that allowed them to communicate globally with others within minutes; sending orders and other written information.

As recently as the early 1990s there simply was no technology for global communication with the power and flexibility of the Internet.

New technology leads to new words, some of which can mislead us. In particular with the Internet is the notion of *cyberspace*. Even though the Internet has wrought truly dramatic changes in communication, it is important to remember that cyberspace is not a real place, and that people and the things they use to communicate through the Internet all continue to exist in real countries, in the real world. All those countries, people and activities continue to be governed by laws.

* This chapter is not legal advice and should not be relied on as a substitute for legal advice.

The legal principles governing conduct and commerce on the Internet are still in a state of flux. Nevertheless, it is wrong to believe that there is no law on the Internet. The truth is that the task of determining the law of the Internet is primarily a task of applying basic principles of law to the new landscape of the Internet. Individuals and companies who face Internet legal issues are generally concerned with issues of who can do what over the Internet:

- Can I use another person's graphics on my Web page?
- Can I create a page about why I dislike Madonna?
- Can I keep someone from stealing my new idea for conducting auctions over the Internet?
- Can I own the mcdonalds.com domain name without getting into trouble with McDonalds Corporation?
- Can I keep people from gathering information on me during my use of the Internet?

All of these examples involve the law, and most of the answers to these questions are based upon the application of existing law to the Internet. In many cases, this process is straightforward. For instance, copyright infringement is still copyright infringement, even if it is committed over the Internet. In other cases, lawyers simply make informed guesses on how a Court would decide the way the existing law applies. Sometimes this is not straightforward, for example, it is unclear whether one company can prevent another company of the same name from using their common name as a domain name.

In this chapter, we will focus on the traditional 'intellectual property' areas of copyright, patent, and trademark law, as well as the law of defamation. More than any other areas of laws, these topics most directly affect the central question of who can do what over the Internet. We will find that the basic concepts in these topics provide a great deal of guidance for users of the Internet. We will also look at how the Internet is altering these legal doctrines, as courts and legislatures occasionally find that the law must adapt situations unique to the Internet.

In addition, the chapter will discuss several legal areas that are largely being developed from scratch as a direct result of the Internet. In particular, we will look at possible legal problems with linking to the Web sites of others, at the confusing issue of whose law applies to transactions over the Internet, and finally at the law of privacy on the Internet.

Our examination of these issues, will primarily be in the context of the laws of the United States and European states. In most cases, the laws of the industrialised countries have become quite similar, so that the examination of laws in one country provides a good indication of the broad effect of laws in another country, but there are always important differences in details and practices. This is especially true in the intellectual property areas of copyright, patent, and trademark, since international treaties have unified many different aspects of these laws. In addition, the United States and Europe have led the way in legal principles on the Internet. Other nations routinely look to the approaches of these jurisdictions to guide them in the development of their own laws. So while this focus will limit the international applicability of this chapter, we believe that no other approach can describe the state of the law of the Internet in as succinct a fashion.

## Copyright

No topic is more important to understanding the law of the Internet than copyright law. At its most basic, the law of copyright gives the person entitled to the copyright the legal right to prevent the unauthorised copying of 'works of authorship', such as documents, images, and sounds.

Most countries now grant a copyright on a work as soon as it is created. Since no special applications or actions are required to secure these rights, national copyright laws and international copyright treaties protect almost every document, image, and sound file on the Internet against unauthorised copying. This is true even though a primary benefit of the Internet is the ability to copy and distribute documents and files with ease.

Every time a Web page is viewed in a browser, a copy of some or all of the contents of the page is made, even if only temporarily, on the browsing user's computer. It is safe to say that every time a person uses the Internet some copying of copyright works will be happening, whether the page contains text, a video, a music track, or any combination. This copying is only lawful under copyright if it is permitted by the owner of the copyright.

Many copyright owners, wanting to collect royalties for their creations, believe that the Internet is a challenge to their legal rights. Some feel that the threat is so great that either the law or the Internet itself must be changed to ensure that authors receive royalties every time a copy of their work is made. Others feel that information 'must remain free', and therefore resist any limitations on their ability to copy and distribute files on the Internet. Most legal observers feel that existing copyright laws, with some recent updating to reflect the realities of the Internet, already provide a good balance between the rights of authors and the needs of Internet users.

## COPYRIGHT AND PATENTS — THE DIFFERENCE

In this section and the section on Patents we examine two of the most important theories of law that protect the fruit of human creativity. To do this it is vital to understand two distinct types of protection that flow from these theories.

**Copyright.** Copyright law gives the owner of a work the right to prevent others from *copying* the work. It does not stop others from independently creating the same work. It also does not prevent the use of the ideas expressed in her copyrighted work. To obtain a copyright, it is usually not necessary to do anything other than to 'fix' the work by writing it down or saving it to some electronic medium. Copyright usually lasts for many years (up to 70 years after the author's death).

Thus, while an article describing a new way to obtain unlimited electrical energy from the sun is protected by copyright from the moment it is written, the new idea—how to obtain energy from the sun—is not protected. So if someone were to photocopy the article, this act would infringe the copyright owner's rights. However, the copyright owner could NOT prevent someone from taking the idea found in the article and selling devices based on that idea.

**Patent.** A patent is a monopoly right which a country gives to an inventor to prevent others from making, using, or selling an invention. Patent rights are obtained only after an application is filed with and granted by a patent office. To qualify for a patent, the invention must not have been publicly disclosed and must be novel and non-obvious. This process usually costs many thousands of US dollars, and usually takes more than eighteen months to complete. A patent will last for a shorter period of time than a copyright, usually for 20 years or less.

If the author of the article had obtained patent protection for her technique of obtaining unlimited electrical energy from the sun, she could prevent others from taking her invention. This right would extend only to the countries where a patent had been obtained.

## Copyright principles

Copyright law provides protection against all forms of unauthorised reproduction, distribution, and display of works of authorship. Copyright law was originally devised to protect printed works. Over the years, the law has adapted to changing technologies. Today, copyright law has expanded so that it is now copyright infringement to photocopy a book, to copy a computer software program, or to use someone else's graphic file on a Web site. It is not necessary to copy the entire original work for copyright infringement to occur. All that is necessary is that the copying be of a 'substantial and material' part, which is a qualitative not quantitative test.

Copyright law also allows authors the right to prevent others from making derivative works. A work is a derivative work if it is based upon an earlier work, even though it does not directly copy the earlier work. Derivative works usually transform, recast, or adapt the original work in a new way. For instance, the adaptation of a novel into a motion picture is considered the creation of a derivative work. In the computer industry, the translation of a software program into a different programming language or operating system is generally considered a derivative work of the earlier version.

While each country can determine what types of works are protected by copyright, most countries protect the following types of works:

- literary works, which includes software code and other programming
- musical works, which includes both melodies and song lyrics
- dramatic works, including any accompanying music
- pictorial, graphic, and sculptural works
- motion pictures and other audiovisual works, and
- sound recordings.

Thus, copyright law protects text, still and moving images, sound files, scripting, and programming – almost everything found on the World Wide Web.

Copyright protection exists at the moment a work becomes 'fixed'. For example, a song is protected by copyright as soon as it is first recorded on paper or cassette tape. For copyright to 'exist' in a work there is no need in most of the world to file an application for copyright protection, or to place a copyright notice on a work. Although notice is no longer required under US national law, most people continue to place copyright notices on their works. The notice allows them to take advantage of the international protection afforded by copyright treaties, as well as to remind others that the work is protected by copyright law and inform others of who owns the copyright. The notice usually takes the form of the copyright symbol ©, the year of publication, and the owner of the copyright. For example:

© 2000 Macmillan Press Ltd.

In addition to the fixation requirement, a work must also be 'original' before it will be protected by copyright law. However, the amount of originality required is extremely small. The work cannot be a mere mechanical reproduction of a previous work, nor can the work consist of only a few words or a short phrase. For instance, the phrase 'Life's a Beach' is too short to be protected by copyright. Trademark law best protects short phrases such as this. Beyond these few exceptions, almost any work that an author creates will meet the originality requirement.

Interpretations of 'originality' for the purpose of copyright law vary between countries, and some have categories of protection for works that are not considered worthy of copyright protection. Our comments here reflect the position under the laws of the US, the UK and other countries which follow the same legal approach.

## Copyright rights versus ownership of a copy

In most countries, copyright law is governed by a statute that grants certain exclusive rights to the owner of a copyright in a work. These exclusive rights are different from the rights given to a person who merely owns a copy of the work.

For example, when a person purchases a book through Amazon.com, she has received a property right in a copy of a copyrighted work (namely, the book). As owner of that copy of the book she may then resell the book, or even destroy it, since she owns the physical copy of that book. However, when she purchased the book she did not receive any ownership of the copyright in the book. Instead, the author holds all of the legal rights of copyright until the author specifically transfers them.

Consequently, the owner of a copy of a book may not use a computer to scan the book and then upload the text to the Internet, since the right to copy a work is one of the exclusive rights granted under copyright law. This distinction allows a copyright owner to sell copies of a work, or even the original work itself (such as a sculpture), without forfeiting any rights under copyright law.

## Fair use

The doctrine of fair use developed over the years as courts tried to balance the rights of copyright owners with society's interest in allowing copying in certain, limited circumstances. This doctrine is based on the belief that not all copying should be banned, particularly in socially important endeavours such as criticism, news reporting, teaching, and research. Some traditional examples of fair use include:

- taking a small excerpt from a book for use in a book review
- using quotations from a speech in a news report
- quoting sections from a book in a student's academic paper, and
- making a parody that includes some elements (but not all) of the work being parodied.

The doctrine of fair use is somewhat complicated, and it can be difficult to determine when an otherwise infringing activity can be considered fair use. Perhaps the most useful rule of thumb is that if a copy is made for educational or news reporting purposes, the copy will generally be considered a fair use unless it substantially affects the value of the original work. In contrast, if the copy is made for commercial purposes, courts will be less likely to find the copy to be a fair use.

## Ownership

One of the most important concerns in copyright law is the determination of copyright ownership. The general rule is that the author of the work is the owner of all copyright interests in the work. However, where two or more parties create a work together, they may create something that the US Copyright Act labels a 'joint work'. If a joint work exists, then both authors are co-owners of an undivided interest in the entire work.

### 'Work for hire'

In the US, in situations known as a 'work made for hire,' the author of the work is no longer the individual who created the work. Instead, the 'author' is the entity that hired the creators of the work (such as a corporation for whom the author works as an employee). Generally, wherever an employee creates a copyrighted work, the work is a work made for hire. Consequently, the employer is considered the author, and the employee has no copyright interests in the work.

In the US, a work can also be considered a work made for hire if a contract with an independent contractor specifically states that the work is made for hire AND the work falls under one of nine categories of works listed in the Copyright statute. Although there is some debate about this, most attorneys believe that software programs and Internet Web sites are not among the nine categories of works listed in the Copyright statute. As a result, if an independent contractor is hired to create a software program or Web site in the United States, she will be considered the author of the work. This is true even if her contract specifies that it is a 'work made for hire'.

## WATCH POINT: OWNERSHIP OF INTERNET WEB SITES

Web sites written by employees hired to create Web pages will usually be considered works made for hire. Consequently, the employing company itself will be considered the author of the Web pages written by those employees, and ownership will properly reside with the company. It is prudent, where US law applies, nonetheless to have employees sign agreements whereby they agree to assign all copyrights in materials they develop to the company. The reason for this prudence is that the determination of who is an employee requires an analysis of many factors and might cause unexpected results in rare cases. In addition, the work made for hire doctrine requires that the work be done 'within the scope of' the employee's employment. Generally, Web pages developed by a programmer or marketing employee will be within the scope of his or her employment, but it is best not to rely upon such an ambiguous phrase.

In addition, companies hiring outside consultants to develop a Web site must be especially careful. Outside consultants will usually not fall under the work made for hire doctrine. It is best to draft an agreement with the consultant that requires the consultant to agree to assign the copyright to the company. It is also important to make sure that the copyright ownership passes all the way from the individual creating a Web page to the consulting firm hired by the company. Therefore, companies should review not only their agreement with the consulting firm, but also the agreements by which that firm hires individual Web designers.

Some consultants are reluctant to assign all copyright in the work they develop to their clients. For example, there may be components in the work they create that are part of an existing 'stock' of code which is reused for other clients, and should not be owned by one client. In those cases, an agreement must be carefully drafted to ensure that the business retaining the consultant has a continued right to maintain, update, and alter its Web site.

Copyright law treats the work of employees differently in other countries. In the UK, for example, the copyright in the work of an employee will be automatically be the copyright of the employer. In contrast, the work of an external contractor or consultant will always remain their copyright, unless there is a written agreement signed by them expressly transferring the copyright they have or will create.

## Copyright infringement in Web sites

One of the most common examples of copyright infringement on the Internet is the use of another's graphics, music, text, or scripting in the creation of a Web site. Unfortunately there is currently almost no foolproof way with digital media for a non-technical client to know whether a work is original or has been copied without permission. Web designers who cut corners by appropriating text, scripting, or images from another Web site are probably infringing the copyright of the true owner.

An example of this was a publisher who wanted to issue a CD of clipart. To obtain the clipart the publisher organised a competition for readers to submit suitable work, which would, under the rules of the competition, become copyright work owned by the publisher. The winner happened to have used a scanner to submit a copy of a work by a published artist, without their permission. Without exhaustive checking the publisher could not have known this, but the CD could not be published with the winning entry without infringing the copyright of the artist.

Images for the Web are normally created in a drawing or other image creation program. In doing so, however, it is best to start from scratch rather than from someone else's creation. Even if an image is significantly altered, the new image may infringe upon the copyright in the first image by being a 'derivative work'.

## Strict liability and Internet copyright infringement

One of the recent debates in copyright circles has centred on a principle known as strict liability. Strict liability is a legal principle that holds that someone is liable for their actions regardless of whether they acted knowing what they did was unlawful. Copyright infringement is one of the areas in which strict liability is used. A person is considered to have committed copyright infringement whenever they copy a protected work, even if they did not know that the work was protected. For instance, if a newspaper reporter copies large portion of someone else's article for her own story, she is guilty of copyright infringement. In addition, if her newspaper then places the story on its Web site, the newspaper itself is committing an infringement. Moreover, if a wire service picks up the story, all of the newspapers around the world that print the story will commit a copyright infringement. This is true even if the newspapers had no reason to suspect that the article was copied.

Although this rule seems rather harsh, it has been the governing principle of copyright law for many years. However, when the rule is applied in the Internet and online contexts, some disturbing results have occurred.

One of the first cases involving strict liability for copyright infringement in the online context was *Playboy* v. *Frena*.[1] In this case, Mr Frena ran a bulletin board service having many different sections, including an area where users were allowed to upload and download adult images. Playboy sued Mr Frena when it discovered that his users had uploaded images copyrighted by Playboy Enterprises. Even though Mr Frena was not aware of the images until contacted by Playboy, the court used the doctrine of strict liability to hold Mr Frena liable for copies on machinery under his control.

In 1996, the Religion Technology Center of the Church of Scientology tried to apply the theory of strict liability to Internet service providers (ISPs) when it sued Netcom for the activities of one of its customers. A man by the name of Erlich had used Netcom's services to post on the Internet some materials that the Church claimed were protected by copyright. The Church argued that Netcom's ignorance of the infringement should be irrelevant under the doctrine of strict liability, since Netcom provided the computers that contained and facilitated the copying and distribution of the materials. Most Internet observers felt that if the Church were successful in its arguments, Internet service providers such as Netcom and AOL would be overwhelmed by copyright lawsuits and would have to withdraw from the business. Sensitive to these arguments, the court stated that it would not apply the doctrine of strict liability to ISPs.[2] This decision has recently been enacted into the US Copyright statute in the Digital Millennium Copyright Act.[3]

In 1999, the European Union proposed a draft Electronic Commerce Directive, similar to the Digital Millennium Copyright Act. This draft Directive provides that an ISP will not be liable for the violation of copyright or pornography laws by their customers, whenever the ISP has no prior notice of the illegal activity.

## Patents

In the summer of 1997, the computer industry was buzzing over Microsoft's multi-million dollar investment in Apple. Apple enthusiasts viewed the deal with suspicion, having long seen Microsoft as the largest threat to Apple's continued existence. The rest of the world wondered why Microsoft would bother to invest in Apple at all. What most people overlooked was the additional agreement that was a great benefit to both parties; a promise by Microsoft to pay Apple an undisclosed amount to settle patent claims that Apple had against Microsoft. Some estimated these payments may run into the hundreds of millions of dollars.

As a result of the settlement, Apple received a major infusion of capital, and may have been granted access to Microsoft's own patent portfolio in developing future Macintosh operating systems. Microsoft, in turn, freed itself from years of additional litigation, and the possibility of a single Apple patent bringing down its entire Windows empire.

It is not surprising that many people missed the import of the patent settlement. Apple's patent rights existed only because of recent changes in patent law. Twenty-five years ago, the idea of granting patents to software was almost unthinkable. Now, countries are routinely granting patents on software applications, including software programs running over the Internet. In fact, Internet patents are becoming so common that many experts fear that patents will soon severely limit the expansion of the Internet.

The purpose of patents and the important differences between patents and copyright are explained in the previous section on copyright in this chapter, under 'Copyright and Patents – the difference'.

### Protection granted

Because patents will soon play such an important role in the Internet, it is important to understand some basic principles of patent law. Although laws differ in details from country to country, the issuance of a national patent will almost always give the patent owner the right to prevent all others from making, using, or selling the patented invention in that country. In effect, the patent owner obtains a monopoly on her invention. Consequently, if a patent were issued on a certain software technique, the owner of the patent could prevent all others from making, selling, or using software that contained that technique.

Patent protection applies even when another party independently develops a patented technique. Thus, a software or Internet developer faces the risk of infringing another's patent even when they did not copy or know about the earlier patented development.

### Unisys example

In 1985, Unisys obtained a US patent[4] on a technique of compressing data known as the Lempel Ziv Welch (or LZW) technology. The LZW technique was developed in the early 1980s, and has become one of the most widely used data compression algorithms on the Internet. Among its many uses, the LZW technology is currently used to create and display GIF and TIFF image files and PDF documents, all of which are widely used on the World Wide Web.

Because of their 1985 patent, Unisys has the legal right to prevent anyone from making, selling, or using a software program that uses the LZW technology. In 1994, Unisys discovered that the GIF image format developed by CompuServe was using the LZW technology. Once Unisys made this discovery, it entered into negotiations with CompuServe. Rather than fight the patent, CompuServe agreed to pay a royalty to Unisys.

Other companies soon followed CompuServe's lead and took out licences under the patent. Microsoft agreed to a licence in 1996, perhaps seeking to avoid a repeat of its 1994 patent infringement trial. In that trial, Stac Electronics successfully sued Microsoft for infringing its data compression patent, winning a 120 million dollar verdict.

As of 1999, over 1500 companies have licensed the LZW technology from Unisys. Experts believe that the LZW patent is the most widely licensed patent in history.

## Software patents

Many people still believe that computer software is not patentable subject matter. However, Patent Offices in Europe, the United States, Japan, and many other countries have now affirmed that, if it meets the other requirements for patentability, computer software can be patented. Because of the strength of its computer industry, the United States has led the world in legal developments determining the patentability of computer related inventions.

For many years, the US Patent and Trademark Office (PTO) refused to grant patents on inventions relating to computer software. Up to and through the 1970s, the PTO avoided granting any patent if the invention involved a calculation made by a computer. Their rationale was that patents could only be granted under the Patent Act to processes, machines, articles of manufacture, and compositions of matter. Patents could not be granted to scientific truths or mathematical expressions of it. The PTO viewed computer programs and inventions containing or relating to computer programs as mere mathematical algorithms, and not processes or machines. As such, software related inventions were considered 'non-statutory' and ineligible for patent protection.

In the 1980s, the United States Supreme Court forced the PTO to change its position. The Court found that software related inventions were patentable as long as the invention was not *merely* a mathematical algorithm. Thus, an invention for curing rubber was patentable, even though the only novel feature of this invention was the computer software program used to time the curing process.[5] On the other hand, the Supreme Court had earlier found that a software method of converting numbers from one form to another was unpatentable as it was *merely* a mathematical algorithm.[6] This earlier decision was still considered to be good case law, which left most legal observers confused. No one was quite clear how to determine whether an invention was 'merely a mathematical algorithm' or not.

Throughout the 1980s and most of the 1990s, inventors knew that some software programs were patentable and some were not. Unfortunately, no one knew exactly how to make that distinction. After years of confusing court decisions and inconsistent action, the PTO issued new guidelines for its patent examiners in 1996. These guidelines allowed patent attorneys to craft applications that were more likely to be considered patentable. When these guidelines were combined with pro-patent court decisions from the late 1990s, inventors could finally be confident that most software related inventions were patentable.

In Europe, a similar move to allow software patents has taken place. On the 4th February, 1999, the Boards of Appeal of the European Patent Office handed down a decision[7] that appears to remove the doubts that surrounded the possibility of obtaining patents for software-based inventions in Europe. The Boards of Appeal explained the decision by pointing out that they are not bound by the

Guidelines of the European Patent Office (which contained the key phrase 'A computer program claimed by itself or as a record on a carrier, is not patentable irrespective of its content'). The Boards of Appeal proceeded to give their own, definitive interpretation of the troublesome Article 52 of the European Patent Convention: programs for computers 'as such' are not patentable, but 'programs for computers must be considered as patentable inventions when they have a technical character'. It seems likely that Article 52, which contains other provisions that have become obstacles to patenting software inventions will be repealed altogether, to bring Europe in to line with international patenting practice. This decision opens the doors for patenting software-based and Internet inventions in Europe.

## Obtaining a patent

Unlike a copyright, which protects software or an Internet Web site as soon as it is created, patent protection only exists after a patent is officially issued by a national patent office. The additional steps of obtaining patent protection are designed to ensure that patents are granted only to inventions that are new, useful, and non-obvious.[8] An invention is considered new if it has not been previously known or used in society. Most inventions will be considered useful, although inventions in the medical and chemical areas must meet fairly stringent requirements.

Finally, even if an invention is new in the sense that the exact invention was not previously known, a patent will only be issued on the invention if it is also a *non-obvious* improvement over what was previously known. This determination is made by an examiner at the patent office deciding whether the invention sought to be patented would have been obvious 'to one of ordinary skill in the art'. In other words, the patent office will compare the invention to what was previously known. The office then determines whether the differences in the new invention would have been obvious to a person having ordinary skill in the type of technology used in the invention.

Patent offices issue patents only after the inventor files an application that meets very strict guidelines. The creation of a patent application can be a demanding and expensive process although Patent Offices have made great improvements in reducing the costs of filing a patent. The application must include a complete description of the invention and conclude with one or more claims. The claims are complex sentences that describe the scope of the patent. Because of the complexity of patent applications, most inventors hire patent attorneys to create the application. Typical legal costs for creating and filing a software or Internet patent application range from US$5000–20 000 at the time of writing.

A successful application may take two or more years to complete. This delay is one reason why many software companies decide against filing for patent protection. When a new product has an expected life span of one to two years, the two-year wait for enforceable patent rights is considered excessive. However, in many countries[9] the patent 'dates back' to the date it was filed. In these countries, if competitors used the invention without a licence, they will be liable to claims from the patent owner for licence fees from the date of the application.

## Internet patents

The increased availability of patents for computer software programs has coincided with the rise of the Internet. As a result, many of the patents being issued today relate directly to activities and commerce taking place on the Internet. The US Patent Office estimates that over 1500 Internet specific patents were issued in the United States in 1998, a tenfold increase from 1995.

Some of the first patents that were brought to the attention of the Internet community were actually developed for unrelated purposes. The Unisys LZW patent, for instance, was a general compression patent filed in 1983, well before the advent of today's Internet. Most companies, however, have now accepted the applicability of this patent to the Internet, and have agreed to pay royalties to Unisys in exchange for a licence under the patent.

In 1995, a company now called E-Data Corporation purchased a patent[10] that covered the downloading of electronic data to kiosks in retail stores. One month after purchasing the patent, E-Data wrote letters to more than 75 000 companies conducting online transactions. The letters alleged that the companies might be infringing on E-Data's patent. E-Data claimed that its thirteen-year-old patent covered all sales over the Internet in which users purchase and download electronic data (including music, software, or newspaper articles) to their computers. Within four months, E-Data had brought lawsuits against more than forty companies alleging patent infringement. After almost two years, the court has recently held that the patent did not cover sales on the Internet, and dismissed the lawsuit. E-Data appealed the decision in April 1999.

While Unisys and E-Data attempted to apply earlier patents to the Internet, it was only a matter of time until patents emerged that were drafted with the Internet in mind. In March 1998, Open Market Inc. surprised many in the Internet world by announcing that they had been granted three patents covering fundamental technology used in Internet commerce. The first patent[11] covers secure, real-time payment using credit and debit cards over the Internet. Open Market claims that most Web sites that allow credit card payments are in violation of this patent. The second patent[12] covers the use of the 'shopping cart' technology in Web sites, a technique used by thousands of the commercial Web sites on the Web. The last patent[13] covers the ability to analyse how users browse through content on a Web site, which allegedly is infringed by most major Web sites that analyse user actions.

Unlike E-Data, Open Market did not rush to the courts to enforce its patent rights. Instead, Open Market tried to encourage companies to voluntarily sign up for licences by offering what it considers generous royalty terms. However, companies did not rush to take licences under these patents. One year later, not a single company had signed up.

Other recent Internet patent announcements include the claim of Priceline.com that their new patent[14] pre-empts all others from conducting reverse auctions online. Reverse auctions allow a buyer to submit a purchase offer at a certain price, which one of multiple sellers can then accept. Priceline.com uses this technique to allow users to name a price that they are willing to pay for airline tickets, which various airlines can either accept or reject. Much like Open Market, Priceline.com sees its patent as having broad applicability, and hopes to raise money through the licensing of its technology.

---

### WATCH POINT: BAD INTERNET PATENTS

When a software patent application is filed, it is examined by a patent examiner to ensure that the invention meets the new, useful, and non-obvious requirements. In this examination, examiners compare the new invention to 'prior art' – the information that is already known to society. To find this prior art, patent examiners in the US are trained to research previously issued patents. Unfortunately, in the area of software and Internet inventions, most of the prior art has not been patented since software was not even considered patentable until recently. Therefore, when the patent examiner reviews previous patents to determine whether or not the invention is obvious, unpatented software and Internet programs are not taken into account. This may lead to the patent office granting a patent that should not be granted.

Projects such as that undertaken by an organisation known as the Software Patent Institute are attempting to make more software prior art available to patent examiners. However, bad software and Internet patents continue to be granted. These patents cause problems for the software and burgeoning Internet industry, since those accused of patent infringement must do their own research into the prior art to prove that the patent is invalid. In addition, the owners of these patents are disadvantaged, since the validity of their patents can be more easily challenged than patents that are granted in non-software areas. Finally, the existence of these bad patents has turned many software and Internet developers away from the idea of patenting their inventions. However, this problem should eventually be overcome as databases of pre-existing software and Internet applications become more complete and as patents on these technologies become more common.

## The ongoing debate

The emergence of software patents has not been universally praised. Newsgroups are filled with debates among Internet and software developers over the desirability of patent protection. Internet publications bemoan the negative impact that these broad Internet patents will have on the growth of the Internet. They argue that competition will be unfairly limited if a company such as Priceline.com can use the patent system to keep all competitors out of its core business.

In contrast, many argue that copyright protection for computer programs has become excessively narrow. They suggest that the only hope left for protecting software and Internet programs is through the patent system. While some inappropriate patents may slip through the patent office, the courts are able to invalidate these patents if needed. They feel that the Internet startups of the world should be given the same protection given as companies like Polaroid, who successfully used their patents on instant photography to keep Kodak out of their marketplace.

While the debate over the appropriateness of Internet patents continues, one thing has become clear: the doubts of the past as to whether these inventions are even patentable are gone. For good or for evil, these patents are here to stay, and they will continue to have a major impact on the Internet.

## Trademark rights

Choosing between similar products when making a purchase is an experience almost everyone has had. Often an unconscious but unquestionably key element in purchasing decisions is the recognition of the brand name or trademark associated with the product.

Very often a purchaser will prefer an item that carries a brand they know, even if this involves paying more. On the Internet, purchasing goods and services will involve selecting products at least as much by reference to brand as in conventional transactions, arguably more so because there will be less opportunity to examine the product. Being able to use such a brand (and prevent others from using anything similar to that brand) is clearly an important value to the business manufacturing and supplying the product.

The law in most countries of the world recognises the ownership and protection of names and brands used in trade, referred to here as 'trademark'. Through a long development of laws in many countries, trademarks are today registered by 42 different categories of goods and services, known as 'classes', which are internationally defined. Rights for the same mark can be separately owned in each of these categories. For instance, there can legally be registrations for the mark 'Water' by over forty different owners. In addition, a trademark must be registered in each country in which protection is desired. In some countries, such as the European Community Trade Mark members,[15] it is possible to make a single application that will be treated as an application for the same trademark in all the member countries. Either way, the trademark protection provided by the registration extends only to the national boundaries where the registration is made. Thus, it is possible for multiple companies to have registrations for the mark 'Water' in the same category, but in different countries.

## What is a trademark?

A trademark can be more than just a word or symbol used in business. In many countries, sounds, three-dimensional shapes and even smells are protectable as trademarks.

In ethical terms, one may say that a trademark is the means by which the owner can build up the trust of customers in products that are associated with that brand. This trust may be more than simply a 'good feeling'. For example, in the case of vehicle spare parts, the use of some trademarks can assure the purchaser that what they are buying will be safe. In commercial terms the value that a trademark has is referred to as 'goodwill'.

In the English case of Mercury Communications[16] the judge, Laddie J, said, referring to the owner of a registered trademark as a 'proprietor':

> the rights acquired by a proprietor who registers a mark... [enable a proprietor] to restrain any trader who uses the same or a sufficiently similar mark on the goods covered by the registration... even if in the marketplace no confusion is being caused... [and even if the proprietor] is not using [the proprietor's] own registered trade mark.

Although some countries' laws will protect the 'goodwill' in a brand without registration as a trademark, for a name to be effectively protected in a way that may be quickly established across many countries, a brand must be registered as a trademark. Unlawful use of registered trademarks can in some cases lead to imprisonment or a fine, as well as to payment of compensation ordered by a civil court.

What makes a brand capable of being protected as a trademark? Trademark law requires[17] that the mark to be registered must be capable of distinguishing the goods or services of the proprietor from those of another.

The Internet suffers from a fundamental mismatch with trademarks in the way in which domain names can be registered. A domain name is unique; there cannot be two www.water.com domain names registered. By comparison, the name 'Water' could be registered[18] in more than 40 classes of goods and services in the same country, and by multiple owners in different countries in a single class. On the Internet with domain names, this is technically impossible, as even individual registrations by country, for example www.water.co.fr, www.water.co.uk, www.water.co.de and so on, could only have one registration per country. The domain name registration system makes no attempt to deal with 'examination' of names to establish whether they are confusingly similar to existing registered names. So a competitor wishing to register a name in Germany would be able to obtain a registration using a national language translation of an existing registration in another country (such as, in our example, www.wasser.co.de) without objection from the registration authority.

Although much of the publicity around domain name legal disputes has involved the activity of registering well known trade names as domain names by companies and individuals with more or less convincing reasons for doing so (for example the recent *One in a Million*[19] case in the UK), there is a more worrying, longer term issue for the Internet community. Businesses with established names may be prevented from using those names on the Internet simply because another business, possibly in an unrelated sector of the market, has registered the same domain name.

Outside the commercial sector, if there should ever be a top level domain '.per' or '.fam', for personal or family registrations, is it acceptable that the first person(s) to register www.chiu.per or www.singh.per or www.smith.per will prevent all others by the same name? Given the fact that the domain name registration system is technically more limited than the trademark registration system it is inevitable that this will lead to an increasing number of disputes.

One case in particular highlights the limitations and differences between the systems of registration for domain names and trademarks: the *Playmen*[20] case. This involved an Italian publisher, Tatillo, of Playmen magazine against whom Playboy Enterprises Inc. obtained, in 1981, an injunction preventing use *in the United States* of the name Playmen or any confusingly similar word on a magazine of the relevant type published or sold in the United States.

Tatillo set up a Web site some time in 1995 with the domain name www.playmen.it, from which e-mail subscriptions to a closed area of the Web site were available. Soon after this was discovered by Playboy it asked a Court in the United States to rule the Italian publisher in contempt of the original injunction.

What was significant about the ruling was that the Court considered it relevant that the Web site could be accessed from the United States (even though it was not physically located within the United States) and that the publisher accepted subscriptions from the United States. It was irrelevant that users themselves initiated the access to the Web site which was outside the United States. The publisher had 'actively solicited' United States customers to its Web site and had, by doing so, distributed its products in the United States. This was held to breach the injunction and attracted, among other orders of the United States Court, a fine of $1000 a day.

---

## AMAZON VERSUS AMAZON.COM

The United States is one of those countries that will protect unregistered trademarks in addition to registered trademarks. All that is required to obtain so-called 'common law' trademark rights in the United States is use of the mark. As a result, it is impossible to find out if anyone else is using a mark simply by checking the US trademark registers. Amazon.com recently discovered this when a Minneapolis, Minnesota bookstore operating under the Amazon name sued the Internet retailer in April of 1999 for trademark infringement. The local bricks and mortar Amazon bookstore was well known locally for many years, but had no reputation outside of the state of Minnesota and had never registered its mark. Nonetheless, unless its delay in filing the lawsuit is held against it, Amazon's local trademark rights may pose a significant legal problem for Amazon.com.

This lawsuit also reveals one of the difficulties in applying trademark law to the Internet. It is nearly impossible to have an Internet presence that is not viewable everywhere in the world. As a result, even though Amazon.com could normally choose to overcome its legal problems simply by not operating in the Minneapolis area, such a resolution is not available to it over the Internet. Internet retailers must typically operate around the world under the same name.

---

## Defamation

One of the natural features of the spoken word is that, at least until technology permitted it to be recorded, it was almost as transient as our thoughts. Only the report of a witness could tell what words had been said on any occasion, which meant that the reliability of the account and the interpretation the hearer placed on the words they heard or thought they heard had to be factored into any assessment of what was in fact said.

In many senses this lack of certainty over the spoken word acted benignly, well captured perhaps by the old English saying 'Sticks and stones may break my bones but words will never hurt me'. Today, with technology that makes every word of every message persist almost indefinitely, words do hurt. In particular, they can hurt as a result of the legal liability they create for the persons and organisations whose systems the messages are held on or pass through.

## Common law elements – slander and libel

In 'common law' countries (such as the US, Australia, UK), statements that damage another person's reputation *in the estimation of right-thinking people* are called 'defamatory statements'. Four key legal elements must be grasped for an understanding of what is defamatory:

- **The statement must be 'published'.** For a successful claim that a person has been defamed, the statement must have been communicated to a third person, that is someone who is not the person making the statement or the person defamed. This means that it is not defamation if someone is rude to another person (but only rude about them) in private and no one else hears what was said. In order for defamation to occur the statement in question must be 'published' in the legal sense of the word, which means communication to a third person. On the Internet, publication can take place by an e-mail or bulletin board forum, as well as by a public Web page.

- **Each republication of a defamatory statement is defamation.** Each time a defamatory statement is repeated, the person repeating the statement is responsible for that repetition. An Internet Web site owner, a newspaper, magazine, or television broadcaster, that republishes a defamatory statement is, with certain exceptions, as liable as the author or speaker of that statement, regardless of the lack of any personal knowledge regarding the statement. A person who merely sells or prints a newspaper or a video tape is considered only a secondary publisher, and is liable only if he or she had knowledge of the defamation.

- **The statement must identify the claimant.** A statement is not defamatory of the person claiming if they cannot prove, on the balance of probabilities, they are identifiable from the statement.

■ **The statement must be untrue.** It is a complete defence to a claim of defamation if the statement is, in substance, true (that is, if the 'sting' of it is true, even though certain matters of detail may not be). It is also a defence if the statement is 'fair comment' and in the public interest or made under the protection of privilege, but these defences and special types of libel, such as criminal libel, are beyond the scope of this chapter.

The technical legal term, in the common law countries, for a spoken or transitory defamatory statement (assuming it is not recorded) is 'slander', and a written or permanent statement is 'libel'. This distinction between slander and libel has significance in the burden of proof required: a person claiming they have been *slandered* will have to show they have suffered actual loss (for example financially), although there are some exceptions (such as statements relating to their trade, profession or calling, alleging a serious crime or infection with some types of disease).

In the United States, concern over the freedom of the press has limited the ability of public figures to sue for defamation. The US Supreme Court has ruled[21] that public officials or other public figures must prove malice before a claim for slander or libel can be brought. In this context, malice can only be shown by showing that the author of the statement had actual knowledge that the statement was false, or acted in reckless disregard as to whether it was false. The spite or ill will of the author alone is not enough to show malice.

## Defamation in the digital world

The law of defamation developed recognising the difference between, on the one hand, spoken, transitory words and, on the other, written, permanent words. But is this difference properly reflected now informal communications, such as e-mail, which are of course written, are legally considered not to be transitory? The persistence of informal messages on the Internet arises only by reason of the technology of messaging – copies are held for recipients or browsers to read and will often remain in caches, archives and back-up media for years if not decades. In many instances, if you asked the author of a message whether they wished the message to be preserved indefinitely, or to be freely passed on to and read by others, the answer would be 'no'.

This aspect of the Internet has introduced a fear among employers and system operators and imposed a burden on the user. She or he can not assume anything they say or send informally in digital form is, or will be, only informal and will not be given indefinite life within the digital media of the systems it has passed through, let alone any printed copies that are made.

In some respects this may be considered an unacceptable burden. There is no generally available way in the digital medium one can choose to say something that is automatically and irretrievably deleted as soon as it has been read by the intended recipient.

Under the Defamation Act 1996 in the UK the period for bringing a claim of defamation has been reduced from 3 years to 1 year after the publication, although unlike any other period of limitation for the UK, the Court has a discretion to allow the period to be extended in certain circumstances. While this may help users of digital media by reducing the risk to the maker of a defamatory statement, it does not address the issue of communications made via digital media being treated as libel where otherwise there would only be slander.

For service providers and others whose systems simply pass on or store messages and Web pages, who are likely to be wealthier targets for claims, the issue of liability for defamation raises the question why they should be liable. In the UK, although a common law defence already existed, the Defamation Action 1996 introduced the specific statutory defence of 'innocent dissemination' and extended it to operators of and access providers to communications systems where there is no effective means of controlling the transmission of defamatory statements. However the defence also requires that reasonable care was taken and the person relying on the defence did not cause or contribute to publication. A recent case in the UK against Demon Internet saw an unsuccessful attempt to use this defence where the service provider had been notified of the defamatory statement and did not act promptly to remove it.

Similarly, in 1996 the US Congress passed the Communications Decency Act. The most widely publicised portions of this Act attempted to limit the transmission of indecent material over the Internet. The US Supreme Court declared these sections to be unconstitutional in 1997. However, the remainder of the Act remains in force, and serves in part to protect providers or users of 'interactive computer services' from being treated as the publisher or speaker of any information provided by another. Recently, this section was used to prevent America Online from being found liable for defamation as a result of the statements made by a columnist available through AOL.[22]

## CAN THERE EVER BE A DIGITAL DISCUSSION GOVERNED BY THE 'CHATHAM HOUSE RULE'?

Sometimes people from different organisations meet together to discuss subjects that may involve giving opinions or even indirectly disclosing confidential or sensitive information about their work or the workings of their own organisations.

Such meetings can be vital to achieving understandings that benefit wider communities. For example they can be the only opportunity to relate and have corrected reports or rumours that have caused concern, any of which could potentially be defamatory.

To enable these discussions to be free from fear of later disclosure of comments made, the Royal Institute of International Affairs in the UK developed the so-called 'Chatham House Rule', which is widely used. The substance of the rule is:

> participants are free to use the information received [from the discussion] , but neither the identity nor the affiliation of the speakers, nor that of any other participant may be revealed; nor may it be mentioned that the information was received at a meeting.

With Internet technology it is possible for a similar discussion to occur by means of text-based 'chat forums' or even audio or video forums or simultaneous conferences. Inevitably users, their employing organisations and the providers of hosting and data transmission services may preserve copies of any of the messages, audio or video contributed during the discussion. By doing so they make permanent the statements, exposing the participants to the risk of libel claims, and not honouring the intention of the participants when they adopted the Rule that their comments will have *impermanence and anonymity.*

### Is it only words that count? When does defamation occur?

Defamation can occur through pictures, images, gestures and other methods of signifying meaning. So, for example, a picture, of a person that had been scanned and changed by merging another image[23] suggesting something defamatory could make anyone who then passed that message on liable to a claim for defamation by the person concerned.

Equally a Web designer inserting in the source code of an HTML page a hidden defamatory statement that was only visible to people who read the source code of that page could be considered defamation.

In law, if the person who publishes a statement is the person defamed by the statement, there can be no defamation. But here the nature of identity on the Internet introduces another complicating element – it is of course possible to 'spoof' the identity of the author of a message. In the recent 1999 case in the UK brought by British physicist, Laurence Godfrey, against Demon Internet, the defamatory statement was contained in a message that appeared to come from Godfrey in the Internet newsgroup soc.culture.thai. In that case Godfrey asked Demon to remove the message but Demon refused.

## Problems with linking and metatags

Linking is the heart and soul of the World Wide Web. If linking were disallowed or made illegal in the abstract, the Web would no longer exist. Although, no court or legislature would consider a ban on all linking in the Web, there are circumstances in which linking can present legal issues.

### Copyright – derivative works

It is possible through linking for a Web site to incorporate a graphic stored on someone else's Web server. In this case, the Web site creator does not copy the image; only the end user creates a copy. This does not mean that the Web site creator escapes liability, however. Copyright law provides that one who knowingly makes an infringement possible can herself be held liable under a theory of contributory infringement. In addition to possible copyright violations, it is considered a serious breach of Net etiquette to link to another's image without permission.

### Defamation

A link to another's page or image could also be part of a defamatory statement, and hence subject someone to legal liability. An example defamatory link could be: '*This man killed my son, cheats at work, and has venereal disease*'. The statement alone does not identify anyone in particular, and hence is not defamatory.

If the statement contains a link to a page where an individual is identified, however, the link provides the context that turns the statement into defamation.

## Trademark infringement

Any link that falsely leads the end user to conclude that the Web page author is affiliated, approved, or sponsored by the trademark owner could lead to a claim of trademark infringement. Very recent cases are also raising the possibility that the inclusion of metatags in a Web page to make one's own page appear in a Web search against a competitor's trademark, may be an infringement of trademark.

## The *Shetland Times* case[24]

The *Shetland Times* newspaper operates a Web site containing some of its articles. A competitor, *The Shetland News*, decided to include on its Web site the headlines from the *Shetland Times*. The headlines were directly linked to articles on Web pages created and maintained by the *Shetland Times*.

Although the court ruled in favour of the *Shetland Times*, the relevance of this preliminary decision to linking on the Web turns on a technical aspect of UK copyright law. As a result, the ruling shows that the courts have not reached a clear statement on the status of linking and copyright but it may be that some kinds of linking will be declared illegal.

## Microsoft/Ticketmaster dispute – deep linking

In this US court case, Ticketmaster complained that sites operated by Microsoft illegally linked to pages 'deep' within in the Ticketmaster Web site. Microsoft was linking directly to pages dealing with musical concerts that were of interest to Microsoft's users. Ticketmaster objected that by deep linking within the site, the user was able to bypass the advertisements that Ticketmaster had placed on its home page. Although legal observers felt that Microsoft had a good chance of prevailing, the case was settled when Microsoft agreed to link only to the Ticketmaster home page.

# Whose laws govern?

While much of Internet law can be determined by examining existing laws, some aspects of the Internet stretch fundamental legal concepts beyond recognition. For example, the traditional concept of location has been severely altered by the Internet. The pervasive access provided by the Internet makes for a kind of 'omnipresence', where all participants on the Net wherever located can be actors in any other part of the Net. For example, a bookseller based in the US can, overnight, become a global bookseller just by establishing a Web site. A book purchaser in Australia has suddenly engaged in international commerce by purchasing from that Web site. When the purchaser and the bookseller have a dispute, whose law governs – the United States or Australia? Does the US bookseller have to abide by Australian advertising laws? Can the officers of the US bookseller be held criminally liable if one of his or her books violate Australian pornography laws?

Unfortunately, these questions form the outer boundary of Internet law, and are still mostly unresolved. Courts have been increasingly willing to apply local laws to remote parties because of their Web sites. As explained above, the US court in the Playboy and Playmen dispute held that the Playmen Web site was subject to US laws because they had US customers. Consequently, Playmen was considered to have violated a court order that prevented them from doing business in the US under the Playmen name.

Most Internet lawyers now believe that if a Web site conducts business with customers in a particular country, there is a good chance that the operators of the Web site will be subject to the laws of that country. This result could subject Internet companies to conflicting regulations, where some countries require certain behaviour and other require the opposite behaviour. This area of the law is still being developed, and we must wait to see how issues like this are resolved.

# Privacy and the Internet

Although it has sometimes been said that technology outpaces the law, raising the question of whether law can operate effectively in a technological environment, it should be noted that legal standards based on fair information practices, rather than the regulation of particular technique, have actually withstood the test of time fairly well.

This conclusion, from Marc Rotenberg, Director of the Electronic Privacy Information Center, USA,[25] represents a leading perspective on the importance of the law and legal privacy standards internationally in the age of burgeoning technological advances, in which the Internet now leads the way.

The argument is made that legal standards for privacy have been in development (since at least the US Privacy Act of 1974) and must be strengthened by being better applied. Ironically the latest European Union data protection law does not recognise the United States as providing an adequate legal regime for the protection of personal data. This is primarily due to the fact that the United States has so far avoided government standards and is instead trying to rely on private industry to develop and implement adequate privacy measures.

However, it may be argued that the Internet involves a steep change. An example may help to illustrate this and perhaps point us to something deeper in the discussion of privacy laws and treatment of the individual in the digital world.

In the United Kingdom, the Data Protection Act has been in force since 1984, and a new Act implementing the EC Data Protection Directive that applies to all member states of the European Union will come into force in 1999. However, even with this Act in force, it might not be a violation of the Data Protection Act to make available a Web page on the Internet, for anyone to use, with access to a database containing the names and home addresses of every Director of a UK registered company. One could envisage this could be searched, so that by simply entering the family name of a person one would immediately have a list of people of that name, and their home addresses.

But is such a level of exposure acceptable? In law the residential address of a company officer is considered a matter of public record or was, at the time in the late 1980s, that the law regulating companies in the UK was last consolidated. Is it reasonable that a company director has the address where they and perhaps their dependants live available to be found within a second's searching by a person that may never be identified as having looked up their address? What if that person were a contract killer? Is it possible for certain kinds of access to or dissemination of information to be excessive even though there is no defamation or infringement of data protection law?

The focus of much of the law in this area so far is on the rights of the individual over information that defines and identifies them. This focus does not deal although with another factor: the degree of exposure of the individual. Whether the individual be a public person, or a private individual whose life is invaded by members of national or world media, following some disaster, we as a society may soon take additional measures to assure the protection of the individual As never before the individual is open to have her behaviour monitored and exposed via the Internet to an extent that can be described as unconscionable.

## Notes

1. 839 F. Supp. 1552 (M.D. Fla. 1993).

2. *RTC* v. *Netcom*, 907 F. Supp. 1361 (N.D. Cal. 1996).

3. Pub. L. No. 105–304 (HR2281), 112 Stat. 2860 (1998).

4. US Patent No. 4 558 302, which will expire in the year 2002. Patents on this compression technique were also obtained by Unisys in the United Kingdom, Canada, Japan, France, Germany, and Italy.

5. *Diamond* v. *Diehr*, (1981) 450 US 175.

6. *Gottshalk* v. *Benson*, (1972) 409 US 63.

7. IBM's application [European Boards of Appeal case T 0955/97].

8. The new, useful, and non-obvious requirements come from the US Patent Statute. Other countries follow similar principles, although the language used to express those principles can vary. For instance, the European Patent Convention requires that an invention be 'susceptible of industrial application... new, and... involve[s] an inventive step' before it can be patented.

9. Including Japan and Europe, but not the United States.

10. US Patent No. 4 528 643.

11. US Patent No. 5 724 424.

12. US Patent No. 5 715 314.

13. US Patent No. 5 708 780.

14. US Patent No. 5 794 207.

15. Austria, Belgium, Denmark, Finland, France, Germany, Great Britain, Greece, Ireland, Italy, Luxembourg, Netherlands, Portugal, Spain and Sweden.

16. *Mercury Communications Ltd* v. *Mercury Interactive (UK) Ltd* (1995) FSR 850.

17. Trade Marks Act 1994 in the UK.

18. This is an example for illustration – if marks are to qualify for registration, they must be distinctive and not purely descriptive of the particular product or service to which they apply.

19. *British Telecommunications Plc* v. *One in a Million and Others* (1998) 4 All E.R. 476.

20. *Playboy Enterprises Inc* v. *Chuckleberry Publishing Inc* (DC SNY, 79 Civ 3525, 19 June 1996).

21. *New York Times* v. *Sullivan*, (1964) 376 US 254.

22. *Blumenthal* v. *Drudge*, (1998) No. 97 – 1968 PLF (DDC, April 22).

23. For an interesting case, on the point of 'merged' images see the UK case *Charleston* v. *News Group Newspapers Ltd* (1994) EMLR which turned on a newspaper publishing digitally composed photographs taken from a 'sordid computer game' of two personalities apparently in an indecent act.

24. *Shetland Times Ltd* v. *Dr J Wills et al.* (1997) F.S.R. 604 (Ct. Sess.O.H.) (Ireland).

25. 'Preserving Privacy in the Information Society', Rotenberg, M. Electronic Privacy Information Center, USA (undated).

# 6 The Internet and Varieties of Moral Wrongdoing

JEROEN VAN DEN HOVEN

## Introduction

In the decades to come, many more people will get access to the Internet. They will go online to search for information and provide others with information, shop and pay, advertise products and services, exchange thoughts or just chat, express themselves politically or artistically, convince others, deliberate and amuse themselves. The Internet offers wonderful opportunities to reach out to our fellow human beings, but the darker side of human nature will certainly also migrate into cyberspace. It will not take very long before the full spectrum of immorality will be covered online: war atrocities, violence, crime, deception, greed, aggression, rudeness, inconsiderateness, impoliteness. Before the turn of the millennium, we have already seen the first signs of cyber-warfare, cyber-terrorism, identity theft, the targeting of pro-abortion doctors, Auschwitz lie rhetoric (that is, the denial that the Nazis killed millions of Jews and the (pseudo) historical research which aims at supporting this denial), racist hate speech, organised crime, brutal child pornography and questionable forms of hacktivism (a combination of hacking and activism, which is usually directed against company Web sites in order to debunk or ridicule their claims and policies).

This chapter addresses the moral evaluation of individual online behaviour. It does not provide an exhaustive listing of moral questions nor does it provide definite answers to the moral questions discussed. It provides a conceptual framework in the context of which questions and answers can be articulated. Sincere moral questions about individual online behaviour are always appropriate, just as in the offline world, but in taking this perspective two caveats are in order. First, a focus on the moral evaluation of individual actions and behaviour may obscure structural features of the Internet which may determine the range of options open to individuals. Studies in the sociology of science and technology reveal the socio-political backgrounds to the design of information infrastructures. It has been shown in a number of studies that values are embedded in hardware, software (Friedman, 1997; Winner, 1986) and technical standards (Feng, 1999). Research on the politics of search engines

(Nissenbaum and Introna, 1998), for example, indicates that biases are built into the search algorithms, which present the user with less than objective search results. Studies in the political economy of networks and analysis of path dependence in the development of information infrastructures uncover limitations to the freedom, autonomy and personal responsibility of the individual Internet user. Monopolies develop in winner-take-all markets, which lock-in individuals so as to seriously limit the choices and options open to them. A micro-ethical perspective as exemplified by the question 'what should he/she do?' is therefore not always an adequate and fruitful starting point if one wants to chart and understand the moral dimensions of a new socio-technical domain such as cyberspace. Second, the pace of the technical development of the Internet and the novelty of the phenomenon make it unlikely that we can reach strong moral convictions and claims to moral truths about individual cases. More is to be expected from an ethics of the Internet that is reflective and exploratory than from an engineering approach to ethics that seeks to apply existing ethical theories routinely to Internet quandaries in a search for unique answers.

As Jim Moor and Bernard Gert have observed with respect to the nature of applied ethics, the 'ground preparation', that is the conceptual analysis and (re)description of the problem area or moral case, is often more important than the logical application of a moral theory (Moor, 1995). The result of 25 years of applied ethics is, among other things, that the idea of starting out with a tool kit of either deontological or teleological or virtue ethical normative theories is based on a misguided conception of applied ethics (Van den Hoven, 1997a).

## Four problems

An overly simplistic conception of applied ethics will be inadequate because any serious attempt to reflect on the moral aspects of the Internet will have to deal with the following four general problems:

- problems of jurisdiction and projection
- problems of application
- problems of individuation
- problems of moral ignorance.

## Problems of jurisdiction and projection

The Internet cuts across the territorial borders of sovereign nation states, which makes geographical boundaries as delineations of jurisdictions inadequate. Whereas physical borders between countries have always determined which set of normative rules apply to individual behaviour it is now unclear under which jurisdiction one's actions fall and which laws apply to one's actions. As information is divided, packeted and routed in numerous and untraceable ways, the geography underlying traditional legal thinking proves to be useless. Which rules do we follow, which principles do we obey when sending encrypted messages, downloading pornographic material, sending pictures protected by proprietary rights, forwarding personal data? The Internet constitutes a truly international and global realm of action for which it is practically impossible to successfully impose national laws and regulations. Let us call this the problem of jurisdiction (Johnson and Post, 1997).

In the early stages of the development of the Internet, governments of sovereign nation states tried to solve the problem of jurisdiction by solving what could be dubbed the 'problem of projection', that is the problem of mapping or projecting national laws of geographically defined jurisdictions or normative regimes onto cyberspace. German authorities for example have tried to force CompuServe to disable access for German residents to pornographic material on servers abroad. The state of Tennessee has tried to force a California-based electronic bulletin board to screen off offensive material for Tennessee residents. The Dutch government has tried to limit access to gambling sites on servers located in remote countries. Advanced filtering technology, cyber-policing, extensive logging and accountability contracts of governments with Internet Service Providers and combinations thereof may provide ways to explore how far one can go in mapping geographically based jurisdictions on to cyberspace and establishing an isomorphism of borders in cyberspace and borders in real space.

Another paradigm for thinking about the scope of legal and moral norms on the Internet has been proposed (Johnson and Post, 1997), which seems to solve both the problem of jurisdiction and the problems of projection. It has been observed that in geographically based jurisdictions, the exit option is costly for an individual. If a US citizen would prefer Luxembourg as a country to live in, he could move, but that would be expensive. The costs of moving to one's favourite jurisdiction in the real world are often so high as to be prohibitive. In cyberspace, however, the cost of exiting a particular online community, discussion list, or alpha world is almost zero. The free and unhindered movement of individuals between jurisdictions is easy and inexpensive. This could trigger an artificial evolution or process of speciation of jurisdictions, the boundaries of which are software protocols, instead of rivers and barbed wire.

## Problems of application

A second problem in moral thinking about the Internet relates to our need to twist and stretch the traditional concepts that we are accustomed to use when thinking about information technology. This conceptual twisting and stretching may produce puzzlement and moral perplexity. In practically orienting ourselves in a new domain we use expressions such as *cyberspace*, *informational privacy*, *virtual reality*, *data theft*, *telecommunication* and *virtual community*, as if we were already clear about the meaning of 'space', 'privacy', 'reality', 'communication' and 'community'. The use of expressions which have the prefixes 'cyber', 'virtual' and 'informational' suggests that we know what we understand by them, but this is misleading, since in fact their function is to indicate that we want to talk about 'a new sort of community', 'a new sort of space', 'a new sort of privacy' and 'a new sort of reality', thus taking out a mortgage on future reflection about the nature of those new phenomena. Second, and not unrelated to the foregoing issue, there is another peculiar feature of information technology that prompts conceptual disquiet. Information technology is instrumental in simulating, duplicating and replacing human beings, and mediating their interactions. Now that we no longer need to interact face-to-face to communicate, we begin to wonder what the essence of communication is. Now the real thing is no longer required to give us the impression of it, we are at a loss about what reality is; now more and more people tele-work and collaborate over the Internet, we wonder what a 'colleague' is and what is a 'community'. The concepts that used to structure our moral life-world and used to provide us with moral guidance are not only problematic in their application to Internet contexts, but the Internet transforms the very practices and institutions to which it is applied.

Finally, Internet technology may give us reasons to reconsider and reconstruct our major moral concepts and the terms of art in ethics, as we find that their conditions of application no longer obtain. Moral philosophers are still building their ethical theories on the presence of a real human face, without giving thought to the fact that their ethical theories should now also apply to a world where many decisions are taken without a real human face ever being present. Alternatively, moral philosophies are advocated that are inspired by Aristotle's moral virtues, while not addressing the fact that virtues are dispositional properties of persons, the development of which require a relatively stable social environment, plenty of time, repetition, and a robust set of moral exemplary situations. Furthermore, the idea of human rights is proposed without dealing with the problem of jurisdiction (see above) and the fact that many human rights apply to human beings as biological organisms, referring to nourishment, shelter, movement, captivity, torture, and so on. Sometimes the notion of care is given a central role in a system of ethics without taking into consideration the fact that caring relationships between people are increasingly mediated by information and Internet technology of all sorts, which may require a different conception of care. Finally, obligation and duty are made the central concepts of ethics and no thought is given to the way moral commitment and trust, as carriers of obligations, may be compromised by the fact that in our dealings with others, meeting up with good old-fashioned natural persons in three-dimensional space will be the exception. [HONG KONG **1**] It is clear that we are in a difficult predicament when thinking about moral problems and the Internet since our traditional ethical concepts no longer apply in a straightforward way.

## Problems of individuation and moral ontology

A third problem adds to these difficulties. The evaluation of individual action on the Internet departs from evaluations of real world action. The latter are typically clear-cut situations that can be described by means of expressions such as 'John saw to it that the door was closed'. The paradigm cases of traditional human agency allow us to individuate (that is to define as individuals and to count) the entities that exemplify the basic ontological categories of our choice. We manage to distinguish with relative ease between different agents, macro-physical objects such as doors, and assign to actions and objects uncontroversial spatio-temporal coordinates. Moreover the causal context is usually transparent. We are usually able to figure out what caused what. These presuppositions concerning traditional moral ontology become highly problematic in cyberspace. What is an agent? What is one object? What is an *integrated product*? Is that one thing or two sold together? What is the *corpus delicti*? If someone sends an e-mail with sexual innuendo, where and when does the sexual harassment take place? Where and when it is read by the envisaged addressee? Or when it was typed? Stored on the server? Or as it was piped through all the countries through which it was routed? And what if it was a forwarded message? Where is the agency or the agent if software robots or autonomous agents are sent out on the Net?

### Problems of moral ignorance

The problems of moral epistemology, that is, problems concerning our knowledge about the moral status of what one is doing online, may be put as follows:

There are problems that result from the unforseeability of consequences of our actions given the interdependencies in networks and the concurrent actions in a causally intransparent network environment. Individuals may simply be unable to predict the future consequences of their individual actions.

Users act through software applications, so their actions are assigned external functionality by the software they operate. We may not know in the morally relevant sense exactly what we are doing in terms of the consequences of what we think we are doing. What we are bringing about is a function of the software we use. To many of the ordinary users this function is hidden or 'black-boxed'. A special case of this occurs in a trivial sense, when we are unaware which transactional data are generated as we surf the Web. As Reiman observed in his analysis of road pricing systems (Reiman, 1995), 'driving from A to B' is transformed into 'driving from A to B and creating a record of that passage'. Similarly, retrieving information from a Web site is transformed by extensive logging procedures and Web site analysis tools into 'accessing a Web site and creating transactional data about that access, as well as a host of other data'. For many of the things we do, we are familiar with a range of relevant descriptions under which we can be said to do them. When 'I am mowing the lawn', I probably also realise that I can be said to be 'taking some physical exercise of sorts' in addition to 'preventing the fellow in the neighbouring garden from taking a nap'.

We may not know what we are doing in the sense that we do not know what principles or moral concepts, rules or criteria apply (see problems of application). We may furthermore have trouble figuring out what the moral ontology is of the phenomena we are thinking about (problems of individuation).

## Classification of moral issues

Not all moral issues concerning the Internet are hard cases. Some are more special than others. In order to distinguish between the simple cases and the more difficult ones it may prove useful to distinguish between the following four types of issue.

## Internet-related issues

First there is a type of issue where the Internet environment is neither necessary nor sufficient for the issue to arise. Good examples of this type of issue, which I will call Internet-related issues, concern for example questions about truthful advertising on the Internet and fraud in e-commerce transactions. The fact that push media or portals are involved, or Electronic Data Interchange protocols, does not add to the moral problems as such. The same holds for child pornography on the Internet. The very same moral issues concerning truthful advertising and honesty in business and the use of children in the production of pornographic material are typically involved in traditional media as well. Their morally problematic character arises in exactly the same form in the offline world, the moral core being 'deception' and 'child abuse'. When Con.com does not deliver the goods, the moral issue is 'wrongful appropriation', 'deception' or 'negligence' not 'Internet fraud' in any special sense. The Internet is not involved in its quality of advanced network technology, but in the character of business environment. The Internet is thus not necessary for this moral problem to arise, but neither is it sufficient for the occurrence of the moral problems in question. We can picture the Internet without fraud and deception. This type of issue therefore represents the lowest grade of involvement of the Internet in moral issues.

## Internet-dependent issues

Another type of moral issue must be distinguished from the Internet-related issues: Internet-dependent issues. In Internet-dependent issues, the relevant network technology is necessary for the moral problem to arise, but not sufficient. Therefore, the various forms of trespassing in networks and the various forms of hacking where illegal access to data is obtained, or viruses are spread cannot take place without computer networks and security technologies. Computer viruses provide a good example of Internet-dependent issues. They are pieces of software that cause a machine to perform actions it was not originally programmed to execute. They spread through computer networks by copying themselves. Internet technology as we know it is a necessary condition for their occurrence and their digital epidemics. To put it crudely: without the Internet, no viruses, no spamming, no flame wars, no hacking. Nevertheless, it is logically possible to have these forms of Internet technology and at the same time not have these moral problems. The online world could be free of them, if only its inhabitants choose to have it that way. New technologies offer additional options for morally wrong behaviour, but these forms of moral wrongdoing – if that is what they are – do not occur as a matter of course.

## Internet–determined issues

Next, Internet-dependent issues have to be distinguished from what I call Internet-determined issues. In Internet-determined issues the moral problems are bound to arise if the relevant computer applications are introduced or put to work. Internet technology in these forms is sufficient, although not necessary for them to occur. A good example of this type of issue is the problem of 'equal access' and the problem of 'moral responsibility for the quality of online information'. As soon as we introduce Internet-like technology – assuming a certain level of routine use – there is *ipso facto* a moral question with regard to who has access, and who is responsible for the quality of online information. Although sufficient, the Internet is not necessary for this type of moral question to arise, since we encounter the same moral problems of equal access and responsibility for the quality of information in card catalogues and books.

## Internet–specific issues

Finally, there is a peculiar type of moral problem, where the Internet in its relevant application is both a necessary and a sufficient condition for the problems to arise. That is to say, the problem does not arise anywhere else outside the Internet domain in this form, and, second, it is bound to make its appearance as soon as the relevant Internet applications come into existence. Problems related to emergent values (Steinhart, 1999), emergent artificial intelligence and artificial life on the Net in the form of autonomous agents or softbots belong to this category. If we could create artificial agents (rich, robust and resourceful avatars) and mental states in computational artefacts, that would surely land us in the middle of the most peculiar set of moral problems that we can imagine. We would be dealing with agents that might decide to do things on their own. Such problems are bound to arise, given the state of the technology, and have not been encountered anywhere else.

## The Internet and ethics

Traditionally two fundamentally different and mutually exclusive conceptions of the moral evaluation of individual actions stand out in the history of moral philosophy. One is to subsume a case or issue under independently justified principles of the right. The idea here is to follow the principles that articulate what is morally right irrespective of the consequences. The other is to look for the course of action which maximises the good. This approach involves determining which action yields the best consequences measured in terms of some standard of the good. What is good could be conceived of in terms of happiness, basic needs, shares of primary goods, desires or preference satisfaction, or welfare.

In moral thinking about the Internet one could thus – along the lines of the first approach, which is usually referred to as *deontological* – start out with some one or more moral principles and see what these say about particular cases. Alternatively, one could attempt – in accordance with the second approach, which is usually referred to as *teleological* – to frame what is good for users, and spell out what is wrong with actions that interfere with their attempts to get it.

Both of these approaches, when considered in isolation and taken as exclusive and absolute ethical points of view, represent overly simplistic accounts of moral deliberation and decision making and need to be supplemented or enriched to be adequate as an ethical framework for the moral evaluation of individual cases and actions. Two recent cases may serve to illustrate their insufficiency when considered in isolation. Helen Nissenbaum (1995) discusses the problem of software piracy and contrasts the consequentialist and the deontological approaches to copying software and finds neither of them leading to conclusive and satisfactory answers. This result is corroborated by Gert (Gert and Moor, 1998) albeit for different reasons. Eguchi Satoshi (1999) argues that one of the most influential opponents of hacking Eugene Spafford (1995) is confused about the nature of his own arguments. Spafford thinks of them as deontological whereas they are in effect consequentialist in nature. These and other cases clearly illustrate the limited usefulness of the deontology/teleology conundrum.

I shall discuss four different approaches that provide a richer ethical framework. They are very different, but have some important features in common that should interest us in the context of a study of the ethics of the Internet: first, they all try to move beyond standard and simplistic positions in ethics, and second, they are formulated with a clear awareness of the urgency of political and policy questions. In some sense they all cut across the standard deontological/teleological distinction in their attempt to accommodate the complexity and richness of moral questions. Each of these views allows us to recognise a great variety of different types of moral reasons, which can be made to bear upon an individual case.

These approaches are first, a pluralist objectivist (neoaristotelian) theory, as proposed by Amartya Sen and Martha Nussbaum; second, a pluralist axiological account, as proposed by Thomas Nagel; third, a sophisticated deontological framework as described by Bernard Gert (applied to information technology by Gert himself, and Jim Moor); and finally a responsibility account, as proposed by Robert Goodin.

I will situate Internet cases in the context of discussions of these views in order to illustrate how they may help us to shed light upon some of the moral questions raised by the Internet.

## The Internet and the idea of human flourishing

The Internet is a new and relatively autonomous domain of human action and experience which can be characterised in terms of a set of related public goods. One way of grounding our moral appreciation of what happens on the Internet is to look at what is good for human beings, not in any deep metaphysical or essentialist sense, but in terms of their functionings and basic capabilities to function. The Internet accommodates our need for information, communication, coordination, transaction, and personal relations. There is a great variety in what people want and value in these respects, but it is relatively uncontroversial that all human beings attempt to realise practical goals in social contexts and that access to information, and opportunities for communication, coordination, transaction, and personal relations are extremely important to them. The Internet thus supports critically important aspects of human flourishing. Online acts and rules of conduct are subject to moral assessment precisely because they make a difference to whether people flourish within (offline and online) communities (Schmitz and Goodin, 1998).

According to conceptions of the quality of life articulated by Amartya Sen (1985) and Martha Nussbaum (1993) there are several functionings and basic capabilities, that is, possibilities of functioning, in human lives that form the main object of our attempts to achieve fairness of distribution and equality. These provide us with a substantive conception of the good life and are constitutive of any life that is going to be rich enough to count as fully human. This teleological conception of ethics defines what is right in terms of what is good, instead of defining – as deontological theories do – what is good in terms of what is right.

The (objective) list of aspects or functionings of worthwhile human lives does not entirely apply to the Internet environment, since it is concerned in part with human beings as biological organisms and the needs of embodied persons, such as needs for food, drink, shelter, mobility and sexuality. These aspects of persons are the least prominent on the Internet, with the exception of the last. Further the capacity for pleasure and pain also regards human beings primarily as embodied individuals. Human beings have various capabilities; such as perception, imagination and thinking, practical reasoning, emotion, relationships with other human beings, humour and play. Human lives are worthwhile and can be characterised as well-rounded, rewarding and good to the extent that they contain these functionings and the capabilities to function. Lives without them can be regarded as impoverished.

To the extent the Internet offers us opportunities to exemplify these basic capabilities, it should be regarded as a morally significant environment. Actions which interfere with it can be seen as morally wrong in principle, since they diminish its value in this respect.

**Dimensions of flourishing: information, knowledge and reflection**

Since information acquisition and dissemination is the first and most prominent function of the Internet, and the acquisition of information is obviously of great importance to human beings, we need to look in some detail at the value of information and the importance of being informed or having access to information in the lives of individuals. Many forms of online action are morally objectionable because they impede persons in these informational aspects of their functioning, for example, by distortion, deception, dissemination of inaccurate data.

First, information is valued for the fact that it is instrumental in adding alternatives to the choice set of the individual, informing about things he might have preferred if he had only known about them. To the extent that it is better to have more choice than less, it is better to have more information than less. More information in this sense contributes to the welfare of individuals by increasing the probability that they will satisfy their desires. Second, people may obtain satisfaction from processing information, deliberating, and exercising choice. Third, by confronting real choices that result from the cognitive processes associated with information processing, persons may learn about themselves.

What does seem to have value is having access to information, but also the fact of being recognised as the kind of creature who is able to process information, and deliberate and choose on the basis of that information. Choice and information, as two sides of the same coin, can even be construed as constitutive of a certain ideal of a good life. Being informed and having approximately veridical representations of the world that allow us to plan for ourselves are probably considered goods of incomparable value.

Fourth, the value of information can also be derived from its potential to help discriminate between known alternatives and to reduce the number of unconnected preferences. Someone may prefer clean air to smog, and at the same time prefer living in Mexico City to living in Helsinki. Information about pollution in both cities may enable him to connect both previously unrelated preferences. Increasing the amount of information available to individual citizens as rational persons may thus expand their choice set, thereby increasing the chance that they get what they want, and help them to connect preferences defined in the choice set.

Fifth, information is valued for the fact that it helps people to coordinate actions. A mutually beneficial exchange opportunity may remain unexploited, because both parties are unaware of the opportunity.

Sixth, information is also instrumental in the allocation of rights. James Coleman (Coleman, 1990) provides a good example of how this may occur. For example, the right to smoke in public places, once held by smokers, has been transferred (and reversed) to persons in the vicinity. Two types of information are relevant, first the information about effects on the smokers themselves, and second, information about the effects on others in the smoker's vicinity, so-called passive smoking.

### Other functionings and basic capabilities

People express themselves emotionally, politically and artistically. There is a deep-seated drive to express our inner lives and thoughts and share our hopes and feelings with other human beings of our choice. It is clear that the Internet offers fabulous opportunities to do so. Also interactive and hypertextual fiction and virtual reality offer new modes of artistic expression. Apart from practical, scientific, artistic and commercial purposes, we also communicate in order to deliberate about political issues and common causes. Human beings, as Aristotle correctly emphasised, are political animals. The short history of the Internet makes it perfectly clear that it offers opportunities to revitalise democracy and shape the idea of a political community. Games of all sorts abound on the Net and thus provide a panoply of opportunities for play and humour. Cybersex and pornography offer many occasions to satisfy one's curiosity and one's sexual desires. [HONG KONG **2**] There are boundless opportunities for affiliating and socialising on the Net. A great variety of these modes of sharing, relating and caring can be encountered online. Telemedicine and telecare allow children in hospital to stay in touch with their families at home, their pets and class-mates. Patient groups get together and exchange experiences and offer mutual support. Also the Internet offers highly mobile employees the opportunity to regain the sense of collegiality. These are all aspects of human flourishing and represent in principle valuable modes of being and experiencing. If an individual seeks after them, then the burden of justification is with those who prevent him or her from achieving it.

## The fundamental moral values

Thomas Nagel (1979) has proposed a pluralist theory of value, which cuts across the standard division of teleological and deontological theories. His typology of values provides a sensitising framework that may be helpful in the moral evaluation of individual moral decisions and actions online. It points to salient moral considerations by drawing attention to different types of values that may be brought to bear upon individual cases. The problem is that these fundamental values are incommensurable and often lead to incompatible moral advice, whereas we have nothing else than practical wisdom to adjudicate between them. These different types of value reflect the fact that human beings can take different perspectives and can switch between them, as if standing on a rail track and being able to think of the tracks as merging at the horizon, or instead to think of them as running parallel beyond the horizon. Both points of view are accessible to us. We may think of a problem or situation from a self-interested and personal stance, but also from the point of view of humanity, timelessly, or from the point of view of ourselves as social beings with roles and a position in a social network of relations. Some of the fundamental values are outcome oriented (utility), some of them abstract from the consequences of actions (obligations and duty), some of them are personal and agent-centred, others impersonal.

### Special obligations

First of all there are special obligations and duties that we have on the basis of our position in a community or social network. There are special obligations between employers and employees, between parents and children, between neighbours, between a service provider and individual Internet users, between a systems administrator and those depending on him or her for services and assistance. We incur these special obligations sometimes as a result of voluntary relations, sometimes in the context of relations that happen to us. Often we have special obligations towards people or groups of people who are vulnerable, dependent upon us, or at least for whom our actions can make a difference. Internet Service Providers seem to have special obligations because of their position and knowledge of individual online behaviour.

Traditionally this idea of agent-relative responsibilities is associated with the idea of moral division of labour; those close to us (in terms of geographical, physical and emotional nearness) can be said to have a stronger claim to our attention and care than those who are more distanced. In the online case, however, proximity in this traditional sense seems to have become an irrelevant criterion. We can establish special relations with all sorts of people all over the world. People from countries at war, victims of terror and violence, oppression and exploitation may seize the communication cord and reach out for help. News about what happened at Tiananmen Square in Beijing and news from Kosovo reaches us via the Internet. It seems that in establishing e-mail contact a morally relevant relation is established. The same applies to ongoing relationships that are established via chat rooms, and which may culminate in real world encounters and enduring relationships.

As people establish special relationships online, relations of special obligations come with them. They can be easily disrespected, for example when legitimate expectations of confidentiality are not met, when our e-mail is forwarded. For example, consider a case of identity deception, as when someone over a period of years has had a sustained and caring relationship with a 35-year-old handicapped woman who in reality turns out to be a male 65-year-old psychiatrist. This is commonly perceived as identity deception, and a transgression of the special obligations that have been established between the participants in the course of that relationship, in which the deceived party has exhibited genuine and authentically felt care and compassion for the fate of the young handicapped woman.

## General rights

Second, there are general rights that everyone has as a human being. These can be negative or positive, such as the right to be free from coercion (negative), or free to do certain things (positive), such as freely expressing one's thoughts. Important general rights that individual users have on the Internet are freedom of speech, freedom of information, privacy, right to private property, freedom of conscience, individual autonomy and self-determination.

General rights to private property, privacy and freedom of speech represent sources of valid moral reasons. Their scope of application and their meaning however may not always be clear, as was indicated in our discussion of the problems of jurisdiction, application and moral ontology. In some cases we must reconstruct the rights to be able to use them in assessing and evaluating individual moral wrongdoings. An example of a general right that may to be decomposed is the right to privacy. In order to produce a fine grained moral account that helps us think about moral reasons for limited, differential and conditional access on the Internet, the privacy concept must be broken down into less vague and less controversial moral wrongdoings (Van den Hoven, 1999).

A straightforward one is the harm (dis-utility) at stake in data protection. We want to prevent harms (these can be called *information-based harms*) done to individuals on the basis of the abuse of their personal data, and therefore we adopt regimes of limited access to personal data. We know that people will be stalked, murdered and raped if too much information about them is freely available. The second reason we may have for limited access to personal information is that we want to establish an equality of arms in the process of commercialisation and marketing of personal data on the Internet. Protective measures in that case aim at providing the individual online with the tools to strike a fair bargain in trading their data for discounts or access. P3P (a platform for configuring privacy preferences of Web browsers) and other privacy enhancing technologies (PETs) that allow users to configure their privacy preferences and engage in dynamic negotiation with Web sites are good cases in point. These are Internet applications that offer consumer protection and establish individuals as fair party to the deals in which they have a legitimate interest. A third reason we may want to limit access is because we want to prevent information from one context, sphere, sector or jurisdiction from being used in another and thus reducing the efficacy of the individual. Educational, psychiatric or medical information may not be appropriate in the political or commercial sphere, and vice versa. A broad range of types of discrimination come under this heading. Finally, individuals – especially on the Internet – like to experiment with identities. Too much free-floating information facilitates labelling and categorisation, and induces moral judgements that could easily become impediments to experiments with identity and the fashioning of one's life, which is widely regarded as one of the attractive features of the Internet.

## Utility

A third source of value is utility. That is the consideration that takes into account the positive and negative effects of one's actions on everyone's welfare. Welfare can be construed in terms of money, happiness, or well-being, preferences satisfied or in terms shares of basic goods. The usefulness of science and education can for example be defended on the basis of utility. All moral discussions cast in terms of benefits and harms appeal to utility in some form. In the online world we have to anticipate that people will try to harm each other. Utility is an impersonal and outcome-oriented value. The debate about whether it is permitted for employers to read employee e-mail is a case where claims in terms of the utility of monitoring worker's communications clash with claims in terms of a universal right to privacy. Surveillance may be demonstrably economically superior to non-surveillance, but that does not mean that a general right may be overridden in this case.

Functional utility

One of the most clear forms of wrongdoing can be identified on the basis of violations to the public goods which the Internet provides.

Dorothy Denning (1999) articulates, by way of introduction to her discussion of information warfare, a theoretical frame of information resources and their value. She distinguishes between the following information resources: containers, transporters, sensors, recorders and processors. Information resources have different operational values that are characterised by Denning as a function of five factors.

1. A person's concerns and commitments at a given time.

2. The user's capabilities, which include knowledge, skills and tools, but exclude accessibility of the resource. An information resource such as a Web

site or ftp server only has value if the prospective user has the appropriate skills to access it.

3.  The third factor is availability, which is a measure of the degree to which the resource is accessible. This aspect of accessibility is taken by Denning to include among other things the degree to which a resource can be manipulated and its content specified, whether it can be viewed, processed (downloaded) altered, copied, distributed and sold.

4.  Another factor is integrity as a measure of the state of wholeness or goodness of the resource or the degree to which it is accurate complete, genuine and reliable. Value is usually directly proportional to its integrity.

5.  A final factor is time. The value of a resource is dependent on the time it is available. But like any other public good, such as logistic infrastructures or public transport, the information infrastructure cannot function if too many individuals abuse or misappropriate it. If we all send bulk mail, engage in flame wars and produce garbage, then the primary functionality of the Internet would soon be on its way out. Behaviour that diminishes or negatively affects information resources or speed, bandwidth, computational power or storage of the infrastructure and its application needs to be justified in terms of overriding moral reasons. Users are not only annoyed when they find their activities interfered with by people who are new (newbies) and have not taken the trouble to find out what the rules of the game are, and are for example sending out inadvertently long e-mails to multiple lists; they are also *justifiably* angry, since these people waste scarce and valuable resources: time, attention and information.

## Economic utility

Some forms of behaviour, such as spamming or bulk mail, may not only affect the functional utility and have serious consequences for the primary function of the information infrastructures, but may also negatively affect the legitimate economic and commercial interests that individual and collective actors have in the Internet. Spamming may be seen as generating transaction costs and negative externalities. An action induces negative externalities if the costs of that action are imposed upon others than the agent of the action. Bulk mail or spam imposes economic costs in terms of waste of attention, time and functionality of information resources on the receiver. This is particularly true when the action is considered on a cumulative basis. Opportunity cost is another form of economic damage that may result. The time, attention and resources spent on data trash and garbage cannot be spent productively or to the receiver's economic benefit.

Epistemic utility

There are many obvious advantages relating to the use of the Internet for scientific research, fact finding, inquiry and information gathering in the form of newsgroups, e-mail, preprint archives, video conferences, online databases, Java and virtual reality applications.

Alvin Goldman (1992) has proposed standards to evaluate how well social practices contribute to attaining true beliefs and to assess their epistemic success, while Paul Thagard (1999) has convincingly shown that the Internet does well by these standards. The first standard to evaluate epistemic success is the *power* of a practice, that is its ability to help people find true (for those among you who dislike 'true', you may think of 'interesting') answers to the questions that interest them. *Fecundity* of a practice is its ability to lead to large numbers of true beliefs for many practitioners. Computers and Internet connections are not free, but may be cheaper than travel to libraries, subscribing to journals, and buying numerous books. *Speed* of a practice is determined by how quickly it leads to true answers. Its clear that with respect to speed, the WWW and Internet have enormous advantages. The *efficiency* of a practice is how well it limits the cost of getting true answers. The Internet is rapidly becoming more efficient. The last and perhaps most important standard is *reliability*, that is the ratio of truths to the total number of beliefs fostered by the practice. Reliability seems to be one of the problems with the WWW and the Internet at present. We all know about the rubbish, the availability of outdated and inaccurate information, and the propagation of disinformation on the Net.

Reliable epistemic practices that enhance human intellectual functioning by means of computers and electronic networks may be said to 'epistemically empower' users and researchers, that is upgrade their capacity to reason and make decisions by means of computational devices and communication networks. The limits of epistemic empowerment converge with the limits of our scientific imagination in cognitive psychology, artificial intelligence, mathematics, software engineering and microelectronics: intelligent filters, autonomous agents, data mines, data distilleries and knowledge refineries are becoming part of reality.

## Perfectionist values

Fourth, perfectionist values derive from some conception of the perfect human life or ideas about the intrinsic value of things. Scientific discovery and artistic creations are examples. Much of the hacker ethics is cast in terms of perfectionist ends. Hackers report the excitement of creating a virus with a particular set of properties, satisfying a set of technical constraints. This is seen by some as a mathematical discovery and an exercise worthwhile in itself. Sometimes hackers refer to the usefulness (utility) of their work, since it draws attention to security and privacy leaks, or raises the awareness of our vulnerability in general in the age of the Internet. Sometimes they think of themselves as having special obligations because of their knowledge and skills.

Moral objections to virtual reality applications are perfectionist in nature, that is they do not have bad consequences, they do not violate general rights. They are just distasteful or at variance with what most people consider to be appropriate. Maiming as many children as you can in a VR game, spending most of one's time in MUDs, being thrilled by the nth version of Doom, or online indulgence in some of the more unusual paraphilias can easily upset other people, or strike them as not fitting, improper and signs of an impoverished life. As we observed above, it is difficult to limit the freedom of individuals with regard to these activities on the basis of perfectionist values alone.

## Commitment to one's own projects

Finally, there is commitment to our own projects. This consideration also has *prima facie* moral value. We want to finish our projects that we think are important for some or other reason. So when deciding a hard case, we may want to bring to bear upon the case the fact that we want to pursue a path that we have taken, simply because it is valuable to finish what one has set out to do. There are forms of moral wrongdoing online that affect people's commitments to their own projects. Some people may have embarked upon online projects only to find, after investing emotionally in building communities and sites, contributing to conversations and discussions, that these projects were terminated by others, usually commercial parties. Some online communities have turned out to be data harvest sites, which were harvested and terminated without regard for the interests of those who committed themselves to these projects.

Different types of moral theories epitomise a singular type of value, excluding or playing down the importance of the others. Utilitarian theories for example focus on utility, excluding all others, deontological theories focus on obligations and rights, egoistic theories concentrate on commitment of persons to their own projects.

## Moral rules on the Internet

Moral rules can incorporate, express or serve the values identified by Thomas Nagel. It is useful to distinguish between two types of moral rules governing online behaviour. First order moral rules identify our moral obligations online. Good examples of first order rules are netiquette rules, and codes of conduct. Second order moral rules or 'recognition rules' allow us to identify what is moral and what is not. A recognition rule enables us to recognise the properties in an action or decision that we have reason to endorse (Hart, 1961). Maximise the happiness for the greatest number of people or 'follow the instructions' or 'read the signs', or 'familiarise yourself with the netiquette' are examples of recognition rules. 'Be polite in e-mail correspondence', 'always tell the client the truth' and 'make yourself look good online' are examples of first order rules.

There are many different lists of rules of netiquette, that is the recommended ways to behave properly online. Virginia Shea (1999) lists the following rules:

1. Remember the human

2. Adhere to the same standards online that you follow in real life

3. Know where you are in cyberspace

4. Respect other people's time and bandwidth

5. Make yourself look good online

6. Share expert knowledge

7. Help keep flame wars under control

8. Respect other people's privacy

9. Don't abuse your power

10. Be forgiving of other people's mistakes.

Most of theses rules are concerned with two things, first, respect for other human beings (1, 2, 3, 8, 10), and second respect for information resources (3, 4, 6, 9). Of common concern to both parts is the ease with which e-mail is sent, wrong attachments are appended, the effects on the interests of individuals are forgotten because of the technological mediation and absence of a real human interlocutor, a sense of anonymity. They also draw our attention to care in spelling, expression, layout as means to maintaining good relationships. Neglect of these factors can lead to flame wars, that is episodes of escalating, rude e-mail correspondence. Flame wars add injuries to insults, since in addition to the insults that are made, disrespect is shown for things that are scarce and valuable to other people (time, attention, information resources).

## Common morality

Bernard Gert has proposed an elaborate system of ethics that he calls 'common morality'(1998), which he has applied to the field of IT together with Jim Moor (1999).

Gert (1999) proposes ten justified moral rules:

1. Do not kill

2. Do not cause pain

3. Do not disable

4. Do not deprive of freedom

5. Do not deprive of pleasure

6. Do not deceive

7. Keep your promises

8. Do not cheat

9. Obey the law

10. Do your duty.

The moral point of view requires impartiality and a moral attitude towards the moral rules. *Moral impartiality* requires that one's actions are not influenced by considerations as to who is benefited or harmed by these actions. The *moral attitude* requires that one obeys the moral rules except when a fully informed rational person can publicly allow violating it. The rules together with impartiality can be said to constitute the deontological element, the moral attitude to represent a teleological element in Gert's system of common morality. He discusses the case of 'violating intellectual property law by making copies of software for one's friend'.

Given the fact that existing intellectual property law is not grossly unjust and that in the standard case no great harm is prevented by copying software for one's neighbour, impartiality requires that one does not select the laws one happens to like from the laws one happens to dislike. One should be willing to defend in public, and have it made publicly known, that it is all right to violate existing copyright law in order to benefit an individual of one's choice.

In order to answer the question whether a rational and fully informed person would allow a particular violation of a moral rule, the situation should be described in terms of morally relevant features only. Among other things, moral relevance includes what harms are prevented by the violation, whether there are alternative actions that are preferable, is it done intentionally or knowingly, is it done in an emergency situation, what are the benefits?

Identity theft and deceiving people online with respect to one's identity seem to violate rules 6, 7 and 8. However it seems quite common and accepted practice in chat environments, where it could be publicly allowed (and is in fact known by all participants), whereas in e-commerce environments, assuming false identity would be morally wrong, since it could not be publicly allowed in that context.

## Moral responsibility

Several moral philosophers have recently tried to articulate a responsibility-based ethics. In professional ethics and applied fields, such as medicine, business and technology, framing moral permissions and obligations in terms of responsibilities has advantages to more abstract moral vocabularies. They can be easily integrated in a description of social and professional roles, seem to bridge the gap between cognitive recognition of the truth of certain moral propositions and the motivation to act in accordance with them and are easily convertible into legal vocabularies in terms of accountability and liability.

Some authors have criticised traditional, blame-oriented, backward-looking conceptions of responsibility (Ladd, 1988). An adequate conception of responsibility, they argue, makes it possible to apportion responsibilities, and does not construe it as an all or nothing matter and as exclusive, in the sense that the responsibility of one person rules out that others may also be held responsible for the same outcome. Responsibility conceived along these lines is agent-relative and consequentialist in nature. In contradistinction to duties, which take specific actions of persons as their object, responsibilities are outcome and result orientated. David Schmitz (Schmitz and Goodin, 1998) has proposed a conception of responsibility that is similar to this one in as far as it is future oriented. Economists say that a decision involves a negative externality when someone other than the decision maker ends up bearing some of the decision's cost. Responsibility is externalised when people do not take responsibility for the problems they cause or find themselves in, and when they regard the solution to the problems they are part of as someone else's business. Responsibility is internalised when agents take responsibility for the future consequences of their actions. There is a constant urge to externalise responsibility, as Sartre sharply observed in his discussion of bad faith, that is the condition in which human beings deny their own freedom and responsibility because it weighs too heavy upon them. The Internet environment with its relative anonymity, mobility, tangled joint causation and unfamiliar and emergent properties seems to foster this tendency in individuals.

We may distinguish between responsibility for doing, knowing and expressing on the Internet.

**Responsibility for doing**

With respect to actions online, we may distinguish between the following responsibilities of all parties and types of agents involved (Goodin, 1985). First there are *task responsibilities*. The fact that A has a *task responsibility* for X implies that A ought to see to it that X is brought about. If A has for example a task responsibility to subscribe or to send an attachment, he has the obligation to see to it that this is done. But associated with each task responsibility is a so-called negative task responsibility concerning X. A negative task responsibility concerning X is an obligation to see to it that no harm is done in seeing to it that X is brought about. So in seeing to it that the attachment is sent one has the negative task responsibility that the attachment is not at the same time sent to the wrong people, or that SUBSCRIBE is not sent as text to all subscribers. The System administrator A (moderators of discussion lists, and those taking care for the continued existence of cyber-communities) has what we may call *supervi-*

*sory responsibilities*, in which case A ought to see to it that X (where X denotes a state of affairs in which some other, B, does – or refrains from doing – something and B is not identical to A). This notion is meant to cover cases where A and B range over natural human persons, but could also be construed as ranging over artificial agents, such as bots, or software, such as HTML links. We may thus be said to have *supervisory responsibility* for software artefacts. An ISP may also be ascribed supervisory responsibility for links to forbidden material. Many debates concerning the moral status of ISPs are concerned with their supervisory responsibilities.

In addition to these types of responsibilities all those online have *self-monitoring responsibilities.* 'Seeing to it that X' requires, minimally that A satisfy himself that there is some process (procedure, application or activity) at work whereby X will be brought about; that A check, from time to time, to make sure that that process is still at work, and is performing as expected; and that A take steps as necessary to alter or replace processes that no longer seem likely to bring about X.

When someone has failed in his task responsibilities we say that he failed to discharge his responsibilities; when he has failed with respect to his self-supervisory responsibilities we say he acted irresponsibly, that is, he was insensitive to his responsibilities, as it were.

I want to draw attention to another type of responsibility the user has. It may be referred to as his or her *meta-task responsibility,* associated with task responsibilities in information environments (Van den Hoven, 1998). Person A has a meta-task responsibility concerning X means that A has an obligation to check whether 1) conditions are such that it is possible to see to it that X is brought about, 2) conditions are not such that it is impossible to see to it that no harm is done in seeing to it that X is brought about. If someone justifiably can be said to have the task responsibility for sending out documents to a list of people, then he must check whether his workplace, facilities, and system are such that he can discharge his task responsibility and negative task responsibility.

### Responsibility for knowing

Next to responsibilities for doing, we have responsibilities for knowing (epistemic responsibilities). We thus also have responsibilities for knowing on the Net. We have already seen that information is all important in the people's lives. Should the use of the Internet, online databases, preprint archives be seen as a responsible way of forming beliefs? Is it responsible enough to result in beliefs that deserve to be called knowledge? Is it responsible enough to take full moral responsibility if something goes terribly wrong when people act upon the information thus acquired?

Traditionally knowledge was defined as *true justified belief*. The quality of the justification for a purportedly true belief is therefore all important. If it is not good enough, one could have knowledge by luck. Therefore it is usually required that in order to have genuine knowledge the person him or herself should be in a direct causal or observational relation to the evidence supporting the belief and be able to articulate it him or herself. This seems to be exactly the problem of gaining knowledge on the WWW. The problem for users of information systems concerns the *justification* of the relevant proposition or the presented data. Modern information consumers are dependent on authority. They are no longer able to present the supporting evidence for their claims to know things themselves.

The Internet exacerbates a strong tendency to a division of intellectual labour and cognitive interdependence in modern science. Some examples will clarify this claim. At the Los Alamos National Library, Paul Ginsparg created a database of new physics papers, By 1996 this archive served more than 35 000 users, over 70 countries with 70 000 electronic transactions per day. CERN makes extensive use of WWW: The Delphi project (**DE**tector for **L**epton, **P**hoton and **H**adron **I**dentification) involves about 550 physicists from 56 universities and institutes in 22 countries. The Human Genome project is another collaborative research project that would be impossible without the WWW. The Human Genome centre at MIT's Web site has been accessed 100 000 times in two years. On-line Mendelian Inheritance in Man (OMIM) contains genome maps, information on genetic diseases and traits, is updated almost daily and is widely accessed by many researchers around the world.

Traditional views of knowledge have not paid attention to this essential social dimension of knowledge, and could therefore be considered too narrow and at variance with online scientific research practice. Most people would, for example, claim to know that smoking causes lung cancer, although they could not possibly present – let alone reproduce – the biochemical, histological and epidemiological evidence themselves. Trust grounds the rationality of our epistemic enquiries nowadays. This solution calls into question and sets limits to individual control and autonomy in the domain of knowledge acquisition, since trust implies a leap of faith, a reaching outside our grasp.

The difficulty we may have in accepting this picture stems from an individualistic bias in epistemology. We find it hard to accept the fact that we are 'epistemically vulnerable'. The modern knowledge enterprise is an intricate but delicate web of trust: cooperation, not intellectual self-reliance, is the key virtue in any scientific community. Epistemology is thereby rendered as requiring ethics, insofar as knowledge can only be based on certain kinds of relations between people. So it seems that in using electronic media in collaborative research we can be held morally responsible for seeing to it that we can assess the extent that it was reasonable for us to assume that sources were worthy of trust.

The problem is that in an early modern conception of knowledge there is perfect alignment of epistemic responsibility and moral responsibility. The knower by definition is also the one who can be held personally accountable if anything goes wrong. But now the responsibility for knowing and the responsibility for doing seem to have come apart. The knower can give no other account than in terms of the structure of the epistemic network and by pointing to trustworthy nodes in the epistemic value chain. But we like to think that when placed in the hands of scrupulous, diligent and prudent researchers, or when we put a high quality Internet2 in place, or institutionalise certification or quality assurance tools, rating services, much can be done to increase the Internet's reliability.

## Responsibility for expressing

In addition to responsibilities that flow from the functional, economic and epistemic value of the Internet and its practices, there are responsibilities for expressing (Kernohan, 1998). Racism, hate speech and violent pornography are expressions on the Internet that have a very problematic status: we cannot condone them, but neither can we simply ban them, as the case of the Communication Decency Act indicates. The general right of freedom of speech may be perceived as overriding. Some things that induce disgust in one person may not do so for others. Often evaluations of these matters involve perfectionist values (as described above), that is, views of how human beings should experience their sexuality or how they should ideally behave. These perfectionist values and ends are highly problematic as sources of justification for limiting the freedom of others to express themselves. Mill's harm principle still forms the moral bottom line here: only the prevention of harm justifies the limitation of individual freedom by government. [Hong Kong **3**]

Joshua Cohen has argued that hate speech, pornography and racism may be construed as harmful (1993). He distinguishes between *direct harms*, such as defamation, and *environmental harms*, or as Feinberg has called them *accumulative harm*s. These are caused by expressions that 'pollute' the communication environment gradually. Each individual expression does not damage the environment, but the accumulated expressions do, because they create an oppressive, hostile, or – depending on the case – an obtrusively moralistic environment. The environment then becomes one where it will be difficult for example to respect general rights, or to seriously discharge one's special obligations to female colleagues. The third form of harm caused by expressions are *indirect harms*, for example when the expression persuades users to do something harmful; to make a bomb, plan a terrorist action, or just go kill somebody. It can be argued that the somewhat elusive accumulative or environmental harm can be construed as implied in the harm principle, thereby offering a way to think of this type of expressions as moral wrongdoings.

Using Robert Goodin's concept of a *negative task responsibility*, we may say that both recreational and professional users have a negative task responsibility in doing what they ought to do on the Net, which consists in seeing to it that one prevents *expressive harm* (direct, indirect and environmental) to others.

## Comments

This is truly a very bleak picture of the life to come. In a fiercely dynamic and personal territory such as Hong Kong, where the culture promotes face-to-face relations and supports notions of collectiveness, where physical isolation from others is extremely problematic given population densities (perhaps unless you are in prison in solitary confinement), I find it very hard to imagine a time when most people telecommute and we hardly ever meet anyone else in 'three-dimensional space'.

**HONG KONG**

This may be true, but it must also be taken within the social, legal and cultural context in which the user chooses to access the materials. It may be that accessing cybersex or pornographic materials will not only satisfy you, but also land you in jail or worse. With respect to games, consequences other than enjoyment may include losing your job or frittering away your life – personal choices to be sure, but perhaps not very positive ones. It is inadequate to consider only the positive consequences of the various applications on the Internet without considering their possible side-effects that may be rather more detrimental to one's 'health'. An additional aspect is to consider resource utilisation. Given limited and costly Internet resources, which is true in many developing countries for example, should one consider the uses of the Internet that benefit society at large, rather than only the individual?

**HONG KONG**

**HONG KONG**

**3**

I agree with the importance of preventing harm, but it seems unlikely that we will agree on what harm is, and is not. From the paragraph above, I could argue that if I am sufficiently disgusted by the sayings of another person (their freedom of speech), then I am harmed, especially if I am addressed directly. In this context, it is necessary to challenge the overriding right to freedom of speech, given its implications. Is it so sacred that we cannot even contemplate its abolition? Could we protect the rights of the majority without the right to freedom of speech? Perhaps it comes back to perfectionist values, to tolerance, to humanity. Why do we have laws, if not to prevent the descent into anarchy, which some on the Internet seem not too concerned about?

# Japanese Comments

Hacker: Van den Hoven's use of the word 'hacker' has a broad sense from the virus writer (without infection) to the Web site intruder. His image of a hacker is a patchwork and hard to define what a hacker is. Though your prepared glossary seems to describe both hacking and cracking, there is no entry for hacker.

The Hacker Ethic: As Van den Hoven described 'the hacker ethic' without definition, the hacker ethic also must be defined. Steven Levy's definition is famous, but it is vague and the context has changed. I propose the definition of *The New Hacker's Dictionary* 3rd edition (MIT Press, 1996).

# American Comments

Comments on this chapter from the American commenting author, Terrell Ward Bynum, proved much longer than those of any other comments in this book; indeed, their 1800 words form an entire essay. However, as the essay is relevant and likely to enhance discussion, it is included here in full.

## Comments on Chapter 6 – Terrell Ward Bynum

In the late 1940s and early 1950s, visionary mathematician/philosopher Norbert Wiener single-handedly created computer ethics as a field of academic research. In his monumental book, *The Human Use of Human Beings* (1950, 1954), Wiener spelled out a powerful and practical method of applying ethics to computing technology. Even today, in the era of global information ethics and the Internet, the concepts and procedures that Wiener developed fifty years ago still provide an effective method of analysing and resolving ethical questions associated with ICT of all kinds. Wiener's ground breaking book provides a number of practical ideas that could be added to the present chapter.

Wiener based his foundation for computer ethics upon a 'cybernetic' view of human nature that leads readily to an ethically suggestive account of the purpose of a human life. From this, he derived 'principles of justice' upon which every society should be based. Finally, he spelled out a practical strategy for identifying and resolving computer ethics issues wherever they might arise.

Wiener's cybernetic view of human nature emphasised the *physical structure* of the human body and the tremendous potential for learning and creative action that human physiology makes possible. To underscore this fact, he often compared human physiology with that of less intelligent creatures like insects:

*Cybernetics takes the view that the structure of the machine or of the organism is an index of the performance that may be expected from it.* The fact that the mechanical rigidity of the insect is such as to limit its intelligence while the mechanical fluidity of the human being provides for his almost indefinite intellectual expansion is highly relevant to the point of view of this book... man's advantage over the rest of nature is that he has the physiological and hence the intellectual equipment to adapt himself to radical changes in his environment. The human species is strong only insofar as it takes advantage of the innate, adaptive, learning faculties that its physiological structure makes possible. (Wiener, 1954, pp. 57–8; italics in the original)

On the basis of his 'cybernetic' analysis of human nature, Wiener concluded that the purpose of a human life is to *flourish* as the kind of information-processing being that humans naturally are:

I wish to show that the human individual, capable of vast learning and study, which may occupy almost half of his life, is physically equipped, as the ant is not, for this capacity. Variety and possibility are inherent in the human sensorium – and are indeed the key to man's most noble flights – because variety and possibility belong to the very structure of the human organism. (Wiener, 1954, p. 51)

A good human life, according to Wiener, is one in which 'great human values' are realised – one in which the creative and flexible information-processing potential of 'the human sensorium' enables humans to reach their full promise in variety and possibility of action. Different people, of course, have various levels of talent and possibility, so one person's achievements will differ from another's; and it is possible to lead a good human life in an indefinitely large number of ways – as a public servant or statesman, a teacher or scholar, a scientist or engineer, a musician, an artist, a tradesman, an artisan, and so on.

Wiener's view of the purpose of a human life leads him to adopt what he calls 'great principles of justice' upon which a society should be built – principles that, in his view, would maximise a person's ability to flourish through variety and flexibility in human action. (Wiener, 1954, pp. 105–6). To highlight Wiener's 'great principles of justice', let us call them 'The Principle of Freedom', 'The Principle of Equality' and 'The Principle of Benevolence'. (Wiener himself does not assign names, but merely states them.) Using Wiener's own definitions for these key ethical principles, we get the following list:

- *The Principle of Freedom* – Justice requires 'the liberty of each human being to develop in his freedom the full measure of the human possibilities embodied in him'
- *The Principle of Equality* – Justice requires 'the equality by which what is just for A and B remains just when the positions of A and B are interchanged'
- *The Principle of Benevolence* – Justice requires 'a good will between man and man that knows no limits short of those of humanity itself'

Wiener's cybernetic account of human nature leads to the view that people are fundamentally *social* beings who can reach their full potential only by actively participating in communities of similar beings. Society, therefore, is essential to a good human life. But society can be despotic and oppressive, and thereby limit, or even stifle, freedom; so Wiener introduced a principle to limit as much as possible society's negative impact upon freedom. (Let us name it 'The Principle of Minimum Infringement of Freedom').

■ *The Principle of Minimum Infringement of Freedom* – 'What compulsion the very existence of the community and the state may demand must be exercised in such a way as to produce no unnecessary infringement of freedom.' (1954, p.106)

If one accepts Wiener's account of human nature and the good society, it follows that many different cultures, with a wide diversity of customs, religions, languages and practices, can provide an appropriate context for human fulfilment and a good life. Indeed, given Wiener's view that 'variety and possibility belong to the very structure of the human organism', he presumably would expect and encourage the existence of a broad diversity of cultures around the world to maximise the possibilities for choice and creative action. The primary restriction that Wiener would impose on any society would be that it should provide the kind of context in which humans can realise their full potential as sophisticated information-processing agents; and he believed this to be possible only where significant freedom, equality and human compassion hold sway.

So-called *ethical relativists* often point to the wide diversity of cultures in the world – with various religions, laws, codes, values and practices – as evidence that there is no global ethics, no underlying universal ethical foundation. Wiener, on the other hand, has a powerful and creative response to such sceptics. His account of human nature and the purpose of a human life *can embrace and welcome the rich diversity of cultures and practices* that relativists are fond of citing. At the same time, Wiener can advocate an *underlying ethical foundation* for all societies and cultures.

Wiener's suggested methodology for analysing and solving computer ethics questions is one that, essentially, assimilates new ethical judgements and new cases into the existing cluster of laws, rules, practices and principles that govern human behaviour in the society in question. The key elements of this approach are the following:

■ *Human Purpose* – Ethical judgements and practices must be grounded in the overall purpose of a human life: a society and the rules which govern its members must make it possible for people to flourish – to reach their full potential in variety and possibility of action.
■ *Principles of Justice* – The Principle of Freedom, the Principle of Equality and the Principle of Benevolence should guide and inform every person's judgements and practices; and society must neither permit nor impose unnecessary limitations upon individual freedom.
■ *Clarity of Concepts and Rules* – The meanings of ethical concepts and rules, in a given situation, should be clear and unambiguous. If they are not, one must undertake to clarify their meanings to the extent possible.
■ *Precedent and Tradition* – New ethical judgements and cases should be assimilated into the existing body of cases, rules, laws, policies and practices.

Given these elements of ethical analysis, Wiener's methodology can be construed as including the following three steps:

■ Step One: Identify an ethical question or case regarding the integration of ICT into society.
■ Step Two: Clarify any ambiguous concepts or rules that may apply to the case in question.
■ Step Three: Apply existing principles, laws, rules, policies and practices which govern human behaviour in the given society. Use precedent and traditional interpretation in such a way as to assimilate the new case or policy into the existing set of social policies and practices.

For any given society, there will be a 'cluster' of existing laws, rules, principles and practices to govern human behaviour within that society. These form a complex and extremely rich set of overlapping, criss-crossing policies that constitute a 'received policy cluster' (Bynum and Schubert, 1997). This received cluster of policies should be the starting point for developing an answer to any computer ethics question.

If a given case or question does not fit easily into the existing set of rules and policies in one's society, then one must either (1) make adjustments in the old policies and rules to accommodate the new case, or else (2) introduce a totally new policy to cover the new kind of case. Presumably, if such a new case were to arise, one would have to use the overall purpose of a human life, together with the fundamental principles of justice, to create and justify new laws and policies consistent with the old ones. Such a case would be an example of James Moor's classic 'policy vacuum' for which one must formulate and justify new policies. (See Moor, 1985)

It is important to note that this method of doing of computer ethics need not involve the expertise of a trained philosopher. In any society, a successfully functioning adult will be famil-iar with the laws, rules, customs, practices and policies that normally govern one's behaviour in that society and enable one to tell whether a proposed action or policy would be considered eth-ical. If the introduction of ICT creates new possibilities and opportunities that do not fit neatly into the existing policy cluster, those affected and those responsible for implementing the new technology should use customary means of assimilating new cases to existing precedent and interpretation. Thus, all those in society who must cope with the introduction of ICT – whether they are public policy makers, ICT professionals, business people, workers, teachers, whatever their role in society – can and should engage in computer ethics by helping to integrate ICT ethically into society. Computer ethics, understood in this broad way, is too vast and too important to be left only to academics or to ICT professionals.

Wiener makes it clear that, on his view, the integration of ICT into society will constitute the remaking of society – the 'second industrial revolution' – destined to affect every major aspect of life. It is bound to be a multifaceted, ongoing process, one that will take decades of effort and will radically change everything. In Wiener's words, we are 'here in the presence of another social potentiality of unheard-of importance for good and for evil'. (Wiener, 1948, p. 27) The defining goal of computer ethics, then, is *to advance and facilitate the good consequences of ICT and prevent or minimise the harmful ones.*

The computer revolution – predicted by Norbert Wiener fifty years ago – is now unfolding worldwide. The 'information age' is emerging; and the Internet is playing a central role in its birth. The ethical foundation for computer ethics that Wiener laid down five decades ago can still provide effective tools and guidance as we confront globally significant ethical issues on the Internet.

**Endnote:** These comments are derived primarily from Bynum (1999). Quotations from Wiener's *The Human Use of Human Beings* are all from the 1954 Second Edition Revised.

# 7 Information Integrity

RICHARD A. SPINELLO

## Introduction

The primary axis of discussion in this chapter is an important question that confronts any organisation connected to the Internet: how does it preserve and safeguard information integrity in a networked environment? The precise meaning and scope of 'information integrity' is a matter of some debate. For our purposes information integrity implies that proprietary or sensitive information under one's custodial care is kept confidential and secure, that information being transmitted is not altered in form or content and cannot be read by unauthorised parties, and that *all* information being disseminated or otherwise made accessible through Web sites and online data repositories is as accurate and reliable as possible. Failure to take this obligation seriously could result in harm to data subjects, that is, the affected individuals or those about whom the data are relevant. Or it could result in harm to the organisation itself especially if sensitive information such as trade secrets are misappropriated.

In the opening section we dwell on the imperative to keep proprietary, sensitive information confidential; we will see how this issue intersects with the theme of privacy already discussed in Chapter 4. The next several sections focus on the challenge involved in keeping information secure on the Internet; this begins in the second section with a review of why this challenge has become so formidable. In the third section we turn to the various specific threats to a secure environment such as viruses and worms, unauthorised access, and so forth. The fourth section discusses the countermeasures which organisations can take to protect their information assets and to secure the transmission of sensitive electronic documents. These include encryption schemes, antivirus software and firewalls. In the next section special attention is given to the use of digital signatures because of their critical role in ensuring the integrity of data being transmitted over the Internet. In the sixth section we consider the moral dimension of this security issue, which is often overlooked. We make the case here that security is both a moral imperative and a fiduciary obligation to an organisation's stakeholders. In the subsequent section we examine a more subtle threat to information integrity: neglect or carelessness that can result in online data of poor quality. The Internet has increased the mobility of data and the complexity of data management, and this in turn magnifies the challenge of safeguarding accuracy and reliability. In the final section we consider the problems encountered by those who publish or disseminate information in cyberspace along with their potential liability for libel. In the final section we emphasise our conclusion: information is the lifeblood of the Net-centric organisation and hence it must be vigilantly protected with a coherent strategy that judiciously seeks to minimise security risks at a reasonable and manageable cost. No organisation or individual can afford to be cavalier about the integrity and viability of its critical information resources.

## Preserving the confidentiality of proprietary information resources

A recent report in *Forbes* magazine described how easy it has become to spy on one's competitors. The reason is not gaping security holes in IT systems but instead the corporation's penchant for revealing too much information on its Web sites. This includes detailed executive biographies, research papers, job postings, price lists, discussions on new product developments, and descriptions of strategic alliances. Is it possible that the ease of publishing information on the Web has made some organisations too forthcoming? Consider this example cited in the *Forbes* article: DuPont's Web site (www.dupont.com) 'offers a list of factories and yarn spinners around the world that work with CoolMax, a synthetic used in athletic apparel.'(Penenbeg, 1999). The Web site includes the addresses of these facilities along with the names and some background about their plant managers. Clearly, the information supplied by DuPont would be of immense help to a competitor interested in producing their own synthetic material. Many companies seduced by the public relations benefits of elaborate Web sites make the mistake of making too much information public, forgetting that competitors and cyberspies will also be culling this material. Information such as research papers, patent applications, new product trajectories, and so on should remain proprietary for as long as possible so as not to signal a competitor about the state of one's research and development plans. It is pointless to have high level security systems if companies reveal too much of the information that should be proprietary on their Web sites. Thus, the first requirement of information integrity is to classify information appropriately, making circumspect decisions about which forms of information should remain proprietary and which forms should be made public. Organisations should err on the side of caution in the porous environment of the Internet.

The aggregation of so much personal data on the Internet and the emergence of online data brokers poses another potential threat to information integrity. Once again a careful decision must be made by these data brokers about which types of information should be made publicly accessible. Search engines allow access to these online databases in ways that make it much easier to track down voluminous information about an individual, sometimes for nefarious purposes. Certain Web sites, for instance, permit reverse number lookups so that a user can find a name based on an address or a phone number. Organisations that manage and make available this data are known as 'individual reference services' or 'look-up services' and include companies like Equifax, Lexis-Nexis, and Experian. These companies gather and sell private data such as credit histories or medical records to their clients which include banks and insurance companies. They also make limited amounts of less sensitive data available to the general public through their online databases. As purveyors of data to the public, they certainly have a moral obligation to protect sensitive pieces of information that could be abused if they fell into the wrong hands. An indiscriminate disclosure of confidential and revealing data would manifest serious disrespect for the user's right to the confidentiality of his or her personal information. For example, these online reference services should prohibit the distribution to the general public of social security numbers, dates of birth, or unlisted phone numbers. Social security numbers are a critical link to other data and they could permit opportunities for exploitative data recombination. The issue came to the forefront in September 1996 when Lexis-Nexis, made available mothers' maiden names, social security numbers, and birth dates on its online P-Trak database. The company did voluntarily reverse itself in the wake of a vocal protest, but the incident underlined the need for these reference services to be more disciplined in curbing the public's access to certain pieces of sensitive data whose release could be detrimental to many users. **[HONG KONG 1]**

Thus, if organisations aspire to information integrity they must be more diligent with regard to the information released about their own operations and consistently opt for maximum protection of their information assets. If they are data keepers managing large amounts of personal data, they must prevent the public's access to critical pieces of consumer information that could easily be exploited by providing links to other data that might enable extensive profiling of a someone's background. As discussed in Chapter 4, the increased access to so much personal information online poses a major threat for the preservation of personal privacy. But if there is some measure of self-restraint, a reasonable balance between information accessibility and privacy rights can be achieved.

## The evolving security challenge

In addition to preserving the confidentiality of certain information, organisations must also continually monitor and increase their security for electronic records and online data. There is little doubt that by connecting to the Internet organisations have made their information assets more vulnerable than ever before. The problem is that the Internet is an open network developed for interoperability. It was designed for the efficient transmission of data but not for its security and protection. As the Internet's global diffusion continues, users throughout the world face a dual threat to the security of their data. First, the risks of electronic intrusion and unauthorised access are magnified by connectivity, and so there is a greater likelihood that sensitive data will be pilfered, tampered with, or destroyed. As connectivity continues to increase and as more information is stored on networks, the risk of misappropriation and other mishaps goes up proportionately. In addition, exchanging information in an insecure environment such as the terrain of cyberspace can be a perilous task: rogue technophiles can intercept and alter e-mail messages or otherwise attack commercial transactions.

Attention to security and information integrity issues has always seemed to lag behind the evolution of information technology capabilities. Many organisations have been loath to expend the necessary time and money to minimise their security risks. But prior to the emergence of the decentralised, netcentric organisation, the scope of the security challenge was more manageable for two basic reasons.

To begin with, it was considerably easier to implement security measures in the closed, homogeneous mainframe environments that dominated the corporate landscape in the 1980s. But client server technology and especially Internet connectivity has changed all that. While the Internet makes it far easier to exchange information it also exposes that information to more appreciable risks. In addition, the responsibility for security has shifted from the organisation's IS department, which once exerted central control over computer resources, to individual departments or business units. Thus, the scope of the security challenge expands significantly since every workstation on the corporate network becomes a gateway to the Internet and thereby exposes the whole corporation to risk. Hence, according to Segev *et al*. (1998), 'security can no longer be a sole concern of a security department, IT department, or telecommunications; with the sphere of computing expanding across all areas and levels of enterprise, IS security touches everyone from the custodian to the Chief Executive Officer'. This combination of Internet connectivity and decentralisation of IS responsibilities makes the realisation of security much more complex and difficult, dependent upon both sophisticated technology and careful organisational planning.

## Security problems in a networked environment

Stories about the fragile nature of the Internet's security seem to appear in the headlines almost every day. The Internet's vulnerabilities are underscored by destructive viruses like Chernobyl and Melissa that generated considerable publicity. The latter infected 100 000 computers and cost millions of dollars in containment efforts (Wagner, 1999). Despite tougher laws in some countries such as the amended Computer Fraud and Abuse Act in the United States (1996), hackers seem to be more emboldened than ever before. The newest sport is hacking Web pages. In early summer of 1999 United States Government Web sites were subjected to a series of such humiliating attacks. By surreptitiously accessing their Web servers the sites of both the FBI and the US Senate were altered with digital graffiti; some of it taunted the FBI with questions such as 'Who laughs last?' (Simons, 1999). A recent PriceWaterhouse/Cooper survey reported that 59 per cent of US companies selling their wares on the Web reported similar security breaches during 1998.

Web sites are an especially attractive target for hackers and other mischievous users for several reasons. Attacking a Web server is a public incident that can provoke considerable attention. Further, many Web servers are used for electronic commerce which means that they are receiving credit card numbers, often a focus of hacker activity. [ SWEDEN **1** ] And finally Web sites are increasingly used to distribute proprietary information within an organisation or to strategic partners. This information may be a target for competitors or others with hostile intentions towards a particular organisation.

How can these costly incidents be prevented in the future? Is there a viable way to secure Web servers and protect information on systems that are based on open Internet standards? Before we turn to this important topic it would be instructive to treat in more detail some of the common security threats to information integrity. Once these are more fully understood, we can review the most sensible remedies.

## Computer viruses and worms

During late March 1999, security administrators throughout the world braced themselves for another dreaded computer virus. This one was called Melissa, a macro virus cleverly propagated through Microsoft's Outlook electronic mail system. Recipients of the virus found an innocuous looking e-mail message with the subject line reading: 'Important Message From…' followed by the name of the sender. When the user opened the Word document attached to the message, it activated a macro that looks for the address book on the user's hard drive. Outlook then sent the exact same message to the first 50 addresses that it encountered there. In this way the volume of mail generated by Melissa would multiply exponentially. While Melissa did not destroy data on individual computer systems, it produced volumes of useless e-mail that debilitated e-mail servers. Also, if the user opened or created a sensitive document when Melissa kicked in, that document would be covertly sent to the 50 addresses. In some cases highly confidential memos were sent to these random addresses without any warning.

An even more deadly virus created by a Taiwanese student was called 'Chernobyl'. It infected at least 700 000 computers in the Middle East and Asia in April 1999. In Cairo many large businesses closed because their systems collapsed. Other companies in these underdeveloped areas were especially vulnerable because they have not made the expensive investment in a security infrastructure that has been made by their counterparts in the United States and Europe. Unlike Melissa, the Chernobyl virus did delete significant amounts of data and corrupt programs.

Melissa and Chernobyl are just two examples of the 20 000 known viruses that plague computer systems. But what exactly is a virus? A computer virus is informally and loosely defined as a piece of parasitic, malicious, self-replicating code. More precisely, according to Stubbs and Hoffman (1990), a virus is a piece of code with two characteristics: 1) at least a partially automated capability to reproduce; 2) a method of transfer which is dependent upon its ability to attach itself to other computer entities (programs, disk sectors, data files, and so on) that move between these systems. A virus will not be executed or code replicated until the host program is activated. It can penetrate a system through an external device (such as a floppy disk) or through network links and electronic mail. The most malicious viruses like Chernobyl can efface data stored on the hard disk by overwriting it.

What is most worrisome about the latest breed of macro viruses is the facility with which they can be transmitted over computer networks. This was made painfully evident in the Melissa incident which quickly invaded computer systems and congested electronic highways before it was contained. A macro virus exploits programming capabilities called macros that are built into application software such as Microsoft Word or Excel. While earlier viruses attacked programs, macro viruses can attack documents or templates generated by that software.

Worms are similar to viruses, but unlike a virus, a worm can run independently and travel from one system to another without attaching itself to another entity. Like a virus, a worm is self-replicating – it makes copies of itself that can quickly consume a system's available memory. Worms do not alter programs or overwrite data but they can contain code that does so (such as a virus).

## Unauthorised access and trespass

For our purposes access is 'unauthorised' when the user knowingly and deliberately gains entry to a closed networked computer site or Web site, clearly indicated as such, without the owner's permission.

Networked computer systems are increasingly vulnerable to such access by cybersnoops and hackers who consistently threaten the integrity of the data on those systems. We must first consider how these individuals are able to penetrate supposedly secure electronic systems.

To enter a computer system a username and password is normally required. One of the most popular means of breaking into a system is misappropriating a user's password. Some users carelessly share their passwords with others. Alternatively, hackers can try their hand at 'cracking' passwords. A password can be cracked by sheer brute force trial and error or by using a software program such as CRACK. The former is possible when users are nonchalant about their passwords and use ordinary ones that can be easily deciphered. CRACK and similar programs provide for a more systematic approach. These programs generate a series of words and word combinations that are run against the system password file to find the password for a given location.

Hackers can also exploit security holes in operating systems or network protocols. A group of Russians were suspected of breaking into the site of Aye.net, an ISP located in the State of Indiana in the United States. They randomly deleted files and forced Aye.net to close down its operations for four days. Their break-in was facilitated by vulnerabilities in the operating system of the Silicon Graphics servers that maintain their files. There are also perverse programs such as SATAN that can assist hackers in taking advantage of those vulnerabilities. SATAN's 'attack scanner' was developed to scan one's own site to look for problems, but is now being utilised to probe networks of UNIX computers for their security flaws.

In addition, hackers can employ various methods to gather passwords. They can use programs called 'sniffers' to intercept communications travelling over a network and extract the passwords. A hacker can install a sniffer program masquerading as a monitoring program on an Internet host computer. As information is passed through the network, the sniffer looks for passwords. For instance, when user X logs on to computer A from computer B the sniffer (installed on the hacker's networked computer) can detect the password and thereby give the hacker access to computer B. As the program sniffs out more and more passwords, the hacker can easily gain access to different computer systems linked to the Internet.

Once a system is penetrated, sensitive information in files and documents becomes fair game for the perpetrators. They can do anything from just trespassing and cybersnooping to engaging in data tampering. This data tampering can take two forms: data can be modified or it can be deleted. An employee of the US Coast Guard recently 'loaned out' his password to someone who used it to gain access to the personnel database. Once she succeeded in this intrusion over the Internet she proceeded to delete personnel information. According to reports on this incident it took 115 workers and 1800 hours to restore the lost data at a total cost of $40 000 (DiDio, 1998).

Also computer files can be pilfered by the culprits. This could be a serious situation for an organisation since trade secrets and other valuable proprietary information is clearly at risk. Even military secrets and classified government data may be stolen by hackers or online spies thereby compromising a country's national security.

### Intercepting commercial transactions or e-mail communications

Sensitive data is in even more peril when it is on the move. The threat of security flaws still bedevils the progress of electronic commerce. Buying products on the Internet means that users must give their credit card numbers to the Web site, but many wonder about the security of such transactions. The primary risk is that one's credit card number will be sniffed out as it is transmitted to the Web server. The culprit might then use this number to commit fraud. Some hackers automate their illicit 'sniffing' activities with programs that scan thousands of Web sites and their customers for any sort of security holes or lapses.

The transmission of sensitive information such as confidential electronic documents, health care records, and so forth, via electronic mail is also becoming increasingly common. These communications will need to be highly secure to protect both the sender and the recipient. In most current e-mail systems it is relatively easy to forge the identity of the sender of a message. This could have serious consequences if the recipient is duped into performing inappropriate activities based on that forged message. It is also easy to alter the content of an unprotected message while it is in transit.

Security for these communications should therefore have three distinct but interrelated components:

■ *confidentiality:* the information can only be accessed by the recipient

■ *transmission integrity:* the form and content of the message have not been altered in any way during transit

■ *authentication:* identity of the sender and recipient are carefully verified.

In the next two sections we will explicitly review how a security system can be implemented to ensure that electronic communications are adequately protected from unauthorised interception or alteration.

## Security countermeasures

As intimated in the previous section one of the major new security challenges posed by the Internet is tackling the Web security problem. According to Spafford and Garfinkel (1997), there are three dimensions to Web security:

■ Securing the Web server and the data which it contains. One must ensure, for example. that data on the Web server is not modified without authorisation and is distributed only to authorised individuals.

■ Securing information that traverses between the Web server and individual users, that is, guaranteeing that information supplied by users to that server such as a password or credit card number cannot be read or modified by others.

■ Securing the user's own computer by ensuring that it will not be corrupted by programs or data that are downloaded to it.

There are a number of sophisticated hardware mechanisms and software programs that are designed to protect connected systems and help solve the Web security problem. These will constitute a security infrastructure which should provide organisations with a basic level of protection. It should be pointed out, however, that even the most elaborate infrastructure cannot serve as a substitute for a coherent security strategy. Thus every organisation must work out a plan that will properly balance Internet security with Internet access. Such a plan will include policies and procedures that can be integrated with state of the art technology to provide a unified front of protection that does far more than focus on one or two pieces of the security puzzle. We now turn to a brief overview of the key technical components of this security infrastructure.

## Firewalls

A firewall consists of hardware and/or software that is positioned between an organisation's internal network and the Internet. Its goal is to insulate an organisation's private network from intrusions by trapping any external threat, such as a virus, before it can penetrate and damage an information system. Firewalls, of course, are not foolproof and cannot function properly if there are security gaps or flaws in the overall system such as an unprotected modem pool.

The simplest form of firewall is the packet filter which relies on a piece of hardware known as a router to filter packets between the internal network and an outside connection such as the Internet. It operates by examining the source address of each individual packet along with its destination address within the firewall. If something is suspicious or the source address is considered to be an untrusted site, it can refuse the packet's entry. Most routers already incorporate this type of monitoring functionality. According to Bernstein (1994) 'to safely implement a real-life filtering configuration, all of the permissions and restrictions must be defined in a detailed policy; this policy must be translated to the router's filtering tables'. A more sophisticated, high-level firewall is called an application gateway which includes two routers that create a separate zone between the internal network and the Internet along with specialised software programs that make judgements about specific applications seeking entry.

## Antivirus software

Antivirus software scans a system for malicious code and removes it once it has been located. This software is programmed to look for signs of a virus, such as fragments of code or other errant data. Since new virus forms are constantly being propagated, vendors must update their antivirus software frequently, and users must make sure that they have the latest versions with the most up-to-date protection. The disadvantage of this software is the need for its constant revision. Current versions of this software deal with the newest breed of macro and boot sector viruses.

## Backup systems

Sound backup procedures constitute a vital part of an adequate security system. If data is destroyed through a virus or through intentional file deletion by intruders, an up-to-date backup copy of the file will allow the organisation to restore its information integrity. The more critical and dynamic the information the more frequently backup copies should be made. Backup systems are normally kept off site in case of a physical disaster such as a fire, flood, earthquake or typhoon.

## Probing and intrusion detection tools

Probing tools allow organisations to perform their own proactive penetration testing. This entails the use of these automated tools to probe that organisation's systems and networks for security holes. This will make transparent the system's vulnerabilities. The organisation can then take the necessary steps to plug up these holes.

Intrusion detection systems (IDS) monitor networks for irregular activities such as three successive aborted log-on attempts or packets from a suspicious IP address. They can set off alarms when certain events occur. An IDS can also search for anomalous behaviour on the network, that is, unusual or abnormal activities that appear to deviate from the typical activities of a particular user.

## Filtering systems

In addition to keeping intruders away from sensitive data, organisations must prevent their own employees from exporting that data. Sometimes an organisation may be victimised by insiders who are willing to sell trade secrets or other proprietary information for profit or just for revenge. In order to prevent this, filtering software (such as MIMESweeper) can be deployed to sift through outgoing electronic mail that should not be leaving a particular site. This software is programmed to divert any suspicious looking e-mail into a mail folder labelled 'blocked and captured'. Of course, the use of these filtering systems triggers privacy concerns since employees' outgoing e-mail is being routinely exposed. Should workers have a reasonable expectation of privacy for their outgoing electronic mail? Some organisations may not even recognise such a privacy right for their workers and that brings up a different set of issues that have been addressed in Chapter 4. But other organisations that believe that a strong presumption must be given to workplace privacy rights will need to work through this familiar dilemma between the protection of information and the preservation of those rights.

## Encryption

One way of assuring the safety of information transmitted over an insecure network such as the Internet is to encrypt that information so that it cannot be read or altered in any way. Encryption was defined and discussed in Chapter 4. Recall that data encryption is nothing more than a secret code. It works by taking an intelligible message such as 'the enemy is 100 miles away' and translating it into something which is unintelligible without a key. Automated encryption can be done either through hardware or by means of software algorithms. Although numerous encryption algorithms have been developed, the most popular commercial one is the DES or Data Encryption Standard, which the US government has utilised as its standard since 1977. The DES is currently used in many e-mail and networking packages and was recently recertified by the US government in 1993.

The DES is a symmetric private key cryptography system; this simply means that the same secret binary key is utilised for both encryption and decryption. For this to work properly, both parties, the sender and receiver of the data, must have access to this key. The key itself must then be communicated in a secure fashion or it could be intercepted by a third party or otherwise fall into the wrong hands. This is a serious disadvantage of the private key scheme. It should be pointed out that the longer the key the more difficult it is to crack. (A 128 bit key would be much more difficult to crack than a 40 bit key.)

The other popular encryption technique is known as public key cryptography, which is asymmetric since the keys used by the different parties are not the same. Public key cryptography works as follows: each party gets a pair of keys, one public and one private; the public key is used to encrypt a message while a secret private key is used to decrypt the message. The obvious advantage of public key cryptography is that the sender and receiver of the message do not have to exchange a secret private key before they begin to communicate.

Encryption then is an important tool for protecting information integrity in several major applications such as electronic commerce and electronic mail. E-commerce transactions often involve entering a credit card number on the Internet which opens up the possibility of fraud. If the number is appropriately encrypted it cannot be deciphered by a third party. The Web site server receives the encrypted information, which is then decrypted and verified to conclude the transaction. Netscape's Secure Socket Layer (SSL) is a software program that automatically encrypts credit card numbers that are sent over the Internet. E-mail transmissions involving proprietary information should also be encrypted.

It is worth noting that in many countries, such as the United States, the adoption of strong encryption technology has sparked contentious debate among public policy makers. The government is looking for some measure of control over this technology so that they can decrypt messages being sent by terrorists or saboteurs. One way to accomplish this objective is a key escrow or key recovery system. Key recovery involves archiving a master key with a trusted third party. According to Denning (1998), 'The archived keys are not used to encrypt or decrypt data, but only to unlock the data encryption keys under exigent circumstances'. If a law enforcement agency sought to eavesdrop on a suspected criminal's encrypted e-mail messages, key recovery systems provided by the e-mail software vendor would provide the key to that agency. The United States has long had in place tight export controls which prohibit US businesses from selling strong encryption products throughout the world unless they are accompanied by a key recovery system that would enable the government to decrypt messages. Almost no developed countries have laws that limit the use of cryptography for their own citizens. In Russia, however, encryption users are required to register with the Russian Defence Ministry. And in France the use of any encryption without permission was illegal until early 1999, when the Jospin government decided to legalise 128 bit encryption for domestic use or for export.

The public policy debate about encryption is coloured by many nuances and complexities and a thorough treatment of the issues is beyond the scope of this chapter. But the issue at the crux of this debate can be summed up in one provocative question: should governments be more concerned about their inability to eavesdrop on terrorist communications or about the need for the security and integrity of all Internet communications and transactions?

## Authentication and digital signatures

One way to buttress Internet security is to insist upon knowing the identity of those using the system in question, such as a Web page or an online database. It is also important to verify the identity of those receiving and sending electronic messages. This is known as authentication, which permits the automatic verification of the end user's identity and prevents corruption of the message being transmitted. In the physical world there are many occasions when a person must authenticate his or her identity by producing physical documents such as a driver's licence, passport, and birth certificate. On the Internet electronic authentication serves the exact same purpose.

According to Bellovin (1998), user authentication is normally based on one of three categories: 'something you know, something you have, and something you are'. With this scheme in mind let us review some of the primary methods of authentication:

- *User ID/Password Authentication ('something you know')*: users are required to enter their ID and passwords before entering a site. Subscribers to the *Economist* and its Web site, for example, are not allowed entry unless they first key in a username and password. Passwords, however, are considered to be a weak form of authentication because they can often be cracked or intercepted so easily, sometimes just by watching someone type.

■ *Access tokens/smart cards ('something you have')*: users authenticate their identity through these devices, which hold some secret machine readable information. Since they can be lost or stolen, a user proves his or her ownership by keying in a short password connected with the card which is known as a personal identification number (PIN).

■ *Biometrics ('something you are')*: biometric authentication systems are expensive but growing in popularity. These systems rely upon measurable physical characteristics to identify a user. One product reads fingerprints and compares and matches them against a database of finger prints that have been scanned into a file. This method of authentication is an improvement over password protection since fingerprints cannot be stolen in the same way that passwords can. Forgeries, however, are still possible. Also, the use of biometric identifying mechanisms has ominous implications for privacy rights. Are we ready to accept a system that relies on fingerprints, retinal scans, or even DNA samples to verify the identity of individuals? **[HONG KONG 2 ]**

A digital signature does not fit neatly in any of these categories but it can play a major role in securing electronic communications. According to Keen (1998), digital signatures 'offer electronic validation of the identity of the sender of a message and hence of the authenticity of that message'. When digital signatures are employed properly, Internet communications can be protected from unauthorised access, usage, or alteration. One can send a message to someone and rest assured that it has not been altered on the way.

Digital signatures rely on public key cryptography. They also rely on a process known as a 'hash function', an algorithm that generates a message digest. A hash function creates a condensed version of a message or document, a 'fingerprint' unique to that message such that any alteration could be easily detected. The user first indicates what material or documents are to be included in the 'message'. A hash function then generates a unique hash result or digest of that message. The hash result is then encrypted and signed using the signer's private key. This digital signature and the message is transmitted to the receiving party which verifies it by computing a new hash result of the message using the sender's public key. The recipient checks the new hash result to confirm that the digital signature was created using the correct private key and that the message was not altered in transmission. This will be the case if the two hash results are perfectly identical. Digital signatures can protect the contents of a message against unauthorised disclosure (through encryption) and also provide the recipient with assurance that the message received is identical to the message content sent by the originator. However, there must be some way to guarantee that the owners of private keys used to sign messages are who they say they are. There must be a secure way of binding a key to an individual or to an organisation. This can be done by relying on a trusted third party to certify that the private key does belong to the sender. This third party is called a 'certification authority' (CA) which issues a certificate that verifies an individual's identity and binds the public and private key to that identity. **[SWEDEN 2 ]**

The ultimate security goal for data being sent over the Internet is to ensure authentication, confidentiality, and transmission integrity. This objective can normally be realised by means of digital signatures. Through the use of these signatures we can have confidence that the identified sender really transmitted the message and is who they claim to be (authentication), that the message arrived unaltered (integrity), and that the encrypted message was not read by a third party (confidentiality). Hence, digital signatures go a long way to helping to realise the broader goal of information integrity even in the open and insecure environment of the Internet.

## The moral dimension of securing information

There are many incentives for increasing security consciousness. It is sound business policy, especially for those businesses that intend to make a successful foray into electronic commerce. Security lapses and breakdowns can be major impediments for wary online shoppers. Since online security is such a notable concern for consumers, companies that do not adopt security safeguards will suffer for it in the marketplace.

But there are other reasons why security must be a high priority. Consumers place their trust in e-commerce companies and assume that their credit card numbers will be transmitted safely. **[SWEDEN 3 ]** If such companies are lax about security there could be negative repercussions for these customers who may become victims of fraud if their credit card numbers are intercepted. There is a moral obligation, therefore, to ensure the integrity of online transactions, that is, to take reasonable steps to safeguard the information involved from misappropriation. This obligation is derived from the more fundamental moral duty to avoid and help prevent injury to others. If online transactions are corrupted or sensitive information such as a credit card number is misappropriated, online businesses are accountable for that injury, at least indirectly, especially if this misappropriation occurs through negligence or carelessness. This negligence can manifest itself in several ways such as a failure to acquire the technical knowledge necessary to deploy security safeguards or a disposition to cut corners because security is not regarded as a business or moral imperative.

It can also be argued that there is a fiduciary obligation to an organisation's stakeholders to minimise security risks. In the information age, information is an organisation's most vital asset and this imposes a serious obligation to protect that information from harm. It is unfair to stockholders and others with a legitimate stake in that organisation when its managers put information assets such as trade secrets, customer lists, proprietary product information, into jeopardy through neglect or through lack of vigilance. If such information were stolen, lost, or corrupted the negative ramifications for an operation would undoubtedly be quite severe. Organisations must therefore make a concerted effort to identify their most critical information and to protect it accordingly against threats of viruses, unwelcome intruders, or other misfortunes.

## Information integrity: data accuracy and reliability

Custodians of data also have additional responsibilities of stewardship that go beyond security and confidentiality. The traditional concept of stewardship implies an obligation to look after property that belongs to another, to keep it safe and to ensure its ongoing utility. Thus, a steward is normally charged with taking proper care of the property that has been entrusted to him. In addition to keeping information secure, stewardship responsibility entails maintaining the accuracy and the overall quality of that information. If information under one's control becomes inaccurate and outdated its usefulness and value is questionable, and serious problems could ensue. Stewards must be held accountable for this, especially if such inaccuracies are attributed to neglect, that is, to a wilful disregard for maintaining accuracy despite having the capability of doing so.

The justification for this is grounded in the set of 'information rights' which each individual deserves. According to Branscomb (1995), one of those rights is integrity, that is, the right to control the accuracy and reliability of one's information. This imposes on data keepers an obligation to maintain accurate and up-to-date records of high quality. But how do we determine some reasonable limits for this particular obligation? To what effort and expense should companies go to verify and maintain accuracy, especially when the data in question is highly volatile? How often should records be updated and revised to ensure their accuracy? When grappling with these questions organisations must carefully assess the possible ramifications of inaccuracies, since this will help to determine the amount of resources that should be contributed to prevent those errors (Spinello, 1997a).

The issue of accuracy and reliability has special saliency for the Internet thanks to the widespread availability of online personal information. For example, search engines (see also Chapter 4) such as AltaVista, Excite, and HotBot can supply someone with considerable personal information based on a name search. Similarly, online reference services such as Lexis-Nexis or Information America specialise in making personal information widely and easily available to their clients and the general public by means of the Internet. Much of this information, however, comes from public records and other sources that are not always reliable. If data in one of these online databases comes from inaccurate public records or has been transcribed inaccurately, a consumer could be inconvenienced or harmed in a more significant way. If, for example, the Equifax Credit Information Services Web site contains inaccurate data it could mean that a company using this reference service to check up on a potential customer denies that individual an essential service such as credit or insurance. It could also mean that an employer using the Internet to run a background check on a prospective employee may deny that person a job based on erroneous information. [HONG KONG 3]

The need for accuracy, however, is in tension with the reality of maintaining a dynamic online database with millions of records. According to Mason *et al.* (1995), 'those receiving information have limited capability to ensure that information they receive is accurate and of high quality'. It is impossible, of course, to verify the accuracy of each individual record. Yet what can realistically be done to ensure an acceptable level of accuracy? Several measures can be taken. First, organisations that function as data keepers or reference services should never transfer or make available information that they suspect or have reason to believe is inaccurate. This is the most egregious form of moral negligence which is also illegal in most countries. Second, there should be a mechanism and procedure for correcting errors quickly once they are uncovered and communicated. Third, updates should be done on a regular basis. Fourth, online reference services like Lexis-Nexis should reverse their current policy which does not provide individuals with access to information about themselves maintained in these Web site databases and being sold to clients like mortgage companies or law enforcement agencies. Instead they should let individuals view all of the data in their own files so that they can have an opportunity to correct any mistakes. This prerogative is included in most European data acts but is not the norm in many other countries like the United States. Finally, in some cases when these online databases are the source of information for important matters such as credit or insurance decisions, individuals should be notified of an adverse decision based on their file so that inaccurate data can be corrected or erroneous assumptions challenged. There must be adequate remedies for people who believe that they have been injured by the dissemination of false information in these commercial databases. To be sure, reference services cannot be held strictly accountable for every mistake in an online data repository. But, on the other hand, they should be held morally accountable if they fail to follow these or similar prudent measures which are well within their capacity to carry out. [HONG KONG **4** ]

## Libel in cyberspace

Accuracy is especially important for journalists and other online publishers who are purveyors of news and information on the Web. Thanks to the Web, of course, virtually anyone can be a publisher now. There are many more information sources and it is much easier to disseminate information throughout cyberspace and reach some segment of the cyberspace audience. As the US Supreme Court noted in its recent decision *Reno* v. *ACL* (1997) the Internet enables someone to become 'a town crier with a voice that resonates farther than it could from any soapbox'. Since many of these online publishers will not have the same standards as traditional journalists, there is a much greater potential for inaccuracies and for more libel suits.

When individuals or organisations do disseminate false or inaccurate information they are clearly violating their moral obligation to be truthful and to respect the integrity of information about others. They may also be subject to charges of libel. Libel is a form of defamation and it occurs when a false statement is written about someone that injures that person and brings about his or her disgrace. A libellous message can be posted on electronic bulletin boards or on newsgroups available on USENET which functions as the Internet's worldwide bulletin board. Libellous messages can also be posted on Web sites such as those operated by the new breed of Internet journalists. The most infamous online libel case in the United States has involved journalist Matt Drudge who falsely wrote that a White House aide of the Clinton administration, Sidney Blumenthal, was a wife beater. When Drudge realised that he was mistaken he quickly apologised but Mr Blumenthal still filed a multimillion libel suit.

Libel on the Internet is a growing international problem. It is worth noting that countries have different standards which further complicates matters. In the United States justice system if the plaintiff is a public figure, libel law puts the burden of proof on the plaintiff to prove that there was actual malice involved in making a libellous statement. But British libel law is much more pro-plaintiff, since the defence must only prove that a statement was not libellous. The strongest and most consistently enforced libel laws can be found in Singapore. Both ISPs and publishers are liable for content posted on the Internet. They must register with the Singapore Broadcasting Authority which closely monitors their activities.

The ascendancy of the Internet has subjected libel laws to new scrutiny. Godwin (1996), citing the United States case of *Gertz* v. *Robert Welch, Inc.* (1974), argues that libel law should be facing obsolescence due to the new mode of publishing facilitated by the Internet. In that case the United States Supreme Court upheld defamation laws but asserted that 'the preferred response to a defamation problem is to fix it yourself'. The assumption of libel law is that private individuals who are libelled are victims of the powerful media who control the channels of communication. As a result they cannot 'fix' the damaging impact of a libellous statement without help from the state. But the Internet levels the playing field and gives ordinary users access to an important medium to correct false statements. According to Godwin 'the comparative openness of the Net means that more people who feel they have had their reputations besmirched have access to self-help'. While there is some truth to all of this the playing field is still pretty uneven – if libellous statements are made by a brand name mass media Web site such as www.bbc.com or www.nbc.com the victim's ability to set the record straight by means of a personal Web site is surely inadequate. The only way in which false, libellous statements can be refuted and neutralised is if the victim has access to the same forum in which the libel has occurred, and that is usually not the case. Thus, while libel laws may need revision they are by no means obsolete. Consequently, online publishers must not overlook or underestimate their moral accountability and legal liability for disseminating false information throughout the regions of cyberspace.

## Concluding remarks

We have illustrated in this chapter that information integrity involves the confidentiality, security, accuracy and reliability of information. It includes both information that is maintained at Web sites or in online databases and information being transmitted through applications such as electronic mail. The challenge to information integrity is intensified in the porous digital environment of cyberspace where access to data is easier and security can be more efficiently thwarted. Threats to information integrity can come from many sources including an organisation's temptation to be overly forthcoming in its Web page publications. But the most serious threat comes from security breaches: destructive viruses, unwanted intrusions, and electronic eavesdropping. As a consequence, organisations must implement strong countermeasures that include firewalls, encryption schemes, and authentication systems such as digital signatures. Information integrity also entails ensuring that online data is as accurate and reliable as possible. This means that keepers of online data must have a system in place that will allow users to view their own records, correct errors promptly once they are recognised, and update data on a timely basis. Finally, cyberspace provides a more convenient and effective way for speakers or online publishers to reach a larger audience. These 'publishers' must be especially diligent about accuracy to avoid generating libellous messages.

We have also emphasised here that the emerging netcentric organisation, which has digital networks at its heart, must take systematic and comprehensive measures to protect the integrity of its most important asset, information. As we argued above, there is a fiduciary obligation to the organisation's stakeholders to ensure the ongoing utility and value of that information. Also, given the risks for those affected by security breaches, there is a moral obligation to take adequate steps to ensure information integrity. There is no substitute for an integrated and proactive security plan as the basis for a comprehensive security infrastructure. Unfortunately, developing countries have lagged behind Europe and the United States in implementing such plans due to lack of resources. As a result, they are more susceptible to viruses like Chernobyl and other unwanted incursions. These security deficiencies in developing countries are unacceptable in a borderless world of networked organisations, and yet most organisations in these countries simply have inadequate resources to invest in security. [HONG KONG 5] Perhaps software and hardware vendors need to consider more robust security functionality as an *essential* feature of their products and begin providing it accordingly.

True information integrity may appear to be an elusive goal in the open and free-for-all atmosphere of cyberspace. Yet failure to take this critical objective seriously puts many individuals and organisations at great risk and is well beyond the bounds of ethical probity. Fortified with strong cryptography, elaborate security measures, and sound, conscientious policies, organisations can make substantial progress in protecting the voluminous data that flows through cyberspace.

# Comments

Some hackers, I know, will most certainly jump at this statement. They firmly maintain that hacking is for fun and not damaging, but even looking for credit card numbers, let alone using them, is illegal, immoral and definitely below their ethical standards.

**Author response**
It should be pointed out that every form of hacker activity that involves trespassing of some sort is unethical even if there is no attempt to steal credit card numbers or misappropriate information. People should not go where they do not belong either in real space or in cyberspace. As with most activities, there are degrees of 'wrongness' – it is much more serious to steal credit card numbers than to break into a system just to 'look around', but this does not excuse the latter activity.

**SWEDEN**

1

A digital signature is actually a second step that comes into play after the original ascertaining of a user's identity. It ties the subsequent data to the originally identified user through the use of a key that is only accessible to the identified user. The key can be the password, the secret information in a token or some data that can be accessed once the identification is clear.

**SWEDEN**

2

A real problem with account numbers is that many agents on the Net treat them as some sort of password, which gives the user a right to debit your account. There is no legal foundation for this use in any country that I know of. Actually many countries have laws that forbid such negligent treatment of customer accounts. But it speeds up legal transactions, which makes it rather unlikely that users will complain until they are hit, and then they will not have the knowledge that the law is actually on their side, since the problem is never described in that way in the papers. So the ethical problem is not only how some agents treat data that should not need protection, but does due to normal behaviour on the Net. The problem is also the ethics of companies gladly billing and sometimes prosecuting their customers on a very flimsy base.

**Author response**
I agree completely with the astute comment that the problem with the transmission of account numbers to online vendors goes well beyond misappropriation by miscreant third parties. It can also entail significant misuse of that information by the vendors themselves.

**SWEDEN**

3

**HONG KONG**

What is unclear here is whether the moral obligation to protect privacy should also be a legal obligation. Certainly reference services need to be more disciplined, but I read this as self-disciplined, not disciplined by an impartial regulatory body. The author writes that 'sensitive pieces of information' need to be protected. I could not agree more – but who determines what is sensitive? If there is no national, or international, agreement on what is reasonably sensitive, then such a moral obligation is just a paper tiger.

**HONG KONG**

I suspect that in many countries of the world, this kind of 'privacy' violation is already in place. Hong Kong has a fingerprint database – not solely of criminals, but of the entire population. When an identity card is issued (all adult Hong Kong residents must carry an identity card at all times), fingerprints are taken and stored.

**HONG KONG**

3

I question the advisability of such personal and private information being available in the public domain at all. Not long ago, I applied for a credit card from Citibank. Citibank told me that they would need to contact my employer to check my salary status. They duly did so, and my employer contacted me before releasing that information. I feel much more confident with such a one-to-one checking mechanism than the possibility that Citibank go off to some nefarious Web site possibly located in a different jurisdiction, and over whose accuracy I have no control, if indeed I am aware of its very existence

**HONG KONG**

Moral accountability is one thing, legal liability (to pay damages) is quite another. It is a matter of no small intrigue that the US, surely the most litigious jurisdiction in the world, does not have adequate measures to protect the privacy of data subjects, preferring, or so it would seem, the dubiously effective measures of self-regulation and discipline.

**Author response**

There is an intense debate in the United States about the need for public policy makers to pass comprehensive laws that will adequately protect privacy rights. Europe, of course, already has such laws. In my view, it is preferable to rely on proactive self-regulation rather than on reactive laws imposed by the state. National regulations are inconsistent with the logic of this medium as a borderless global technology. Furthermore, certain technologies such as P3P are designed to give consumers more power and this provides an additional incentive for self-regulators. I do agree, however, that some types of targeted privacy laws are necessary to protect especially sensitive material (such as personal medical records). Thus, the state must provide a baseline level of privacy protection for all of its citizens. In the United States there are some targeted laws (protecting credit data, for example), but there has not been a clear definition of that baseline which should serve as a foundation for those laws.

**HONG KONG**

I am not sure if it is better to tackle the issue of security at a national or organisational level. It may be that some countries have less well developed security of systems than others. But it is seldom the case that a government can legislate that all organisations must conform to a particular standard – certainly in free market economies this is not the case. To say that some countries have lagged behind the US and Europe in terms of security may well be true, but I feel that this misses the point, since it is the component parts – the organisations – that are going to have to improve security.

# 8 Democratic Values and the Internet

DEBORAH G. JOHNSON

## Introduction

Reflections and predictions concerning the social implications of the Internet frequently connect the Internet to democracy and democratic values, although the connection is made in a wide variety of ways. Some claim that the Internet is 'a democratic technology', suggesting that it is *inherently* democratic. Others claim that the Internet can facilitate and enhance democracy – in organisations, in national, state, and local government, as well as on a global scale. Yet others claim that democratic values are at stake in the policies we adopt to shape and regulate the Internet; they claim that the Internet *should be* developed along democratic principles (Ess, 1996).

From a theoretical point of view, the most intriguing idea is that the Internet is (somehow) *inherently* democratic, the implication being that it will, without any intentional shaping or prodding, produce democratic institutions and relationships, and promote democratic values. On the one hand, this idea seems to presume technological determinism, that is, that technology determines social-political organisation (Bijker, 1994). On the other hand, the claim seems counter to the commonly expressed view that technology is value-neutral, for it implies that democracy, a value, is somehow embedded in or, at least, favoured by the Internet.

In the first section of this chapter I explore the idea that the Internet is inherently democratic. I do this by articulating and then critically examining several arguments that seem to be at work in the claim that the Internet is democratic. I argue that the arguments to the effect that the Internet is democratic are valid in drawing attention to capacities of the Internet to facilitate certain patterns of interaction, but they do not justify the conclusion that the Internet is democratic. I draw attention to two anti-democratic tendencies in the evolution of the Internet: a lack of privacy which contributes to the creation of a surveillance society, and the pressure the Internet exerts on national sovereignty. In the second section, I review the democratic values that seem to be at stake in the evolution of the Internet. These include freedom of expression, freedom of association, participation in government processes, equality, and privacy. Here my concern is less with the democratic character of the Internet and more with the kinds of people, relationships, associations, and institutions facilitated by the Internet. Finally, in the third section, I briefly look at the connection between the Internet and democracy in terms of governance of the Internet. I argue here that the Internet has not developed through democratic decision making and this does not bode well for its realisation as a democracy-enhancing technology.

# Section 1

## Is the Internet democratic?

Democracy is at once both a simple and a complex idea, more a cluster of ideas, values, and arguments (theories) than a fixed or well-defined term. The core idea is, perhaps, best expressed as the idea that political power should reside in the citizens of a nation, rather than in a single person (a monarch or dictator) or small group of persons (an oligarchy or aristocracy). In a democracy citizens are the ultimate authority, and government is accountable to those citizens. But this idea has been interpreted in a variety of ways, and has been reinterpreted and modi-fied over time; it has been expressed and realised in somewhat different ways at different times and in different places (Arblaster, 1987; Dahl, 1989). Abramson, Arterton, and Orren (1988), for example, suggest that three competing under-standings of democracy vie for supremacy in American politics, plebiscitary democracy, communitarian democracy, and pluralist democracy.

The moral idea underlying democracy is that individuals are sovereign over themselves, and must, therefore, have some say in the governments by which they are ruled. It follows from this moral basis that not only should citizens have a vote but also a high degree of freedom.

In its more modern expression, in large scale, representative nation states, democracy has meant that citizens have a right to elect representatives to the government. The size of nation states has been a persistent and daunting chal-lenge to the idea of democracy, diluting the power of citizens to influence govern-ment. Some see the Internet as having the potential to facilitate democracy on the scale of nation states and on a global scale.

Indeed, the literature on Internet democracy associates the Internet with a variety of elements connected to the simple idea. If one searches the Web under the topic of Internet democracy, for example, depending on which search engine one uses, the first listings provided are likely to have something to do with free speech. On- and offline, the popular and scholarly literature on the Internet and democracy refers to the following: voting and elections, participation, town meetings, political campaigns, tolerance, equal access, privacy, grass roots organisations, decentralisation.

This is somewhat surprising given that technology has *not* been widely regarded as an important factor in political organisation by mainstream political scientists and public policy makers. To be sure, a small number of technology theorists have been pointing to the connection between technology and political organisation (and social values) for several decades (Ellul, 1964; Mumford, 1964; de sola Pool, 1983; Winner, 1986; Arterton, 1987; Sclove, 1995). But these ideas have not been influential in public policy decision making, at least not in the US. Technology is predominantly regarded (by engineers, policy makers, and the public) as value-neutral.

So, why all this attention to the Internet and democracy? What are we to make of these claims about the Internet being democratic, facilitating democracy or promoting or diminishing democratic values? In earlier work on this topic I identified four ways in which values might be thought of as embedded in a technology (Johnson, 1997b):

■ A technology is said to be infused with value morally through its metaphysical being; the technology was created or produced by an immoral (or heroic) activity and the moral character of that activity carries over into the being of the technology, for example, vehicles designed by Nazis, structures built by slaves.

■ A technology is said to be infused with value in the sense that if the technology is being produced by immoral (or heroic) institutions and practices, then one supports these practices when one buys or uses the technology, for example, rugs made by child labour.

■ A value is said to be embedded in the design of the technology in the sense that the material design carries a value or values. The design of the technology facilitates and expresses certain kinds of activities and relationships that are values, for example, the pitcher contains the value of carrying fluids, the automobile carries the value of human mobility, Long Island bridges carry social hierarchy – since they are built so low as to prevent public buses from reaching beaches used by the wealthy (Winner, 1986).

■ A technology is said to be infused with values in the sense that it has symbolic and expressive meaning, for example, sports cars are macho, information technology is cutting edge. One can read the values in the technology by recognising that technologies always develop and get used in a social, cultural context.

The Internet can be understood as a value-laden technology in each one of these senses, although the literature on democracy and the Internet seems largely centred on the third meaning. That is, the literature suggests that something about the design of the technology – the fact that it connects many individuals to many other individuals – makes it democratic. The web of telecommunication lines connecting people is seen as inherently democratic rather than hierarchical.

In what follows I explore arguments for a strong connection between democracy and the Internet. My strategy here is to articulate the best (and most interesting) arguments that can be made on behalf of the Internet being a democratic technology. Then I critically evaluate these arguments. I argue that the Internet provides us with a mixed picture of democracy-enhancing and democracy-threatening tendencies, and that it will not automatically (because of its inherent design) lead to a democratic social order.

## Argument 1: many-to-many communication

The core idea in many discussions of the Internet as a democratic technology is that the Internet differs from other media and forms of communication in that it is many-to-many communication. Television and radio are one-to-many, and telephone is, for the most part, one-to-one. (Conference calls are, of course, available but are expensive and used less frequently than Internet communication.) The novelty and power of the Internet is that any individual (who has access) can, in principle, talk directly to any and every other individual (who has access). What is new and unusual here is that the power to communicate to many (hundreds and thousands across the earth) is now in the hands of many.

Note here that I say 'many' and not 'all'; it is important to keep in mind that the Internet is not now and may never be available to everyone in the world, although from a technical point of view universal access is possible. It is also worth noting that the uniqueness here has as much to do with the low cost of the Internet and the ease of use as with the physical telecommunications lines connecting millions of sites around the (mostly developed) world. In the past, the power to communicate to many was only available to television and radio stations or, more importantly, to the few who could afford to take advantage of those technologies, namely large companies using the technology for advertising. Ham radio is closer to the Internet in facilitating many-to-many communication but its reach has been limited in part by the low numbers of users and perhaps because of its inconvenience.

From the point of view of democracy, the most important aspect of many-to-many communication is that it is unfiltered, unmediated, and relatively un-institutionalised. What the many say to one another is not filtered by the news media or shaped by a political process that sets an agenda for discussion. Individuals can talk directly to one another and interpret what they hear, rather than listening to media interpretations of polls, first person interpretations of discussions with others, press releases issued by interested parties, and so on. These institutionalised forms of power (for that is what mass media and press conferences and magazines are) are bypassed when individuals can get information directly from primary sources.

Of course, the Internet facilitates the distribution of institutionalised information as well. So, it can be argued that the Internet is democratic in the sense that it facilitates access to many more (filtered, mediated) sources of information. The Web especially does this. One need not, for example, rely on American news sources but can access European and Latin American sources on the Web.

The examples that are often given here to support the democratic character of many-to-many communication, are revealing. Nation states may try to control information flow in and out of their country so as to shape attitudes towards various events in their own or other countries (for example, Tiananmien Square, the Kosovo war) or about proposed legislation. Yet because of the Internet, individuals may have access to information independent of what their country might prefer, for example, information from those who may be close to the event or information from sources with radically different interpretations. Not only is it possible to talk to someone in Yugoslavia about the Kosovo war, it is possible to access news sources in other countries – news sources that may filter quite differently from one's national press. [RUSSIA **1**]

Another important aspect of unmediated, many-to-many communication is that it allows new associations to form (Klein, 1999). The best illustration here is the special interest groups that have formed online due to a common interest, such as a medical illness, a minority political position, a special fetish or (un)popular idea. Of course, a wide variety of special interest associations have been and will continue to form offline. The difference with the Internet is that associations can form across national and international boundaries and yet have fairly frequent and intense interaction. When those who have a common interest are geographically dispersed in such a way that they may not even be able to identify one another, their ability (power) to take action collectively remains fragmented; they have no means of working together, keeping each other informed, making joint decisions, and so on. Separately such individuals or groups are ineffective minorities. The Internet facilitates the joining together of some otherwise fragmented groups. It makes it easier to have frequent contact with individuals who are geographically distant but share an interest. Some such associations remain informal; others become institutionalised. The point here is that new kinds of associations can form whereas in the past there were enormous barriers to association.

## Argument 2: information is power

Before evaluating Argument 1, it will be useful to articulate a second, somewhat overlapping argument with a different emphasis. The emphasis in the second argument is on the idea that information is power. Again the argument plays on the idea of power moving to 'the many', but here the Internet is seen as democratic because it gives *power* to the many. This argument is connected to the debate over the impact of information technology on centralisation and decentralisation of power (see Johnson and Nissenbaum, 1995).

The argument goes as follows:

■ Democracy means power in the hands of individuals (the many)

■ Information is power

■ The Internet makes vast quantities of information available to individuals

■ Therefore, the Internet is democratic (Johnson, 1997b).

In this argument the important thing about the Internet is that it provides information to individuals, be it direct access to other individuals or access to the World Wide Web, be it mediated or unmediated information. The kingpin in the argument is that *information is power* and this idea needs unpacking.

Of course, information is power only if it is accurate information and relevant information. Misinformation is not empowering nor is such a glut of information that one drowns in it. There is nothing about the Internet that guarantees accurate or useful knowledge. One could argue just the opposite, namely that Internet facilitates the spread of misinformation as well as information.

Moreover, there are two valences to the claim that information is power (Johnson, 1997b). The argument for the democratic nature of the Internet works by playing off both. On the one hand, the argument suggests that information goes to individuals and those individuals who *receive* information acquire power. If information is going to the many, then, presumably, the many are being empowered. The more one knows, the more power one has. Again, this is only partially true depending on the quality of the information, its relevance to one's life, and so on. On the other hand, the idea that information is power suggests that the *sender* of the information has power – namely the power to shape attitudes and behaviour by influencing people to see something their way. Television and radio stations are powerful because they shape ideas and influence individuals both in their buying habits as well as in their political and cultural attitudes. According to this interpretation of 'information is power', each of us acquires power when we can send information. We can set up a Web page, send e-mail, participate in chat groups, make postings on bulletin boards, and so on. If the many have the power to send to the many then, in theory, the many have been empowered.

The reality is a bit more complicated than this in that the many do not, by any means acquire the power of a television or radio station, and one's power depends to some extent on one's resources. Nevertheless, there is, at least, some degree of empowerment.

So, in the second argument the Internet is democratic because information is power and the Internet both gives individuals access to information and allows individuals to be senders or providers of information.

## Argument 3: empowering the disempowered, disempowering the powerful

The first and second arguments are combined in some sense in what might be characterised either as a variation of Argument 1 or Argument 2 or as a third argument. According to this argument the Internet is democratic because it gives power to the less powerful and takes power away from the more powerful. The Internet empowers the disempowered and disempowers the powerful. Special interest groups who were not able to find each other or form effective associations before, can now find each other online and by combination gain power. Their lack of power before had to do with their geographic fragmentation or their lack of identity when interspersed in majority groups. The Internet eliminates the barriers to association that existed before and in this way gives power to the otherwise less powerful.

This argument is connected to the second argument in the sense that members of Internet-empowered groups are both senders and receivers of information. The Internet has allowed them to find an audience of like-interested others and allows them to become informed by other members about their common interest. The Internet assists a newly formed group in recruiting other members, and in their acting as a group despite their geographic distance. It assists them as well in contacting political representatives, informing the public, and so on.

## Is the Internet a democratic technology?

Taken together these three arguments claim that the Internet is democratic because: it facilitates many-to-many communication; it facilitates unmediated communication; it provides access to a diversity of mediated information resources; it facilitates the formation of new associations (independent of geography); it gives power to the many to be both receivers and senders of information; and it gives power to the less powerful. What, now, are we to make of these arguments? Are they right? Is the Internet inherently democratic?

Insofar as each argument describes a capacity or capacities of the Internet as currently constituted and used, each argument has validity. [GERMANY **1**] However, each argument takes a further step in asserting that these characteristics or capacities 'are' democratic or 'support' democracy. The second step is highly questionable in each argument. That is, the inference to democracy does not seem justified, and for several reasons.

First, it is questionable whether these characteristics are in themselves democratic. Many-to-many communication, unmediated communication, and access to a diversity of information resources can each be undemocratic depending on the structure and goal of the communication. For example, when many-to-many, unmediated communication means a kind of anarchy in which only the loudest, most aggressive, or richest can be heard or in which the loudest, most aggressive, or richest dominate, then there is nothing democratic about the communication. When there is a wide variety of information resources but all have the same bias, or when all have different biases but all are a form of propaganda, then there is nothing particularly democratic about the diversity of information resources. Hence, it is more accurate to say that the Internet creates the possibility of democratic processes or democracy enhancement, but to make the possibility a reality requires more than simply making the Internet available. To be democratic or democracy-enhancing, the Internet must be structured in ways that support democratic processes and institutions.

Second, the inference from the capacities of the Internet (for certain kinds of communication and empowerment) to democracy is not justified because the Internet is extremely complex and flexible, such that action and interaction in a variety of directions are possible. While the Internet facilitates many-to-many communication, it also facilitates one-to-many communication and one-to-one communication. While it facilitates the formation of new associations, it also facilitates the consolidation of old associations. While it gives power to the less powerful, it also gives new power to the already powerful. Consider that newspaper and television stations as well as large private and public institutions have used the Internet to enhance their power to both send and receive information. There seems no reason to believe that the Internet will support tendencies in one direction and not in the other, or that it will facilitate more of one kind rather than another kind of communication. There are good reasons for predicting that the Internet will do as much or more to facilitate the consolidation of old power relationships than to create new forms of power. [GERMANY 2 ]

The Internet makes possible actions and interactions (information exchanges) that far exceed the capabilities of human beings. When one considers the capabilities of individuals for absorption and use of information, it becomes clear that despite what the Internet makes possible, human beings need help in figuring out what information to access and with whom to form associations. Individuals are likely to, and currently do, use a variety of methods to find the information they want. They use search engines, they subscribe to listservs, they access familiar sources, and so on. Yes, the Internet puts information at our fingertips and makes it easy to review many more sources of information. And, yes, the Internet has facilitated the entry of many new players into the game of filtering and providing information.

Nevertheless, because of the limited capacity of human beings for information, we need institutionalised filtering, selecting and routing of information. Search engines are one example of a new form of institutionalised selection. The designers of search engines have decided how to structure knowledge and order information. Whether or not such tools as search engines are democratic is a subtle question involving how information is selected and ordered. There is no reason to believe that search engines are inherently democratic. In fact, if information is ordered on the basis of how much the source is willing to pay, there is good reason to believe that search engines are not democratic, but rather are tools of domination and manipulation (Nissenbaum and Introna, 1998).

Again, this is not to deny that the Internet facilitates unmediated, many-to-many communication, that it facilitates the formation of new associations, and so on; nor is it to deny that individuals will avail themselves of these opportunities. Rather, the point is that the Internet makes possible a wide variety of patterns of interaction and information access and exchange. It is far from clear whether it will facilitate democratic patterns more than undemocratic patterns of activity.

Even the idea of 'unmediated' many-to-many communication is somewhat of a misnomer, since communication on the Internet is always mediated; it is mediated by computers and information technology. Information technology shapes the nature of communication in a multitude of ways, for example, by favouring text, favouring those who have access, favouring those who have the best equipment, and so on. This is not to mention the ways in which various software and service providers may mediate (or be required to mediate) interactions with others and with information.

Too much emphasis on the idea that the Internet facilitates many-to-many communication skews our understanding of the Internet. It suggests a picture of wires connecting every individual to every other individual. The more accurate picture is one of information flowing from individuals to nodes and then from nodes to other individuals. If we think of the nodes as switching stations, it is possible for information flow to be stopped at these nodes, as we have witnessed in several cases where a country wanted to stop Internet traffic in or out of its borders. If we think of the nodes as service providers, it is fairly obvious that nodes filter information. [HONG KONG **1**] So, the Internet has the potential for a high degree of social control of information flow. [GERMANY **3**] It has the capacity for hegemonic as well as democratic relationships.

Of course, information does not flow to and from every individual in the world or every individual within a nation state. Within each country and globally, there are millions of people who do not have access to the Internet.

A third counter to the arguments from the unmediated, many-to-many communi-cation capabilities of the Internet to democracy is that the Internet is not a hard, obdurate technology. The power of information technology is in its malleability (Moor, 1995). As suggested earlier, the danger of the idea that the Internet is inherently democratic is that it presumes that nothing need be done and the Internet will bring about and enhance democracy. Nothing could be farther from the truth. The Internet lends itself to antidemocratic as well as democratic purposes, and whatever characteristics the Internet has now will not necessarily be there in the future. Intentional efforts will have to be made to retain and actu-alise the democracy-enhancing potential of the Internet.

Indeed, there are several trends in the evolving development of the Internet that are powerfully threatening to democracy. The first has to do with the surveillance capabilities of the Internet. The second has to do with the global scale of the Internet. (Though it may be more accurate to say that global scale challenges our notion of democracy rather than that it threatens democracy.)

As the Internet is evolving, an important struggle is taking shape with regard to the level of privacy one has as one communicates, navigates, and performs a variety of transactions online. One of the seemingly built-in features of informa-tion technology is its reproducibility (Johnson, 1997a). Everything one does on the Internet endures. Traffic patterns as well as content are available to service providers (and hackers) and law enforcement with a warrant. Private marketing agencies also want this information as is evidenced by the creation of cookies.

In an attempt to counter the powerful forces interested in information about Internet use, technologists have been working on a wide variety of privacy-enhancing tools (for example, PGP and other cryptographic techniques). The outcome of this struggle is likely to have enormous significance for the democ-ratic character of the Internet, for without a significant level of privacy in the Internet, the democratic potential of the Internet will be significantly diminished.

Another important democracy-relevant characteristic of the Internet is its global scale. Because the Internet has a global scale, it facilitates international (global) communication, action and interaction. Many see this as democratic because they believe that bringing individuals and countries into closer contact will promote tolerance. On the other hand, just the opposite may be possible. Global commu-nication, action and interaction at the level of many-to-many bypasses national sovereignty. If we assume that every individual should have a say (a vote, influ-ence), for example, in Internet governance, then the authority of nation states may be significantly weakened. From the perspective of nation states, their autonomy is undermined. Thus a major question for the future will be whether recognition of national sovereignty is democratic or undemocratic. In global democracy, are individuals the unit of citizenship or are nation states the citizens?

It is precisely the unmediated character of Internet communication that conflicts with national sovereignty. It undermines the power of nation states by making it difficult to control the flow of information to and from citizens as well as making it difficult to control a wide variety of unlawful behaviour. This is democratic in the sense that citizens have freedom of access to information, but sometimes undemocratic in undermining democratic processes. Remember the Homolka case in Canada in 1993 in which a Canadian judge prohibited the Canadian press from temporarily publishing information on a trial to ensure that a second accused would get a fair trial (http://www.cs.indiana.edu/canada/MediaBan). Information went out of Canada and then came back in through the Internet.

The autonomy of nation states is threatened because the global reach of the Internet seems to strengthen alliances between individuals and businesses across the globe. The global reach of the Internet is also threatening to nation states because a global economy compels nations to harmonise their policies with other countries and, hence, to give up or compromise values that they might otherwise want to preserve.

So the arguments to the effect that the Internet is democratic are highly problematic, although they are useful for uncovering social patterns facilitated by the Internet. The Internet is not inherently democratic, but it has the capacity to facilitate democratic relationships and institutions. Such relationships and institutions will not, however, come about on their own. If efforts are not made to build them, the Internet could just as well move us in the opposite direction.

## Section 2

### The Internet and democratic values

An alternative way to approach the connection between the Internet and democracy is to ask whether the Internet enhances or threatens values that are closely associated with democracy. What are the democratic values at stake when it comes to the Internet and especially Internet policy? Three such values are worth mentioning even if only briefly: freedom of speech, participation, and privacy.

## Freedom of speech

With regard to the Internet, the value that has received the most attention by far in the US is freedom of speech. Free speech is a fundamental precept of democracy and many fear that any control of speech (expression) on the Internet will not only make the Internet undemocratic but will interfere with democracy offline. The event that sparked this debate in the US was the successful attempt by several senators to pass the Communications Decency Act (CDA) in the US Congress. The CDA would have limited certain kinds of speech on the Internet; that is, it would have made it a crime to use telecommunications devices and interactive computer services to disseminate 'indecent or patently offensive sexually explicit material' to children under 18 years of age. Though the Act was later struck down as unconstitutional by the US Supreme Court, its initial passage through Congress made salient the power of the threat to freedom of speech online. [GERMANY 4 ]

Since the CDA was targeted at the protection of children, the debate is far from simple. It brings the value of free speech in conflict with the protection of children and it does so because of the accessibility of the Internet.

Freedom of speech goes to the heart of the Internet–democracy connection in the US because freedom of speech is understood to be essential to government accountability and to citizenship in a democracy. In oversimplified terms, when government has the power to censor information, it has the power to shield its own activities from public scrutiny. Instead of being accountable, the government then has the power to manipulate the public. Moreover, for citizens to vote intelligently for their own best interests and the interests of the country, it is essential that information is readily available and that citizens have opportunities to discuss issues and form opinions. This can only happen when freedom of speech is protected. In other words, freedom of speech is essential for the protection of democratic accountability, and democratic citizenship.

The importance of freedom of speech is also connected to a democratic notion of truth. John Stuart Mill argues that the truth is much more likely to emerge in an environment in which ideas are freely and forcefully debated. True ideas will emerge out of debate and, equally important, will be kept alive rather than becoming 'dead dogma'. In parallel, false ideas will be shown to be false, instead of being suppressed. The falsity of false ideas will be reaffirmed. In other words, people will not forget why true ideas are true and false ideas are false. **[GERMANY 5 ]** If one does not like the language of truth and falsity, Mill's argument is just as powerful when the focus is on good and bad ideas. That is, open discussion and debate is much more likely to lead to the emergence of good ideas. It is much more likely to lead to improvement and progress. Censorship squelches human development and human progress.

The arguments for freedom of speech are very powerful, and there will be powerful resistance to an Internet that does not have freedom of speech. Yet, the Internet is global in scope and, hence, policies are, in effect, global (though they are not being made in a global democracy). It is difficult to see how freedom of speech on the Internet could be limited to one nation and not available to another. **[HONG KONG 2 ]**

## Participation

I have already discussed participation in several contexts. The Internet is seen as democratic because it has the potential to involve many more people in discussions of local, national or global issues. Here the potential involvement seems to have to do with the convenience of the technology. That is, individuals can, while sitting at home, engage in civic discussion, make contact with government representatives, and so on.

However, I have already suggested that whether or not these discussions are democratic or democracy-enhancing has much more to do with how they are structured and who participates than with the sheer number of people who can participate. The point of participation is to have an influence on decision making. Hence, it is important that participation is structured in ways that make a difference. (For example, counting the number of 'hits' on a Web site is hardly a way of creating participation.)

Moreover, as I have already suggested, there is a real problem in who is part of the discussion. Who is participating in Internet democracy? The role of equality in the US is multifaceted. Not only is it understood that each citizen counts the same as another, but there is a commitment to equality of opportunity and equal protection under the law. If a global economy is going to be built on the Internet and if the global economy is going to be supported by democratic institutions and practices, then it would seem that the issue of access cannot be ignored. Who will have access to the Internet? In what order? At what cost? Moreover, these questions have to be answered both at the level of nations as well as individuals. What is universal access? Every country being connected? Or every person in every country? The latter seems very unlikely, and yet the effects of the Internet are likely to impact every individual.

## Privacy

Most concerns about free speech on the Internet have focused on the threat from censorship. This seems unfortunate insofar as the threat of surveillance has been neglected. Freedom of expression can be curtailed as much from surveillance as it can be from censorship. Individuals behave differently when they know they are being watched; in effect, they censor themselves (Reiman, 1995). Yet the surveillance capabilities made possible by the Internet seem to go forward unattended. As mentioned before, technologists are trying to develop new tools to protect privacy, but at the same time, law enforcement and commercial interests make powerful claims for monitoring traffic patterns as well as the content of Internet communication and browsing.

## Are democratic values enhanced?

So the focus on democratic values is not telling as to whether the Internet will enhance or diminish democratic values. Democratic values serve as important categories for monitoring the Internet and for understanding exactly what changes are taking place as a result of the Internet, but the evolution of the Internet can go in either direction, diminishing or enhancing democratic values.

# Section 3

## Is the Internet developing democratically?

A final approach to the Internet–democracy connection alluded to earlier is to ask whether the Internet is being developed through democratic institutions and processes. Perhaps if the Internet were being developed through a democratic structure and democratic institutions, then there would be more reason to believe that its development would result in a democratic technology.

However, no such structure or processes exist. Responsibility for the development of the Internet has shifted and changed several times from its origins in the US military to its development under NSF auspices, to its current management by task forces consisting of representatives from the scientific community and commercial interests.

The Internet's development has been undemocratic in a variety of ways. First, it has been developed almost exclusively in the US despite the fact that the technology has global reach and impacts individuals, countries, and communities across the entire world. Second, even within the US, there has been little public involvement in decision making about the Internet. Generally, even in those task groups where there has been representation, the representation has been very narrow in its spectrum (Garfinkel, 1998; Rogers, 1998).

The Internet's development is probably most accurately characterised as American, ad hoc, and increasingly moving towards private interests and market forces. There is, I should add, nothing that guarantees that markets result in democracy. The shift to private control seems to arise from increasing recognition of the Internet as the medium or vehicle for global capitalism and an intensely global economy. But if the Internet is seen to be primarily an instrument for economic activity, there is again no reason to believe it will enhance democracy or democratic values. The interests of consumers and the interests of citizens of a democracy are sometimes overlapping but they are far from identical. **[HONG KONG 3 ]**

The Internet will not of its own accord automatically lead to democracy, global democracy, or democratic values. It will take a great deal of effort (often against counter forces) to shape the Internet into a democracy-enhancing technology. The questions below need to be asked continually to monitor the development of the Internet:

- How is the Internet governed or how should it be?

- How is the autonomy of nations (states or local communities) recognised in policy decisions regarding the Internet or how should they be?

- Are the economic interests shaping the Internet allowed to undermine its potential to serve political and public interests or should they be?

- Is freedom of expression being protected or should it be?

- To what extent is there privacy on the Internet and to what extent is the medium a medium of surveillance?

# Comments

In this connection, it makes sense to pay attention to one more opportunity given by the Internet. The technology of the Internet allows different kinds of information to be combined – even within the same Web site. Combination of current information (like that from teletype tape, being replenished in sight of a user), on the one hand, with relatively 'static' large analytic papers and formal documents (that can remain in the site for many weeks), on the other hand, is not possible either in 'ordinary' newspaper or in 'old' electronic communications (radio or television). Meanwhile such combination in the Internet seems to be able to contribute to better grounded estimations concerning political events. For example, 'Inforart', a popular Russian site, presents information about NATO's bombing of Yugoslavia in the current information section. In the neighbouring section, they present Igor Ivanov's (Russia's Minister of Foreign Affairs) speech at a session of the State Duma (Russian parliament), where he blames NATO countries for direct violation of the Charter of the United Nations. In the same section, the text of the UNO Charter is presented. So one can (with comparative ease) make use of the UNO Charter's text to see how NATO's action corresponds as well as the validity of Igor Ivanov's accusation. It seems that in cases like this the Internet (in contrast to television) prompts analytic ways of thinking.

**RUSSIA**

The history of technology makes me doubt the validity of this argument. There is no evidence that a certain technological configuration supports certain forms of social communication and hinders others. Today we refer to the telephone as a technology for one-to-one communication and the radio as a technology for one-to-many communication. Indeed, in the very early phases of both technologies it was just the other way round. The radio started as a means of individual communication – in this text also referred to as many-to-many communication – when radio amateurs used the radio to communicate with each other all over the world.

Among the first applications of the telephone in Europe was the transmission of opera and music concerts. In Budapest, Hungary, several thousand people signed up for such a service. The further development of these technologies has changed the dominant way of use. However this shift shows that no certain way of use is technologically rooted in the technology but rather it all depends which kind of use is preferred by the producers. It might well be that in a few years there will be mainly push services in the Internet and on-demand services using only a few frequently visited Web sites of the big publishers and TV networks.

**GERMANY**

I completely agree with this argument and would like to point to similar expectations and hopes with other technologies which have been disappointed, such as two-way cable television, video and personal computers. The personal computer was the subject of the computer lib movement, in particular in California, with the slogan of 'computer power to the people', but then was taken over by IBM and Microsoft. When the video technology was introduced first there was the hope that everybody could make his own video films and that the power of Hollywood would be broken. But today on most of the video cassettes sold we find Hollywood movies.

**GERMANY**

**GERMANY**

The service providers are the critical and uncontrolled force in the game in reality. Remember when AOL closed e-mail accounts of users who had been critical of its pricing policy in the newsgroups. If you have your e-mail account on your business card and then this account is closed, it is like cutting your telephone line. Telephone companies are not allowed to do so without good reasons and without notice, but there is no regulation for ISPs.

**GERMANY**

Readers may well remember the sentence of a German court against a CompuServe manager violating the basic right of free speech. This case occurred before there was special legislation on the duties of ISPs. In the new Teleservices Law, the duty for control is restricted to own contents. If a provider only gives access to contents of others, he is only liable to the extent that he can know with affordable means. (For this legislation see <http://www.iid.de/iukdg/doku.html>; for the CompuServe case see Multimedia und Recht 1988, 8, 19/08/99, p. 429 also http://www.beck.de/mmr/ Materialien/com-puserve-urteil.htm)

**GERMANY**

I think the situation is a bit more complex. Of course there are limits to freedom of speech when other individuals are hurt. Within one culture certain limits to this freedom therefore are accepted. With the international character of the Internet the problem arises that one visits a site and one's own cultural values are offended (what we call sex, many Arabian countries call pornography). While Nazi propaganda is legal in most countries of the world, it is not – because of the particular history – in Germany. This is not just true or false!

**HONG KONG**

It need not be at the level of the country. The City University of Hong Kong recently decided to block student access to certain categories of Web sites, including pornography (hard or soft), drugs, bomb making, terrorism, and so on. This blocking is achieved by means of a filtering list (Smart Filter) set up on a proxy server through which all student Internet connections must be routed. The university's rationale was partly protective, partly resource driven. The unfortunate effect is that such large-scale blocking also leads to the elimination of potentially valuable sites – safe sex practices for example, which come under the 'sex' category.

While some might feel that such filtering curtails freedom of speech or expression, an alternate view is that it upholds the interests of the majority who, by and large, do not wish to be confronted with such information, particularly the more graphical elements. Since the mission of the university is an educational one, and since the cultural values that permeate the lives of the majority of Hong Kong's population do not condone the public display of such material, especially in a centre of higher education, some restrictions on freedom of expression may be appropriate. It is entirely probable that the mass media in Hong Kong would have a field day with stories documenting the accessibility or storage of pornographic materials at a local university. This could have serious implications for the university, including damage to its reputation, its moral standing, its chances of recruiting good students, and so on, none of which are conducive to the university's health.

Sovereignty is a very powerful concept, and not one to be taken lightly. Sedition is punishable by death in many countries - a powerful incentive not to interfere with sovereignty. The line between sedition and freedom of speech, for example, may be very fine indeed. Moreover, knowing exactly where the line lies is not a simple issue.

**HONG KONG**

**2**

I entirely agree. Indeed, I would go further and suggest that there is a potential for the Internet to be run on a hegemonic (plutocratic) basis by the commercial interests of electronic commerce and the associated software application developers. These institutions have vast cash and resource reserves to draw upon, often exceeding the reserves of nation states, whose sovereignty is thereby threatened.

**HONG KONG**

**3**

## Hong Kong General Comment

This chapter is intensely interesting, yet paradoxically also worrying given the assumptions made and the opportunities missed. This paradox was evident even in the title of the chapter – 'Democratic Values and the Internet'. Why democratic? Why restrict yourself to democracy? Why not just 'political values'?

I feel that one could equally well write what would now amount to a devil's advocate chapter titled 'Autocratic/Plutocratic/Meritocratic/Theocratic Values and the Internet'. The Internet could very effectively be used to promote all of these equally valid perspectives of political/religious/economic organisation. Deeper analysis of these systems from an Internet-ethical perspective would be challenging and insightful. It is inadequate to refer only to undemocratic and anti-democratic systems, without doing them the justice of specifying precisely what they are, let alone assessing them for their relative merits.

Computer Professionals and YOUR Responsibilities:

# 9 Virtual Information and the Software Engineering Code of Ethics

DONALD GOTTERBARN

## Introduction and uncertainty problem

The novelty of the Internet has raised some interesting ethical issues. In any new situation, unsure of our ethical footing, we look for standards or models to help us with our decisions. Consider the following situation.

> You are walking down a crowded street when a hand reaches out from behind a door and you hear a pleasant voice say, 'Let me hold your wallet for you.' Even though you are impressed with the trustworthy timbre of the voice, you ask what is to be gained and what is to be lost if you place your wallet into the beckoning hand. From behind the door, the reassuring voice replies, 'There is nothing to be lost. I will hold your wallet so that it will never be misplaced or stolen. You cannot lose it. I will follow you where ever you go and when you need money or anything else from your wallet I will give it to you. I will provide utility and peace of mind.' In response to this explanation, you look at the hand and...

Most people would not turn over their wallets – containing money, personal information, cards that provide access to bank accounts and so on – to a beckoning hand, unless of course the beckoning hand was accompanied by another hand which contained a threatening object. But now consider the following:

> Recently some Web-based organisations have offered to store your bookmark lists for you. They will provide you with access to your bookmarks even while you are away from your home computer. The bookmarks will always be available where ever you are as long as you have Web access.

Many people in response to this type of offer have simply said, 'What a wonderful idea' and have provided their bookmarks to the Web-based organisation.

Why is our behaviour so different in these two seemingly similar situations? The difference between these two stories is that we have significant historical knowledge of deceptive activity directed at gaining access to our money and other things of value. The second situation occurs in a 'new country' (Barlow, 1995) [BRAZIL **1**] where we are not familiar with the norms. Moreover, the technology on which the Internet is based is unfamiliar to most, and this lack of familiarity obscures our understanding of the potential ethical issues related to the second example offer above.

We are feeling our way in a completely new area with seemingly little guidance. Are there any kinds of guidance available to us? Some have argued that the market economy is the most important principle of guidance and use it to justify any activity on the Net. Some have discovered foundations for the minimisation of free speech on the Internet. Tools originally designed to restrict access to pornography are now used to restrict access to political information instead. The apparent absence of ethical standards on the Internet has led to numerous problems listed earlier in this book.

The absence of clear standards and the seeming newness of Internet situations has led some to think that any activity is acceptable on the Internet. Attempts to restrict malicious and immoral behaviour on the Internet have been largely unsuccessful. We will look at a common problem on the Internet – the invasion of privacy in the form of gaining access to personal information – and some attempts to control this behaviour. These attempts are inadequate. It is my contention that one of the reasons for the failure of these approaches is the application of too narrow of a view of ethics needed when working on and with the Internet. There are three levels of ethics when one works as a professional; each level subsuming the other. Many of the problems on the Internet are brought about by only working at the lowest of these levels. To illustrate this let us look at one ethical issue related to the Internet. We will then see how this issue relates to different levels of professional ethics.

## Virtual information and potential solutions

Different types of assaults on privacy have been presented in Chapter 4, and some ways to address those assaults have been discussed in Chapter 6. The newness of the Net and the absence of clear guidance has led to confusion about the nature of privacy, and the way the Internet is related to those privacy issues. To illustrate these difficulties, I will discuss a new privacy issue I call 'virtual information' (Gotterbarn, 1999) and some techniques used to address this issue.

There are many kinds of privacy. Information privacy is 'the right to control the disclosure of and access to one's personal information' (Spinello, 1997b). The Internet has facilitated a significant abuse of these principles of disclosure and access. We can ascertain the physical location of individuals and get maps and directions to locate these individuals. Video cameras are broadcasting images of us; many of these are doing so without our knowledge or consent. Our browsing habits are tracked at home, school, and work. Information privacy is violated when the individual:

- does not know what information is being collected about them

- cannot limit access to what is being collected

- does not control the use and distribution of this information

- cannot correct erroneous data and out-of-date information.

The value of personal information is indicated by the emergence of a new crime–identity theft. This assault on privacy has been expanded to include the gathering of virtual information.

Since their inception, computers have facilitated different levels of assault on and protection of individual information. The concern, in the 1970s, to protect privacy from large centralised databases of personalised information led to gallows humour (Van Tassel, 1976, p. 182), and led to legislation in the US, the 1974 Privacy Act (Edgar, 1997). [SWEDEN **1**] This same concern is mirrored in computer professional's codes of ethics, codes which predated the Internet. For example the guidelines for the ACM Code of Ethics say a computer professional should:

- take 'precautions to ensure the accuracy of data'

- protect 'it from unauthorised access or

- accidental disclosure to inappropriate individuals'

- establish procedures 'to allow individuals to review their records and correct inaccuracies'

- define retention and disposal periods for information.

There are similar imperatives in other codes such as the Canadian Standards Association and in the Australian Computer Society Code of Ethics. For example the Australian Code, Section 4.2 says 'I will consider and respect people's privacy which might be affected by my work'.

The computer has enabled an extensive exchange of such information between different data collectors and across significant distances which can be used positively or negatively. Computer matching (described by Tavani in Chapter 4) has been used by the US Internal Revenue Service to estimate a taxpayer's income by looking at the taxpayer's magazine subscriptions. The Internet has extended the opportunities for data matching; even some major Internet Service Providers do it. 'America Online is matching its active member list with demographic and psychographic *data' (Privacy Times*, May 1997). This exchange of information and the ability to do data matching weakens an individual's control over access to their private information.

Legal mechanisms, peer pressure, 'netiquette' (described by Van den Hoven in Chapter 6), and technical solutions have been used to control the negative effects of computers on privacy. Privacy laws in the US have focused on individual privacy problems – protecting financial information or video tape rental records – whereas, in Europe the approach has been more unified, creating laws and establishing agencies to support those laws. Technological solutions to the privacy problem – passwords, encryption, and so on – have had limited success. **[SWEDEN 2 ]**

The overriding positive value of the Internet is free information exchange. The privacy trade-off is that the window that lets us look out on the world is the same window that lets the world look in on us, and this open window reduces our control over private information. The privacy problem on the Internet has a different flavour from what it had before – individuals now open doors to information about themselves and their computers.

Johnson (1997a) has identified three general characteristics of the Internet which affect ethics: (a) anonymity while browsing, which looks like a very positive support for privacy, (b) the openness of the Internet, which has led to legislation to limit access, and (c) reproducibility, which facilitates the exchange of positive information. Specific technical features of the Net, such as its use of cookies in client-server exchanges, also affects privacy. Information is often collected from Internet users surreptitiously with cookies. Some cookies also allow a site to track your moves without you knowing it. This tracking is often used to build a profile of you.

Etiquette, legislation, and technology have been used to address these new Internet concerns. Some authors have developed netiquette lists (Johnson, 1997a). A variation on Van den Hoven's netiquette approach is to establish a privacy agreement between the Internet user and the Web site that collects the data. This practice has even been institutionalised. The Platform for Privacy Preferences (P3P) and the Open Profiling Standard (OPS) define the transmission of an Internet user's standard profile of personal data. The individual selected the personal data to disclose. But even the formulators of this policy realise its weakness. 'P3P alone does not guarantee privacy or trust' (Principles, 1998). This is the problem with all netiquette approaches. We cannot insure the trustworthiness of information gatherers.

The United States is backing self-monitoring rather than legislation. They have recently (April 19, 1999) strengthened this proposal (Safe Harbor, 1999). This is a form of self-regulation. In addition to the problem that not everyone follows the rules of etiquette, there is a second difficulty with this approach, namely, it perverts the concept of privacy. The right of disclosure refers to our right to be informed about what type of information others are gathering; it does not refer to our requirement to disclose information to others. The right of access is about our ability to access and correct information others have gathered about us. These rights have nothing to do with us supplying information to the data gatherers. The OPS interprets 'disclosure' as the user being expected to build an individual profile of their private information in a specified format, and interprets 'accessible' as that this profile will be made available to Internet providers. This turns the traditional concept of privacy on its head from individual rights of disclosure and access to presumed Internet provider rights to personal information.

In addition to turning the concept of privacy on its head, the Internet has created a broader concept of information. Tavani's data merging is used to make inferences about individuals for marketing purposes. The result of merged data sometimes becomes part of our personal profile – part of our digital persona. (Long, 1997, p. 6) reports that a banker, on a state Health Commission, pulled a list of cancer patients in his area, matched them with the bank's outstanding loans and called in the loans. The banker's action, based on this merging, has created a new 'electronic' fact. It is a fact that these cancer patients had loans called in, and an inference that they are obviously bad risks for loans from other institutions. The 'electronic fact' will now be merged with other facts. The problem is, since this fact is not 'wrong', we cannot have it corrected. Here, the privacy problem is the inference that people will make from this new electronic fact that has been added to the person's digital identity. The Internet has extended this problem.

Internet companies are gathering information about our browsing habits and click streams. Internet companies are making inferences based on your click streams, and providing those inferences to other companies as if the inferences were facts. For example, visitors to a bourbon manufacturer's Web site may be asked by their auto insurance company to certify that they are still entitled to the non-drinker discount. An inference is made from information gathered about Web surfers while they are searching the Internet. From information gathered without our consent or knowledge, an inference is made about us which becomes an electronic fact distributed to an automobile insurance database. Unlike the electronic fact of having a loan called in, this 'fact' is not based on a recorded event but on an inference from other data. Nevertheless, the inference is treated as a fact. I call such inferences *virtual information*. This virtual information becomes part of our 'electronic identity.' We need to be concerned with the privacy and accuracy of virtual information as well as other forms of information. Virtual information, inferences made about your future behaviour, vague personality traits, and so on, is not covered by current privacy legislation. This virtual information is significant because of the near equation of the individual with the electronic information stored about him or her. [SWEDEN 3 ]

The development of 'virtual information' is facilitated by *anonymity* – one of the new characteristics of Internet communications that seemed to support privacy. Because of the open and anonymous nature of communications on the Web, a species of software has been developed and employed with stealth to gather information intelligently. This type of software makes inferences about an individual adding information to and redefining one's digital persona. This is an invasion of one's 'virtual privacy'.

Anonymous transactions on the Web make possible the transparent use of *robots*, which are described in detail in Chapter 2. In the context of the Internet, these are essentially a variety of software programs that perform useful tedious functions, such as seeking out and retrieving information. For example, there is a robot (program) which searches outgoing corporate e-mail looking for inappropriate language or inappropriate humour (Kaplan, 1997). In the same vein there is a slightly more logical species of these robots called *Webcrawlers* or *spiders* which can search Web pages, and send the information they find to the Web site that launched the crawler. They access one Web site, examine it, and follow all the links to other Web sites automatically collecting e-mail addresses or other relevant information. The data they report back and record in their database is based on data matching and merging creating new digital personas. They can travel untraced through a system, unimpeded because of its open and anonymous access. These Webcrawlers do not have the ability to generate 'virtual information' about someone being a heavy drinker, because they visited a Web site selling bourbon, although they can collect the data that is used to make that inference.

There is, however, another species of robot called an *intelligent autonomous agent* (IAA) which is persistent, and applies artificial intelligence techniques to actually make inferences and develop its own Web database. An IAA finds coherence in individually insignificant details. IAAs can work with information that is incomplete, or appears incomplete. An IAA searches the Net, gathering information, making inferences and developing a database for the person who launched the autonomous agent. The IAA's inference is sent back to the host as 'virtual information'. There is at least one product on the market that will search a user's bookmark list. Agents are being programmed into the next generation of Internet browsers that are capable of tracking 'click streams' – all of the screens menus and selections clicked on by a mouse, and the time spent per page. Of course, this 'click stream' could be used to make inferences about you. Your visit to the AIDS information Web site could lead to an incorrect inference about you.

This differs significantly from other forms of data merging. First, the merging and inference building are done by a program not a human being. Second, only the inference is preserved. Since the data on which the inference is made is not preserved, there is no basis to eventually contest the information. Third, the inference becomes a part of our general electronic persona, a digital fact that does not reveal the bias or point of view of the inference maker.

In the light of such intelligent agents and the importance of a digital identity, we need to extend the definition of privacy. It must be extended to include more than the control of the communication of facts and circumstances about an individual. Protection of privacy and of a digital persona on the Internet requires the ability to control virtual information. Control here includes consumer awareness, consumer choice, security, data integrity, and consumer access to virtual information of inferences added to our digital persona.

Asking to control this seems unreasonable. In ordinary life when one makes some inferences about me and relates those hunches to someone else, those hunches can be relegated to the category of rumour. When the computer makes similar inferences, they become part of my digital identity. Without my knowledge, my digital persona has changed. The initial problems about privacy are greater than we thought. How do we respond to the problem of virtual information?

## Responses to an Internet ethics problem

The risks of IAAs are quite real because there are software packages available to develop intelligent agents that can be used by industry to collect any information they may find useful. Internet service providers can agree not to look at files or provide data but this does not meet the privacy threat of IAAs. The activity of an IAA looks like a normal Web transaction.

Etiquette, law, and technology seem inadequate to address this problem. There is a form of etiquette, 'Guidelines for Robot Writers', about how to program the agent. If the top of a Web page is marked 'do not read' then the IAA is supposed to be programmed not to search those pages. However, the IAA's trip to a site is anonymous and unprotected, so these conventions may be ignored easily. From the point of view of the machine being accessed, a hit generated by an IAA is indistinguishable from a hit generated by a human being.

Violations of virtual privacy do not violate any of the standard information abuse laws (obscenity, theft, and destruction of information). Nor do they violate defamation of character legislation (slander and libel). The IAA visits sites in conformance with all US privacy laws. Privacy protection laws do not extend to virtual information. Since the virtual information is based on an accumulation of electronic facts, you have a right to correct the information on which the inference is based, but there is normally no legal right to correct the virtual information.

There are some simple technical adjustments that individuals can make to improve virtual privacy. To prevent searching of a history file by an agent, one can delete the history file frequently. To prevent examination of a cookie file, one can refuse to accept cookies, or if forced to accept cookies, then one can delete them when the transaction is complete. Such actions, however, are inadequate protections of Internet privacy, and they defeat the positive functions of history files and cookies.

The importance of protecting privacy is recognised in all professional computer society codes. The ACM Code of Ethics explanation of the privacy imperative, '1.7 Respect the privacy of others' includes situations like the violation of virtual privacy.

These principles apply to electronic communications, including electronic mail, and prohibit procedures that capture or monitor electronic user data, including messages, without the permission of users or bona fide authorisation related to system operation and maintenance

Until the law and norms of society can catch up, [SWEDEN 4 ] the possibility of the violation of virtual privacy imposes new responsibilities on the software professional to help move the norms of interaction with the Internet forward in a positive direction. Consistent with the goals of privacy protection, a software professional needs to: (a) develop tools which will help the user identify which cookies were recently added, (b) provide means for correcting and limiting access to user profiles, (c) enable users to set retention limits that will be carried in data files, and (d) lobby for enforceable standards on the use of intelligent autonomous agents.

## A professional's code of ethics

The above appeal to a computer professional's ethics code as indicating a way to help address the problem of privacy seems odd. After all, it is those same professionals who developed a system requiring a book on Internet ethics. How can an appeal to a professional's code of ethics help? The facility – the Internet – provided by computer professionals is getting used in ways which violate individual privacy. To answer how a code of ethics can help we need to understand the levels of professional ethics, and who the professionals are when dealing with the Internet. These codes provide help clarify issues and provide a broader and firmer foundation on which to build an ethical framework to start to address these issues, one grounded on a professional standard.

### A profession's ethical standard

One approach to the problem of Internet ethics is to seek out an already established model for behaviour and examine its feasibility as a guide for Internet behaviour. Computer professionals understand the complexity of the issues surrounding the Internet and have developed some techniques to address these difficulties 'technically'. Professionals generally describe their ethical commitment in codes of ethics developed and maintained by a professional society. Recently – December 1998 – the Software Engineering Code of Ethics and Professional Practice was adopted by two international computing societies – the IEEE-Computer Society and the Association for Computing Machinery. The Code they adopted is unique among professional computer codes of ethics because it has been adopted by multiple societies, thus moving it toward a profession's Code rather than the Code of an individual professional society. The development of the Code was an international project with representatives from 14 different time zones. Reviews, re-drafts, and balloting on the Code was conducted in the international arena. It is not unreasonable to say that this Code represents an international consensus of what software engineers believe to be their professional ethical obligations. [SWEDEN **5**]

## Why a code of ethics as a model?

We need to understand the diverse functions of a code in order to understand why we should use a professional code as a model for Internet behaviour, and how a professional code can be related to Internet ethics.

Most professions have developed codes of ethics. The computing profession is no different. There are divergent views about why they develop such codes. These views are related to the different opinions about the nature of professions. Some have argued that such codes are just veiled attempts to generate a positive public image for a profession. Others claim that such codes merely establish a moral minimum and are incomplete. Despite these negative views, codes do serve a number of positive functions for emerging professions. Since some of these functions may be incompatible it is also important to identify and to emphasise those characteristics of a code that are most relevant to the particular profession. To understand the different functions of codes, we need to distinguish between three different types of code – codes of ethics, codes of conduct, and codes of practice – and we need to distinguish three levels of professional ethics.

## Codes of ethics, conduct, and practice

There are three types of code used by professions. The relationships between these types of code form a hierarchy; (1) codes of ethics as distinguished from (2) codes of conduct and (3) codes of practice.

Codes of ethics are more aspirational; they are mission statements for the professional providing, vision and objectives. Statements in codes of conduct are more oriented toward the professional and professional attitudes. They do not describe in detail how to carry out a particular action, but they make clear the issues at stake in different specialised fields. Codes of practice on the other hand fix some accepted state of the art (Berleur, 1996) and relate to current operational activities. The degree of enforcement possible is dependent on the type of code. Codes of ethics, which are primarily aspirational, use no more than light coercion, while codes of conduct violations generally carry sanctions ranging from warnings to exclusion from the professional body. Violations of codes of practice may lead to legal action on the grounds of malpractice or negligence. The type of code used to guide behaviour affects the type of enforcement.

## Levels of ethics

This hierarchy of codes parallels the three levels of ethical obligation owed by professionals. The first level identified is a set of ethical values, such as integrity and justice, which professionals share with other human beings by virtue of their shared humanity. Code statements at this level are statements of aspiration that provide vision and objectives, The second level obliges professionals to more challenging obligations than those required at the first level. At the second level, by virtue of their role as professionals and their special skills, they owe a higher order of care to those affected by their work. This second level of ethical obligation is also shared by every type of professional. Code statements at this level express the obligations of all professionals and professional attitudes. Again, they do not describe specific behaviour details, but they clearly indicate professional responsibilities. The third and deeper level comprises several obligations that derive directly from elements unique to the particular professional practice. Code statements at this level assert more specific behavioural responsibilities that are more closely related to the state of the art within the particular profession. The range of statements is from more general aspirational statement to specific and measurable requirements. Professional codes of ethics need to address all three of these levels (Gotterbarn, 1994).

## Functions

Codes serve many functions, some of which are related to Internet ethics. Professional societies and authors on professional issues for engineers and computers scientists have used codes to serve the following functions:

### Inspiration

Codes might be designed to be inspirational. There are two audiences for such inspiration, practitioners and customers. Martin (1989) emphasises the inspiration for 'positive stimulus for ethical conduct by the practitioner', while Johnson (1994) emphasises a code's function to inspire confidence in the customer or user in the computing artefact and in its creator. The use of language with positive overtones helps to generate both types of inspiration, but such language also introduces a degree of vagueness which limits the ability of the code to help guide professional behaviour. To address this problem, some organisations have developed codes that are accompanied by a set of guidelines to help reduce some of the vagueness.

## Guidance

Historically, there has been a transition away from regulatory codes designed to penalise divergent behaviour and internal dissent, toward codes which are more normative. Such normative codes are only a partial representation of the ethical standards of the profession's members (Anderson, 1995; Gotterbarn, 1996). The statement of the code is used to help the professional examine alternative actions.

These more normative codes, however, are not considered to be exhaustive lists of rights or wrongs, nor are they considered decision procedures to decide what is wrong. The use of normative codes requires moral judgement on the part of the professional. The code may help someone determine a course of action when they are requested to develop a questionable Web application. A sense of moral responsibility is needed for the application of a normative code to concrete situations. Codes are not merely used for guidance in particular cases. They also serve an educational function.

## Education

Most authorities on codes emphasise the educational function of codes. They serve to educate, both prospective and existing members of a particular profession about their shared commitment to undertake a certain quality of work and the responsibility for the well being of the customer and user of the developed product. This includes all Web surfers and developers.

Codes also serve to educate managers of groups of professionals, and those who make rules and laws related to the profession about expected behaviour. A manager's expectations or a legislator's expectations will have an effect on what is asked of a professional, and what laws are passed relating to the profession.

Directly and indirectly, codes educate management about their responsibility for the effects and impacts of the products developed.

Codes also indirectly educate the public at large about what the professionals consider to be a minimal acceptable ethical practice in that field, even if practised by a non-professional.

### Support for positive action

Codes provide a level of support for the professional who decides to take positive action. They provide an environment in which it will be easier, than it would otherwise be, to resist pressure to do what the professional would rather not do. The appeal to the imperatives of a code can be used as a counter pressure against the urging by others to have the professional act in ways inconsistent with an ethical pattern of behaviour supported by a consensus of that profession.

### Deterrence and discipline

This is the other side of the support for positive action. Codes can serve as a formal basis for action against a professional. Some organisations revoke membership or suspend licenses to practice. For example, doctors are encouraged to write prescriptions in accordance with legal guidelines. Recent failures to follow these standards have resulted in 900 physicians in the US no longer being allowed to write prescriptions. The code defines a reasonable expectation for all practitioners. The failure to meet this expectation can be used as a grounds for litigation, even used as litigation against the non-professional.

### Enhance the profession's public image

Some codes specify a minimal standard of conduct. Sometimes this is done at great ethical cost. Codes have been used to prohibit public criticism of fellow professionals, even if they violated some ethical standard.

For an emerging profession, some of these functions are more critical than others. The choice of functions will give the code its own character. The support function is very important. For emerging professions the educational and inspirational functions are also important. At the early stages of a profession's development, the disciplinary function is generally taken over by the law. An example of this is the Data Protection Act in the UK. In most contemporary codes, the attempt to keep a perfect public image of the profession, at the expense of quality professional work, has been abandoned. For example, both the IEEE-CS and ACM codes require that a professional encourages adherence to the code and that she or he calls attention to significant violations of the code. This may hurt the profession's image but it will encourage quality work.

Codes serve to educate multiple constituencies about the ethical obligations and responsibilities of the professional. They educate professionals about what they should expect from themselves and what they should expect from their colleagues. Codes for specific professions also serve to educate society about its rights, about what society has a right to expect from the practising professional.

## Why should non-professionals pay attention to a professional code?

The functions of a code give us some insight into the possible relations between a professional's code and the actions of a non-professional. In addition to circumscribing the sphere of rights and responsibilities, a code also serves to define the minimally acceptable practice from anyone practising that profession. Codes educate the non-professional public in two ways. First, they learn the minimal expected behaviour from a professional. A physician's use of antiseptic when cleaning a wound is a minimally acceptable practice for anyone attending to a wound. Second they also learn the minimal expected behaviour from themselves when working in the professional's domain. A physician would be negligent if he did not use an antiseptic and so would a parent be negligent if he did not use an antiseptic while cleaning his child's wound.

Some codes are more than ethical checklists in that they provide frameworks for ethical decision making. These frameworks can be used by both the professional and the non-professional. The code is important because even the non-computer scientist is engaging in a professional activity when she builds Web pages and supports particular activities on the Web. [RUSSIA **1**] Codes constrain the domain of acceptable behaviour for anyone working in that area.

Software engineering, as an emerging profession, focused on the first four functions of a code; inspiration, guidance, education, and support. The primary functions of the Software Engineering Code of Ethics and Professional Practice were to educate and to provide guidance in decision making for the international community of software developers. The Code clearly defines the responsibility of the profession and the professional to promote and protect positive values.

> Because of their roles in developing software systems, software engineers have significant opportunities to do good or cause harm, to enable others to do good or cause harm, or to influence others to do good or cause harm.

The Internet is like an emerging profession and its users (developers) need guidance. [RUSSIA **2**] I believe part of the difficulty with ethics in this new domain is that most participants fail to see the level of responsibility that they take on when they participate as Internet developers. There needs to be an increased awareness of the enormous power and responsibility involved in working on the Internet. The wake up bell needs to be sounded that we are not merely a *user* of the Internet, but we are also developers of a system that will continue to flounder in an ethical morass until we realise our shared responsibility as user–developers of the Net. The way in which to improve the situation in Internet ethics is to realise that all Internet developers have *all three* levels of professional obligation.

It is sometimes difficult to think about ethical issues while typing at a keyboard. We do not see the person(s) we are affecting, so we do not even think of the first level of ethics. This first level of ethics based on our common humanity is found in most codes of ethics. There is a higher obligation for all professionals. A professional requires a higher standard of care. Because of their special skill and the power that this gives them, physicians owe a higher level of care to their patients. All professionals are bound to maintain their skill in their discipline and cause no harm when they use that skill. Professions differ from one another based on the domain of their knowledge and skills. This third level of ethics is the obligation to those affected by our work to use our skills in the service of humanity. To be a professional is to work toward these three levels of ethics. The third level of ethics requires that I exercise professional responsibility toward all others.

## Conclusion

We have found that the diversity of netiquettes and laws does not resolve the issues with the Net. There are standards of ethics already adopted by software professionals that can be used to guide our behaviour. The Code imposes obligations to develop systems which will limit the ability to collect our click streams, or at least not develop tools which increase the Internet's ability to enable unethical activity. There is an obligation to design systems that do not enhance the potential privacy abuse of IAA, and not to design systems that lessen the security of personal information. The international code mandates that it is inappropriate for some governments to have a lower standard of privacy on the Internet. The recent behaviour of a major computer chip manufacturer, placing privacy violating numerical identifiers in the chip, is unethical by professional standards. To build a browser which surreptitiously has a tracking system would be a clear violation of the code and it would be inconsistent with all three levels of ethics.

The code also helps raise the level of expectations on the Net. Because of its international foundation, the code has a potential impact as an international standard, providing direction for Internet legislation. It at least provides a consistent set of ethical preferences.

The use of a single code, and the adoption of all three levels of professional ethics, does not completely mitigate the inherently open architecture of the Internet that hobbles law enforcement. But a code fulfilling its educational function will change the approach of many to the Internet and provide a counter pressure against the tendency to behave unethically. If nothing more, it will help many realise that their behaviour may be unethical. The standard and this realisation will make them pause and think about the consequences of their actions.

This is summed up in the Preamble to the Software Engineering Code of Ethics and Professional Practice:

> These Principles should influence [Internet Developers/Users] to consider broadly who is affected by their work; to examine if they and their colleagues are treating other human beings with due respect; to consider how the public, if reasonably well informed, would view their decisions; to analyse how the least empowered will be affected by their decisions; and to consider whether their acts would be judged worthy of the ideal professional working as a software engineer. In all these judgements concern for the health, safety and welfare of the public is primary; that is, the 'Public Interest' is central to this Code.

and to an ethically sensitive Internet.

# Comments

SWEDEN

This chapter is written from a US perspective, but it is of general interest to note that the truly international phenomenon of computers and their impact on society has led several European countries to introduce Data Acts in 1973 and 1974, all of which are far more far-reaching than the rather weak US Privacy Act. By now, all western European countries have comparably restrictive privacy legislation and the eastern countries in Europe are rapidly following suit. The European Union also has the Data Protection Directive (95/46/EC), which has caused tightening of laws, already passed or still on their way, in many member countries. The US has many state laws of differing severity, but there is still no general legislation that aims at protecting personal data from misuse by public authorities as well as companies or private persons. These European laws are a clear signal to professionals in the relevant countries, even when they do not directly forbid a certain use of data. Thus they help with some of the problems discussed in the paper, but they are not a full solution, even if we disregard the problems arising from the fact that Internet is international. The situation, then, is radically different in the USA compared to Europe. Actually a US citizen can improve his or her privacy by preferentially using Europe-based Internet services (or services based in another country with similar laws). But this does not remove the need for the ethical codes discussed in the later parts of this chapter.

**Author response**

The respondent is correct about the comparative weakness of United States legislation in the privacy arena. The Internet privacy problem is used here as but one example of how a code can help address ethical issues on the Net. The code I use as a model is distinctive in that, unlike most legislation, it is accepted by many organisations and has a multinational foundation. Until there are multinational laws related to the Internet, transnational codes of ethics are important.

SWEDEN

One obvious reason for the failure of technology to solve the problem is that technology can only provide tools, but it cannot sort out what tools are needed, it cannot govern or restrict the implementation of tools and so on. Thus passwords and encryption can keep information from the eyes of those who are not registered as suitable to see it, but they cannot choose who should see it, and they can not prevent misuse of information by those who have been given access to it. Thus technology has no sufficient solution to the basic problem, only necessary tools to implement some of the solutions. Locks can reduce the risk of being a victim of burglary, but they do not eradicate burglary.

**Author response**

This supports my point.

SWEDEN

This important concept was introduced into the Swedish debate in the early 1970s, under the name of 'data shadow'. A data shadow, just like a person's normal shadow, is a true, impartial image of the real person. Also as the normal shadow, the data shadow shows the person from a given perspective, and it lacks a lot of information that exists in the full three-dimensional figure. The shadow can also be distorted by the surface on which it is projected. The shadow can communicate a lot of useful information about the subject, but you may make serious false conclusions if you do not know the position of the source relative to the subject. The concept has reappeared several times in the international debate under different names (quality of data and so on), but it has never found the sought technical or organisational solution of how to make people aware of the risks of creating and using shadows.

**Author response**

The problem of virtual information is more significant than the problem of 'data shadows'. Virtual information is created by automata and the data on which the virtual information is based is not recorded in the consequential digital persona. The use of IAAs to develop virtual information and the ready availability of software to create IAA virtual information gatherers also make the problem of virtual information very different from data shadows.

---

The laws and norms of society will never catch up. Laws have and should have far more inertia then current opinions of what is 'good' and 'bad' behaviour. Thus laws will always lag behind in non-static situations. The current IT situation is anything but static, and that is a characteristic of technology in general. Thus professionals dealing with the development and implementation of technology will always know of possible consequences in areas where there still are no societal norms. So specific norms too will lag behind what professionals have to decide on. The only remaining support is the more general ethical norms used by professionals in a professional way. That is what ethical codes are about.

**Author response**

I believe that the norms and laws of society will always lag behind the technology, and that the law will always be behind the norms in catching up with technological changes. In many cases the technology and the ethical issues are interwoven. This relationship means that the technological codes will be the closest to the current ethical problems. As the commentator says, professional codes are the only support here.

**SWEDEN**

**4**

---

A professional code of ethics is a very good idea wherever there is a profession and some sort of arena for interaction between professionals. Unfortunately this is not the case for computer programming and computer systems development. The USA is probably the strongest example of a certain coherence and sense of professionalism in this area. But even there pure amateurs, people of the most diverse backgrounds and autodidacts, form a very large part of the actual working force even in very high positions. Most of them are not members of any professional society. But the journals of the American societies are read by very many, and thus have an impact far beyond the registered membership. The problem here is one of 'image'. If the societies are regarded as congregations of real experts in touch with and mastering the real problems, their views and attitudes will be imitated by most people working in the field, 'professionals' or not. If on the other hand the societies are regarded as academic and representative of an alien culture, their views and attitudes will be disregarded and sometimes even the opposite may be sought on every point as a gut reaction. There is no coherent computer profession, even though many working in the field want it to exist. This fact is no reason for a computer society to abstain from creating a code of ethics (on the contrary). But this fact is a warning that the efficiency of such a code may not be at the expected level.

**SWEDEN**

**5**

## Author response

The commentator makes several important points here. In a technical sense computing is not a formal profession. But this should not be confused with an absence of a consensus about professional behaviour. The second point – that for this code to be effective it must be widely circulated and reflect more than an academic stance about computing – is also correct. The code was developed with input from and regular reviews by industry. In fact, the code was adopted as a standard of practice by several software developers and a major computer manufacturer while it was under review by the two professional societies.

**RUSSIA**

The idea to use computer professionals' ethical standards in development of standards that would be valid for a number of Internet users and developers (including non-professionals) is very promising. Availability of computer technology to those who were not computer professionals was an important characteristic of PC that caused mass computerisation of society. Traditionally, responsibility with technology is interpreted in terms of professional ethics. With growth of Internet, ever-increasing number of people become affected by activity of non-professional users and developers. So awareness of all Internet users and developers' responsibility becomes a problem of today. If one wants to explore the problem seriously, he or she should take into consideration ethical standards adopted by computer professionals. However it is important to elucidate not only what professional ethics *can* contribute to the ethics of the Internet but also what it is *unable* to contribute. What rules from ethical codes (like the Software Engineering Code of Ethics and Practice) can be adopted as valid for all 'ethically sensitive Internet' and what rules cannot be adopted? Since the Internet is used by people of different professions, it makes sense to presume that standards of different professions should participate in development of common ethical basis for Internet. How would such standards interact with each other? The Internet is often called a 'global' system. Its users live in different countries; how could different cultures influence a 'globally acceptable Internet Code'? So the assertion that computer professionals' ethics are valuable for development of ethical Internet provokes questions concerning role of other sorts of ethics in this development.

## Author response

There are two points here; one about different professions and one about different cultures. As the commentator rightly points out, those who will be using the Internet are bound by multiple codes of ethics, some of which may be formally stated in a religious credo or a professional code of ethics and some of which may simply be personal standards of ethics. In ordinary life, these standards are, for the most part, additive. The personal standard of 'don't cause pain' and the teacher's goal of 'improving reasoning' are additive in the form of 'don't cause pain while teaching'. The fact that people from many different professions use the Internet fits well with using a software developer's standard to guide the technical portion of one's behaviour on the Internet.

The interesting part is when the principles from these various codes come into conflict. How is one to choose the best action. The authors of the Software Engineering Code tried to address this problem. When faced with conflicting options, choose the option that supports human well-being and quality of life. If the conflict is still between equal alternatives, then support the option that does the most to further human values.

While the parallel between the Internet and a profession is useful, it makes sense to recognise not only their similarity but also their differences. At least two points of difference are obvious. First, normally members of a profession have appropriate education. As a rule this is higher education. But a normal Internet user is not obliged to have anything like higher education in the Internet. He or she is not obliged to have higher education in any field. Even children and students may be users. Second, if an ethical code for a profession comes into existence, its efficiency depends on the power of the professional association that adopts the code, on its ability to accept only those new members who agree with the code and to expel those who do not comply with the code. But Internet is unlike such an association. And any one who is going to develop ethical guidance for the Internet should take into account this dissimilarity.

### Author response

The commentator recognises my point that we are not all expected to be professionals before we touch the Internet and potentially affect millions of lives. The aspect of the code that I appealed to was not its disciplinary power, for at the moment it has none. I appealed to its educational function both for the practising professional and for all others working with the Internet. Until various nations developed laws against spamming, the only enforcement against it was the moral pressure that most people considered it an unethical use of resources; even those who engaged in spamming realised this.

Going further, the Internet is even more than a 'new country'. It is a 'new reality', with new paradigms emerging. Maybe it is a mistake to try to rescue old standards and models to understand and explain this reality. The Internet is almost an entity. We really should open our minds and forget completely the existing rules of the real world and face in a new way the Internet. After all it is a 'new world' that mixes the real and the virtual, people from different cultures and thoughts, the democracy of words, the organisation without an organisation. New rules should appear from and to this unique real virtuality.

### Author response

The commentator offers one of the commonly heard justifications for the lack of ethics on the Internet. It starts out with a hyperbolic claim that 'everything is different on the Internet so we should abandon all of our hard won gains made as civilisation has progressed'. Many who hold this position are so blinded by technology that they fail to see the Internet as just one more evolutionary step in the continuum of human–technological development. The Internet is only interesting in so far as it is used as a communication medium between people, and that as a result of that communication it can greatly affect individual lives, organisations, and cultures. The human beings at the receiving end of this communication have not changed; they feel pain or pleasure, they are satisfied by positive accomplishments, they are capable of receiving and giving love. The fact that one now communicates large amounts of data over vast distances does not eliminate our ethical responsibilities, does not let us throw them away. The Internet has just the opposite effect. We are in contact with more people in new ways, so our ethical responsibility increases. The Internet is a new way to communicate. One must resist taking a truth that there are new and confusing things about the Internet and carrying that truth to such an extreme that it is clearly false, carrying it to the extreme that the Internet is so completely different that we were justified in forgetting all ethics.

# 10 Conclusions

DUNCAN LANGFORD

This final chapter discusses the main themes raised in this book, and brings together the issues, before looking to possible developments in the future.

## Overview

We have seen that the Internet did not come into existence as a carefully organised and designed artefact, but instead was created – and of course is still being created – piecemeal, as a unique blend of high technology and expediency. The physical computers and networks that make up the Internet contain a global mix of material that encompasses every aspect of human endeavour and human failing. This content is revealing of much concerning human society. In the opening years of the second millennium, it may not be an exaggeration to suggest that the Internet may be seen as reflecting a genuine representation of global humanity as it really is, rather than as individuals or even nations might prefer it to be.

While there are many significant issues concerning use of the Internet to be debated, it is of central importance that such debate is founded upon physical realities. Construction of a hypothetical Internet with the intention of encouraging discussion might produce much that is of interest, but it is not an approach taken here. While such an approach to Internet use may seem attractive, if conclusions are to be worthy of application, it is essential for any worthwhile analysis of a technically-based medium to be founded upon technical reality.

For this reason, we began by preparing the ground with a brief study of technical foundations. This described the genesis of what we now call the 'Internet', from its small-scale beginnings as a means for connecting university researchers, to its present state as a global communications network.

One particular problem with the evolution of much, if not all, technology lies in the relative positioning of debate and development, which very seldom take place in that order. While it might seem obvious that public discussion over the use and application of significant scientific developments should precede their actual production, commercial and other pressures tend to make this unlikely. Public debate is consequently frequently triggered only by actual news of outcomes – for example, a much needed discussion on the ethics of cloning was really only initiated after announcement of an actual cloning success: Dolly the sheep. Before the physical existence of Dolly, the whole issue of cloning was considered by many people to belong to the realms of science fiction.

Technical development of the Internet followed this typical path. From the very first, the enormous benefits and potential benefits to be gained from using computers to assist human communications made leisurely examination unlikely. Indeed, pressure for continuing technological development and commercial real-isation of the potential benefits meant that at no stage has there been much time or opportunity for reflection. New development and new ideas are continually pressing, so discussion on exactly what an electronic global network might mean for those individuals and, later, societies who may connect to it, was set aside for later debate. This lack of wider debate left a policy vacuum, which was partially filled by the practical assumptions of first developers. Essentially, little room was left for theoretical discussion on the effects of electronic networking while a headlong rush to physically network the world continued.

Until recently most actual users of the Internet were technically aware individ-uals, who understood the technical background to this form of networking, and who (because of their experience and background) were perhaps biased in favour of academic freedom and individual autonomy. Of particular importance to the early growth of the Internet was a widespread conviction on the part of these established users that individuals could and should be trusted to use the system, and, in particular, that under no circumstances was external supervision or control of the Internet appropriate.

At that time a British Government report summarised the position well:

13. The Internet is perceived to have flourished because it was free to evolve without interference from any powerful self-interested groups (these are inter-preted as including governments and multinational press corporations). This freedom is greatly cherished by Internet users, who believe that access to the valuable information resources that such freedom makes possible is too impor-tant to risk through regulation.

14. Unrestricted data communications are assumed to be vital to the UK's future economic prosperity, and any legislation needs to be framed in this context.

Accordingly, the central principle is that everyone should have unfettered freedom to discuss, but not the freedom to harm others, and that individuals must have the appropriate freedom to choose whether they wish to view items or not. Discretion should be the rule, not regulation.

(COG Report, 1995)

If the early development of the Internet was influenced by the unwritten philosophy of its creators, what of later opportunities for discussion on Internet use, and its potential effects? Despite the expansion of the Internet from local network to worldwide system, there has been only limited analysis and debate. It may be that the technical nature, both of access to the Internet and of the underlying global network, has concealed the need to consider matters not connected with the solution of practical problems. It is certainly true that the explosive expansion of the Internet has in itself created additional difficulties for those committed to an examination of the effects of the Internet on social and other non-technical issues. In particular, the rapidly changing character of the Internet – for instance, its increasingly commercial nature – provided additional discouragement for considered social and philosophical analysis.

Specific aspects of the network, such as the perceived free availability of pornography, have tended to pre-empt what public discussion has taken place. Partly because of this emphasis on certain aspects of the Internet, and perhaps partly, too, because the technical nature of the Internet has encouraged a debate limited to technical issues, there has been little attempt to consider what the introduction of such a global entity, and its associated free flow of information, might mean to human society.

If these difficulties are to be overcome and wider debate to take place, then it will no longer be enough to leave decisions to the technically expert; acquisition of relevant technical knowledge, such as that contained in Chapter 2, should allow informed debate to take place within a far wider circle.

## Themes

The precise nature of the social and philosophical analysis mentioned in the previous section will clearly be dependent upon many different aspects of the global Internet. To assist the process of analysis, it may therefore be helpful to identify some major issues and themes that underlie the debate, and to bring them together here. These themes are, of course, reflected in the shape and contents of this book; it would clearly be necessary for a reader to refer to specific chapters for a fuller discussion of the topics.

## Changing access to information

Once an understanding of the technical nature of the Internet has been gained, it is important to consider the Internet not as something to be viewed in isolation, but as the latest in a series of human artefacts stretching over millennia, allowing potential identification with the effects of other human creations. This approach may be summarised as seeking to identify what there may be about use of the Internet that makes its use similar to other aspects of human experience – with the corollary, of course, that this process should also allow us to see how it may be different.

When considering individual access to information and its transfer between individuals, a major concern has always been one of *relevance*. The perception of the possessor of information concerning the relevance of it to a potential recipient plays an essential part in whether information has been communicated at all. As an old saying goes, 'knowledge is power'. While there are exceptions, from the prehistoric priesthood onward, those possessing information have on occasions appeared to see their primary role as preventing, rather than encouraging, the distribution of knowledge. Again, using a religious example, the promotion of a particular pattern of information can frequently be accompanied by the rigorous suppression of dissenting or competing information.

This position is still largely true. Those in positions of power – commercial power, governmental power, industrial power – guard their secrets jealously. While millions may be spent on the general promotion of desired products, commercial confidentiality can prevent members of the public from finding out more specific data. Too often those organisations possessing information prefer to decide for themselves what should and should not be made available to others.

What, though, of the role of the individual? Here there has been a dramatic change, beginning with the growth of secular education in the sixteenth and seventeenth centuries. Until then, the language of European education was Latin, and, because books and teaching used Latin, those people without a knowledge of the language were automatically excluded from the collective body of knowledge. Such exclusion, of those who do not possess relevant specialist knowledge, is, perhaps, directly analogous to the present manner in which physical access to computers is restricted to those individuals who can afford them, or who work for those who can afford them. Of course, insufficient knowledge of specialist computer skills can also effectively prevent access.

While the introduction of the printing press revolutionised medieval Europe by allowing the spread of thoughts and ideas, the introduction of the Internet has effected a far wider and more rapid revolution, bringing with it the possibilities both of total commercial expression and the complete declaration of personal individuality.

## Are things really different now?

As we have seen in the previous section, free access to information has never been automatic, so restrictions and potential restrictions on information flowing through the Internet are likely to echo previous limitations, inherited from the age of paper publication. What, though, of other aspects of the Internet: when examined closely, might they also carry parallels with previous human interactions?

Chapter 3 looks in some detail at the similarities and differences brought about by communicating through the Internet, rather than by the use of more traditional means – 'traditional' in this context meaning methods of communication up to and including satellite television.

While there are very many aspects of Internet use that possess strong similarities with earlier experience, five aspects are of particular importance:

- global scale
- potential for anonymity
- interactivity
- reproducibility
- uncontrollability.

Briefly, while humans have always been able to communicate with each other, the Internet has introduced a new and very different ability to communicate globally. This may be done by spreading information in a way directly analogous to traditional broadcasting, or publishing on paper. Once distributed electronically, such 'published' information is potentially seen by very large numbers of individuals indeed. Use of ftp or Web publishing permits individuals, for the first time in history, to *globally* publish their views.

Of course, the global broadcasting of views by means of satellite television is already familiar. However, without needing the expensive infrastructure essential for television broadcasts, the Internet not only allows messages to be sent to very large numbers of people, but additionally contains the potential for them to *respond*.

This ability to communicate bilaterally with large numbers of individuals is naturally of considerable potential benefit to those interested in using the Internet for commercial transactions, whereby a single outlet may serve a huge number of very widely distributed individuals. For example, I regularly buy books and DVDs from the online bookshop Amazon.com, which is located many thousands of miles from my home. Actually, beyond knowing it is somewhere in the USA, I have no real idea where Amazon.com is physically located – largely because it does not actually matter. Buying in this way is convenient, and certainly results in a considerable saving – but there are perhaps potential dangers. It has been suggested in Chapter 3 that the longer term effect of such trading may be to limit choice, as the more knowledgeable and richer suppliers may possess advantages over smaller traders. This point is a crucial one in the continuing development of our social fabric, and the issue certainly merits discussion.

International sales and the promotion of national items internationally leads to the possibilities of cultural imperialism, proposed from Australia in Chapter 3 and strongly opposed, in comments on that chapter, from Russia. Is this an old problem in a new electronic guise – does such trading and communication from Western societies open up more vulnerable cultures to the risks of cultural imperialism, or is the risk perhaps overrated?

Discussion on threats to culture leads naturally on to another potential problem – the benefits of global communication may also present the risk of giving global offence. How ought the perceptions and opinions of foreign societies influence the construction of Web pages, and the content of international news postings? Is it essential, or paranoid, to worry about the way your Web pages may appear to geographically diverse cultures?

Of course, the Internet is not limited to communications between members of geographical cultures – it uniquely possesses the ability to develop and maintain new social cultures which have only an electronic location. For example, those individuals who share a common interest, for instance in a specific medical condition, may group together; a low incidence in a specific population may nevertheless result in a large number of individuals globally. The Internet allows such people to communicate directly, in providing support, personal experiences of particular drugs and treatment, and so on. It allows them to work together and gives them the power to act together, perhaps as a pressure group. Of course, this empowerment may also encourage individuals to fight their own individual battles more effectively, because they have the additional 'weapon' of information from the Internet.

Other benefits of communication through the Internet may be less tangible. Those individuals prevented by bodily or other disadvantages from moving freely around the physical world often suffer social isolation. Such isolation potentially may be overcome by encouraging linking to the Internet, with subsequent free movement around the electronic global village, a community of which they can be full members.

There are, naturally, new problems brought about by Internet use, and some of these were also examined in Chapter 3. While anonymity is potentially of great benefit, and far easier to arrange electronically than is anonymity in normal day-to-day activities, it is open to misuse; and global misuse is clearly of greater significance than local misuse. Problems of the law – dealt with in detail in Chapter 5 – are also complicated by the difficulties involved in maintaining a global perception of what may be illegal; understandably, this may vary from society to society, while the material in question may be accessible to all.

## Human issues and the Internet

If we were to consider the effects the Internet is having and may continue to have on our lives, it is likely that the issue of privacy would frequently be raised. However, what exactly does 'privacy' mean in this context, and what might be the implications for the preservation of personal electronic data in the electronic world? For example, it could be argued that to a great extent our online self is the sum of the electronically held information which defines us and gives us an Internet presence; if this is so, to preserve our electronic integrity it is clearly essential for this data to be safeguarded. While our defining data may therefore be vital, how might we protect it, for example from unauthorised changes, or additions?

While we are naturally interested in the technical aspects of the Internet, and the advantages it may offer us in extending our abilities to communicate with others, it is of central importance to consider how the new technology and the implications involved in its use may impact upon our lives. While there may be many potential benefits, it is necessary also to consider what new disadvantages and problems may be brought about by the involvement of the Internet in our lives.

Risk to personal privacy through Internet use is an issue felt by many people to be of particular importance (Wright and Kakalik, 1997) and is therefore one where informed debate is particularly welcome. Herman Tavani, in Chapter 4, has presented a comprehensive treatment of the subject, working from a solid foundation of definition, to discussion of specific areas where the Internet may increase risks to privacy, and even bring about new and Internet-specific privacy problems.

Some issues involving the Internet are, as we have seen in Chapter 3, electronically enhanced versions of problems experienced earlier, in the 'real world'. Others are totally new, and could only have come about through use of the Internet. An understanding of the ways in which the use of Internet-related technology may both enhance risks to privacy, and also protect against them, is surely essential to an Internet user.

While Chapter 4 covers the issues in detail, one previously unknown risk to personal privacy, which I feel is of special importance, concerns the ways in which personal data may be electronically collected without the individual concerned appreciating what is happening, or indeed knowing anything about it. There can consequently be no doubt that the collection of vast amounts of electronic data, together with the parallel ability to mine this data, allows for new areas of concern over personal privacy. The simplest use of the Internet may provide opportunities for the accumulation of information which, when collated and analysed, could supply surprisingly comprehensive personal information – which may even be devastating.

One first-hand example illustrating this aspect of the Internet concerned the DejaNews server, discussed in Chapter 4. DejaNews collects Internet news postings, and then allows its cumulative electronic store to be searched under a variety of headings, including that of 'author'. This means that all postings from a particular person (or electronic address) are able to be retrieved and viewed. Some years ago a PhD student demonstrated the potential risks by using his own name as a search key. DejaNews instantly revealed that he had been posting news items to gay news groups, and sight of these postings – also easily available from DejaNews – made it clear the student was himself gay. Happily, he had deliberately demonstrated this aspect of DejaNews to me as an apposite way for a computer science student to 'come out' to his supervisor – but the risks for a person who might not want to make their sexual preferences known to the world were very clear.

If, in company with Professor Tavani, we believe there should be a presumption in favour of privacy, then discussion on the relationship of privacy to the Internet must be essential. Of course, in human society the issue of privacy has always been important, so the introduction of the global Internet has included old privacy issues in a new guise. However, some aspects of the Internet greatly enhance existing risks, while other aspects additionally introduce new problems – such as the DejaNews example – that could not previously have existed.

Huge numbers of individuals are continuing to gain access to the Internet, while new developments in Internet technology are unrelenting; the future undoubtedly holds further risks to privacy as yet unknown to us. It is essential for the Internet privacy debate to continue.

## The law

Underlying human actions are the restrictions and penalties of the law; but how relevant is 'the law' to Internet activities? Any geographically based action must take place under the jurisdiction of a defined legal system, whatever the precise details of an actual statute – or absence of a statute – may be. In contrast, actions on the Internet may appear to occur in a legal limbo, where the laws able to be applied are uncertain and lacking definition. What then are the relevant legal issues that might appropriately concern users of the Internet – for example, those wishing to undertake Internet-related commercial activities? Whatever the background of an Internet user, there is clearly a need to develop and maintain knowledge of applicable law.

In much the same way that it is necessary to have an understanding of the technical nature of the Internet in order to discuss its use, it is also essential to have an understanding of the laws that are applicable to Internet governance. Chapter 5 therefore contains a concise discussion of relevant law from the perspectives of both Europe and the United States, with additional comment from an Australian specialist lawyer.

We have seen that, although the Internet may at first appear to be a totally new environment, previous 'real world' experience may nevertheless still be valuable, and that such experience is often directly relevant within the electronic world of the Internet. Real world communities are of course normally governed by laws, and it should therefore be unsurprising to learn that within the electronic community the application of laws is also appropriate.

However, when considering the application of law to the Internet the position is not necessarily straightforward, and there are several important points that need to be kept very much in mind.

An anarchic view, sometimes seen expressed in Internet newsgroups, could be described as the appropriation of a cyber outlaw perspective, with the consequent assumption that the electronic frontier has much in common with the lawlessness of historical frontiers. While there is sufficient truth in this assumption to engender debate, for serious discussion the first, and probably the most important, point to be accepted is actually the relevance and applicability of law to the Internet.

The second point is that, in practice, the applicability of law to the Internet is made considerably more difficult for Internet users and information providers by a very basic problem. Even though applying existing statute law to the Internet may be accepted, there remains considerable difficulty in determining what relationships there may be between specific Internet actions and local, or indeed national, laws. As the Internet is, by its very nature, a global, supranational entity, it may logically seem only capable of being controlled by global laws – which at present, of course, do not exist – enforced by a global consensus, which, of course, does not yet exist, either.

A further, related point of considerable importance lies in the dynamic nature of the Internet, and the conflict this must inevitably have with the inescapable 'lead time' necessary for the normal development of statute law.

At one extreme this may mean, at best, that new legal restrictions develop as piecemeal case law, rather than as a response to conscious debate and politically aware decision. However, due to the almost complete absence of specifically drafted Internet laws, and consequent reliance upon development of case law, it may be hard to discover exactly what is, and is not, electronically legal. The lack of precise definition can and does inevitably lead to massive uncertainty on the part of those Internet users who may wish to act within the law, without (in the absence of specific case law) knowing what the law actually is. At the worst, of course, existing law which was never intended for such a purpose might, for the want of anything better, perforce be applied to the Internet anyway.

On the other extreme, the continuing evolution of the Internet is certain to make possible new actions, which, however unacceptable to a society, are nevertheless for the time being technically legal.

There are of course other potential difficulties involved in the application of law to the Internet. However, one final point which may be of considerable interest concerns the next stage – that is, what happens *after* the enactment of national Internet-related law.

Here the problem lies in the applicability of such laws; clearly, they must apply within the boundaries of the country that enacted them; but is it reasonable to expect other countries to act and enforce such laws, as well? Chapter 5 discusses the interesting Italian *Playmen* case, in which a Web site located in Italy and operated by an Italian was nevertheless held to be in breach of US law, on the grounds that it was or could be accessed by US residents. There are very few free access Web sites located anywhere in the world that cannot be accessed in this way. What implications might this case carry concerning the international application of US law? What if the laws of other independent nations are in conflict with those of the US – or of each other?

While immediate practical implications of existing laws are uncertain, so too are the ways in which future Internet-related laws may be developed, as well of course as the manner in which they might be applied. There is undoubtedly much still to consider in the association of international law and the Internet.

## Philosophical foundations

As beings possessing the capacity for reason, we need to move beyond a mechanical appreciation of process to develop an understanding of the philosophical underpinning of our actions and considered actions. How might the application of existing moral theory bear on the electronic interactions involved in Internet use? Such interaction presents new risks and new potential. It is clearly very necessary to determine by evaluation and analysis whether there may be a case for the evolution of a new moral theory specifically concerned with the Internet, or instead whether evolution of existing approaches to the new challenges of electronic interchange is possible.

While we have so far taken a largely practical approach to consideration of Internet use, the application of philosophical theory is of course central to our topic. In the same way that actions within the electronic world of the Internet may reflect actions outside it (with the consequent advantage that previously learned information may be freshly relevant in apparently new circumstances) so the application of previously existing philosophical theory may be similarly applied. It is also true that philosophy is very far from being a static discipline, so that the fresh challenges brought about by the Internet are attracting much thought and attention from philosophers. The combination moves the field of Internet ethics forward, by identifying what may be different about the Internet that makes a difference ethically, and by clarifying which areas of previous analysis might be particularly relevant.

Chapter 6 therefore draws upon varied philosophical research to present a different approach to consideration of Internet use. It specifically examines the moral evaluation of individual online behaviour, and – rather than proposing specific solutions – provides a conceptual framework in the context of which questions and answers may be articulated. The distinctions to be made among various types of Internet-related issues are developed, and a central component – that we are in a difficult predicament when thinking about moral problems and the Internet since our traditional ethical concepts no longer apply in a straight-forward way – explored.

Moving beyond conventional deontological and teleological analysis, the chapter develops and applies a combination of four ethical approaches, that together are structured to form particularly appropriate tools for philosophical assessment of the Internet. This approach undoubtedly provides a richer and more substantial ethical framework for Internet analysis than more overly simplistic accounts of moral deliberation and decision making, which must inevitably be supplemented or enriched to supply an adequate ethical framework for the moral evaluation of individual cases and actions.

These four approaches are very different, but have important features in common that are relevant to this study. All endeavour to move beyond standard and simplistic positions in ethics, and have been formulated with a clear awareness of the urgency of political and policy questions. They may be said to cut across the traditional deontological–teleological distinction, in an attempt to accommodate the complexity and richness of moral questions.

The approaches are, first, a pluralist objectivist (neoaristotelian) theory, as proposed by Amartya Sen and Martha Nussbaum; second, a pluralist axiological account, as proposed by Thomas Nagel; third, a sophisticated deontological framework as described by Bernard Gert (applied to information technology by Gert himself, and Jim Moor); and finally a responsibility account, as proposed by Robert Goodin.

All of these approaches are demonstrably relevant to the operation of the Internet, and in particular have aspects that would benefit debate if their consideration were enhanced by a specific Internet focus. Discussing these views in the specific context of the Internet is consequently likely to provide material for extremely relevant and focused debate.

## The integrity of Internet information

A further important question concerns the validity of electronic information – this may be considered as another central issue, because without dependence on the integrity of electronically contained and transmitted data there can be no reliance upon the Internet at all.

As we have seen, for most purposes the Internet can be seen as a very sophisticated device whose intended purpose, essentially, is to move electronically held data from one geographical location to another. The geographical distance to be covered by data is irrelevant, as is the actual content of the material. While varieties of encoding and decoding will inevitably take place during an electronic journey from sender to recipient, it is axiomatic that neither these codings nor the movement will in any way alter the data; what is transmitted will be exactly what is received.

However, while the theory of global electronic data transmission is easy to outline, practical implementation is likely to reveal potential problems, of varying degrees of seriousness. Most may be summarised under the heading 'data integrity' or 'information integrity'. This implies that those responsible for electronically held information that is proprietary or sensitive will keep it secure, and confidential, that it will not be altered in form or content during electronic transmission, and at all times will be secure from viewing or copying by those unauthorised to do so. Discussion here takes matters a stage further, by emphasising that *all* information being disseminated or otherwise made accessible through Web sites and online data repositories should be as accurate and reliable as possible.

These points may seem straightforward and uncontentious – but all organisations, and (potentially) individuals, connected to the Internet must address the issue of how to preserve and safeguard information integrity in a networked environment. Quite apart from the legal aspects involved in the problem, a failure to take this obligation seriously could result in harm to data subjects, that is, the affected individuals or those about whom the data are relevant. Even closer to home, it could result in harm to the organisation itself – especially if commercially sensitive information is at risk. The risks for an individual whose personal information is no longer confidential are even more obvious.

Chapter 7 considers the central issue of information integrity and the Internet through a study of current practices, paying particular attention to actual examples. The opening section examines the fundamental need, where this is appropriate, to keep electronically held information secure, relating this issue to the theme of privacy, discussed earlier. Further sections focus on the challenge involved in keeping information secure on the Internet, beginning with a review of why this problem has become so formidable. The chapter continues with examination of various specific threats to a secure electronic environment, before discussing the countermeasures which organisations can take to protect their information assets and to secure the transmission of sensitive electronic documents. In view of their critical role in ensuring the integrity of data being transmitted over the Internet, particular attention is given to the use of digital signatures.

The moral dimension of this security issue, often overlooked, is also considered and addressed; security is both a moral imperative and a fiduciary obligation to an organisation's stakeholders. Not all possible risks to information integrity are obvious or straightforward; more subtle threats include neglect or carelessness, which may for example result in online data of poor quality. The Internet has increased both the mobility of data and the complexity of data management, which in turn inevitably increases difficulties involved in safeguarding accuracy and reliability. The problems encountered by those who publish or disseminate information in cyberspace are considered, together with their potential liability for libel – Chapter 5 discussed this issue from a different perspective. The final section of this chapter emphasises its conclusion: electronically held information must be the lifeblood of any Internet-focused organisation, and must therefore be vigilantly protected.

## Is the Internet democratic?

While the Internet is usually experienced by individuals as a series of individual connections, for example in the form of an e-mail, or 'hitting' a WWW site, the whole Internet is surely greater than the sum of its parts. If we then consider the Internet as a whole, we can begin to ask questions concerning the nature of the entity. An example would be whether it possesses any particular bias – as democratic, for instance. Debate here is of considerable importance in determining how we may regard this global network; it is no longer sufficient – if it ever was – merely to use the Internet without thinking through the wider implications inherent in its use.

While we have considered a range of widely differing components which go to make up the technical Internet and its contents, as well as additionally discussing various actual and potential actions by those involved, there is also a need to discuss the Internet as a total entity. This need is, of course, enhanced by other aspects of the Internet, including the varied genesis of today's Internet, its international nature, and its immense size, not to mention its tortuous complexities. While a comprehensive analysis of the entire Internet would be a massive undertaking, there still remains a need to consider the whole, rather than taking it always to be adequately represented by the sum of its parts.

Such discussion could not hope to be comprehensive, certainly in the present state of Internet-specific philosophical analysis, and the current stage of Internet development. However, difficulty of ratiocination is not in itself sufficient excuse to preclude attempts, particularly in view of the obvious importance of bringing forward such discussion. It is clearly important to begin the process of reflecting on issues embracing the global Internet, considered not simply as it might affect individuals or single countries, but as the international entity we know it to be. What might be the nature of this entity? While many pragmatic assumptions concerning its character may have been made, might such presumptions – particularly those which concern its precise character – have questionable validity? Might the geographical origin of the Internet continue to influence its development in ways that may not be immediately apparent? Many similar questions of this kind may be readily formulated.

As a unique creation of humanity, it might be suggested that the Internet should become the focus of a new intellectual, philosophical spotlight, from which we might eventually hope to gain new and revealing insights. While we must await such theoretical discoveries, one central aspect, that of the relationship between the Internet and democratic values, may be immediately addressed. Not only the results of this analysis, but the approach taken and the process itself are potentially of considerable relevance to wider consideration of the Internet, and especially other such globally relevant issues.

Most Americans using the Internet would probably consider it to be a fundamentally democratic artefact. After all, rather than the conventional one-to-many communication of television and radio, it allows many-to-many interaction, and must consequently empower Internet-connected individuals, who are able both to obtain wide-ranging information and to publish their opinions and views on a global scale. Surely, if free speech is the foundation of democracy, then the Internet, which encourages totally free speech, must provide unstoppable encouragement. So if, as most Americans believe, democracy is a Good Thing, then by extension the Internet itself – created by Americans – must also be democratic, and also a Good Thing. Is this so? It may well be thought that further discussion might be needed before firm conclusions are made.

Chapter 8 considers the relationship of democracy with the Internet, and in the process disentangles many unsupported assumptions that may have gained currency. It allows the disadvantages, as well as the advantages, of the established Internet ethos to be examined, and provides a fascinating analysis of the way the Internet as a whole functions and might function. Drawing upon many of the themes considered earlier in this text, the chapter concludes with a series of central questions, which set the scene for a continuing debate on the global entity that is the Internet.

## Your responsibilities

A final theme relates to those responsible for creating and maintaining the Internet – how might they perceive their tasks, and what implications might there be for their successors, and for those individuals who enjoy the benefits of the global communications that have been created?

It may seem from this examination that the pressures and complexities involved in use of the Internet may have to be faced alone. A conscientious person, reading through the previous chapters, may be forgiven for thinking that they must read, discuss and develop for themselves knowledge of what might be considered appropriate Internet behaviour.

However alien the Internet may appear to new or inexperienced users, for such a network to exist there must by definition have been previous travellers and path makers, those people responsible for the technical creation of the Internet itself. While some computer scientists may have been unwilling or unable to consider anything beyond a purely technical brief (Langford, 1995) there has fortunately been a growing movement among professionals to define what behaviour is expected of 'professional' computer people; these expectations have been formulated into solid and well-designed codes of conduct. Further, rather than restricting themselves to the purely technical, specialist contributors to the major professional codes have moved into the area of usage, and have therefore provided valuable guidance and support to those of us who may never design or maintain a computer network, but who will nevertheless spend time in using one.

Chapter 9 brings together many of the themes discussed earlier in this book, and presents them from the perspective of a skilled computer professional. The application of theory to practice can – and here certainly does – provide insights not only into the specific examples discussed, but into the wider application of theory. It is also useful to understand the broader background to the implementation of networked computer systems – and, as had been said before, the Internet is of course the world's largest networked computer system.

It is to be hoped that the lessons learned by computer professionals and discussed in this chapter will be found to have a wider application. After all, when using the Internet, it could be said, to a greater or lesser extent, that we all should become computer professionals.

## Conclusions

Ideally, the end of any written discussion and analysis brings together the issues which have been debated, before extracting from the deliberations one or more conclusions that have been reached. Unfortunately, in the present state of the debate concerning Internet ethics, it is rather too early for firm conclusions to be made. While this book hopefully has made a good beginning, the whole area of Internet ethics is still largely lacking specific analysis. One major difficulty in concluding the discussions in this book is consequently that, rather than presenting a series of neat points which might be readily summarised, we have instead needed to take a more exploratory approach, analogous to marking out the virgin territory that is Internet ethics. We have therefore moved to map out roughly the lie of the land, to identify major landmarks – especially pitfalls – and, when possible, provide help to a future traveller by filling in some explanatory detail.

It is certainly our hope that discussion and debate will continue on Internet ethics, and on the use of the Internet generally. There is no doubt that, in particular, individual and commercial use of the Internet both needs and deserves to be given wider attention, attention that is not necessarily related to the technical operation of the Internet, or specifics such as pornography. As has been discussed, the Internet is of course a global entity, and may be examined as such. One significant example of necessary analysis of this entity was that, despite the expressed democratic philosophy of its American founders, important technical decisions that have been taken in bringing the Internet to its present state could be considered profoundly undemocratic. Those who form the population of the Internet were unable to participate in planning discussions, or contribute to any of the decision-making processes. This situation is broadly unchanged today. Decisions are still being taken which will affect the operation and use of the Internet well into the twenty-first century, but Internet government remains an oligarchy; and this, together with the associated disenfranchisement of the general Internet population, seems set to continue.

Issues of considerable seriousness are in urgent need of debate, for instance, the application of moral standards to Internet behaviour. While there are wide differences in the expectations of peoples in different parts of the world, so, it may be argued, it is unrealistic to expect existing local moral standards and expectations to continue to be relevant within a global electronic community. Would there perhaps be advantages in wiping clean the moral slate, before specifically determining what rules may be appropriate within an electronic community? A community, it must be remembered, whose members may, realistically, never physically meet. The opportunity to debate moral codes from scratch is not a common one, but conflict in the application of varying existing moral standards, and associated need for clear guidance, is very real.

Many further questions, both theoretical and practical, may be raised. Many have been discussed by our authors; some examples include:

- The Internet is rapidly becoming a commercial bonanza, where a global marketplace is attracting a huge range of entrepreneurs. However, should these economic interests that are currently shaping the Internet be allowed to undermine its potential to serve political and public interests?

- The technical underpinning of Internet communications is vital; open standards allow the easy understanding and extension of the Internet. The downside of openness may be an increased vulnerability; for example, is there a viable way to secure Web servers and protect information on systems based on open Internet standards?

- While an immense and growing volume of information is available on the World Wide Web, for this data to be used it must first be located. The only ways of finding previously unknown data are by using established links, or through Web search engines. However, relevant links must themselves first be found, while the design of current search engines is inherently unreliable – it is certainly true, for example, that no existing search engine can locate all pages relevant to a search. How might criteria for the design of these engines be established, and what should their priorities be? In view of their power and influence on international Web use, is there perhaps a case to be made for removing search engines from the commercial sector altogether, and funding them directly by governments?

- Determination of a potential offence is far more difficult when the geographical location of the alleged crime is uncertain. For instance, if someone sends an e-mail with sexual innuendo, where and when does the sexual harassment take place? Where and when it is read by the envisaged addressee? Or when it was typed? Stored on the server? Or as it was piped through all the countries through which it was routed?

- The Internet permits gathering of personal information on a scale never before possible in recorded history. The fears of individuals of the effects this may have on their existing freedoms may well be justified – for instance, how may we respond to someone asking how they might keep people from gathering information on them during use of the Internet? Further, how might the basic concept of individual privacy be threatened by the Internet?

It seems possible to continue generating many such questions indefinitely; in fact, the very ease with which questions on Internet use and behaviour may be generated is in itself an indication of a desperate need for proper discussion.

Whatever our location in the world, we all exist within a society. Throughout history, 'society' has automatically meant a geographically local society, such as a neighbourhood or town, or perhaps a national society, a country. Today, however, there is a totally new possibility – a new electronic society, the so-called 'global village' of the Internet, in which we may all now live. To survive in this new environment, we must develop new rules and new under-standings; we must learn what effects the Internet is having and will have on the lives of those people who will use it.

That is why *Internet Ethics* was written.

# Appendix 1: Glossary of Abbreviations and Acronyms

| | |
|---|---|
| **ACM** | Association for Computing Machinery |
| **ATM** | Asynchronous Transfer Mode |
| **BBN** | Bolt Beranek and Newman |
| **BBS** | Bulletin Board Service |
| **CGI** | Common Gateway Interface |
| **DHTML** | Dynamic HTML |
| **DNS** | Domain Name System |
| **ESMTP** | Extended Simple Mail Transfer Protocol |
| **FSF** | Free Software Foundation |
| **FTP** | File Transfer Protocol |
| **GNU** | GNU's Not Unix |
| **GPL** | General Public License |
| **IANA** | Internet Assigned Numbers Authority |
| **ICANN** | The Internet Corporation for Assigned Names and Numbers |
| **IETF** | Internet Engineering Task Force |
| **IMAP** | Internet Message Access Protocol |
| **IP** | Internet Protocol |
| **IPv6** | Internet Protocol version 6 |
| **IRC** | Internet Relay Chat |
| **ISOC** | Internet Society |
| **ISP** | Internet Service Provider |
| **LAN** | Local Area Network |
| **MAN** | Metropolitan Area Network |
| **MIME** | Multipurpose Internet Mail Extensions |
| **MTA** | (e)mail transfer agent |
| **NNTP** | Network News Transport Protocol |
| **NSFnet** | National Science Foundation Network |
| **NSI** | Network Solutions Inc. |
| **OPS** | Open Profiling Standard |
| **P3P** | Platform for Privacy Preferences |
| **PGP** | Pretty Good Privacy |
| **PICS** | Platform for Internet Content Selection |

| | |
|---|---|
| **POP** | Post Office Protocol |
| **RDF** | Resource Description Framework |
| **RFC** | Request for Comments |
| **SMTP** | Simple Mail Transfer Protocol |
| **SSL** | Secure Sockets Layer |
| **TCP/IP** | Transmission Control Protocol |
| **TLD** | Top Level Domain |
| **UDP** | User Datagram Protocol |
| **URL** | Uniform Resource Locator |
| **UUCP** | Unix-to-Unix Copy Program |
| **VPN** | Virtual Private Network |
| **WAN** | Wide Area Network |
| **WWW** | World Wide Web |
| **XML** | Extensible Markup Language |

# Bibliography

Abramson, J.B., Arterton, F.C. and Orren, G.R. (1988) *The Electronic Common-wealth, The Impact of New Media Technology on Democratic Politics*. New York: Basic Books.

Adam, L. (1996) African Connectivity, Problems, Solutions and Actions: Some Recommendations from Inet 96, 1996. URL:<http://www.nsrc.org/AFRICA/regional-reports/inet.txt>

AIC (1999a) African Internet Connectivity – Continental Connectivity Indicators, June 1999. URL:<http://www3.wn.apc.org/africa/partial.html>

AIC (1999b) African Internet Connectivity – Infrastructure Information, May 1999. URL:<http://www3.wn.apc.org/africa>

Allen, A. (1988) *Uneasy Access: Privacy for Women in a Free Society*. Totowa, NJ: Rowman & Littlefield.

Anderson, R. (1994) 'The ACM Code of Ethics: History, Process, and Implications', in Huff, C. and Finholt, T. (eds) *Social Issues in Computing*. New York: McGraw-Hill.

Arblaster, A. (1987) *Democracy*. Minneapolis: University of Minneapolis Press.

Arterton, F.C. (1987) *Teledemocracy: Can Technology Protect Democracy?* Newbury Park, CA: Sage.

Barlow, J.P. (1995) 'Coming into the Country', in Johnson, D.G. and Nissenbaum, H. (eds) *Computing, Ethics, and Social Values*. Englewood Cliffs, NJ: Prentice Hall.

Bellovin, S. (1998) 'Network and Internet Security', in Denning, D. (ed.) *Internet Besieged*. New York: ACM Press, pp. 117–36.

Benassi, P. (1999) 'TRUSTe: An Online Privacy Seal Program'. *Communications of the ACM*, **42**(2): 56–9.

Berleur, J. *et al.* (1994) 'Codes of Ethics or of Conduct within IFIP and in other Computer Societies'. *Proceedings in 13th World Computer Congress IFIP94*, Elsevier Science B.V., North-Holland, Amsterdam.

Berners-Lee, T. (1991) World Wide Web Seminar, CERN, 1991. URL: <http://www.w3.org/Talks/General.html>

Berners-Lee, T., Masinter, L. and McCahill, M. (eds) (1994) Uniform Resource Locators (URL) – RFC 1738, 1994. URL:<http://www.ics.uci.edu/pub/ietf/uri/rfc1738.txt>

Bernstein, D. (1994) 'Insulate Against Internet Intruders'. *DATAMATION*, **1**: 49–52.

Bijker, W.E. (1994) 'Sociohistorical Technology Studies', in Jasanoff, S., Markle, G.E., Petersen, J.C. and Pinch, T. (eds) *Handbook of Science and Technology Studies*. Thousand Oaks, CA: Sage, p. 238.

Blanchette, J-F. and Johnson, D.G. 'Data Retention and the Panopticon Society: The Social Benefits of Forgetfulness', in Introna, L.D. (ed.) *Proceedings of the Conference on Computer Ethics: Philosophical Enquiry: CEPE 98*. University of London Press, pp. 94–105.

Braden, R., Reynolds, J.K., Crocker, S., Cerf, V., Feinler, J. and Anderson, C. (1999) '30 Years of RFCs – RFC 2555'. URL:<ftp://ftp.isi.edu/in-notes/rfc2555.txt>

Branscomb, A.W. (1995) 'Anonymity, Autonomy, and Accountability: Challenges to the First Amendment in Cyberspace'. *Yale Law Journal,* **104:** 1628–45.

Brennan, W. (1972) *Eisenstandt* v. *Baird* (Majority Opinion).

Bullock, A. and Stallybrass, O. (1977) *The Fontana Dictionary of Modern Thought*. London: Fontana.

Bynum, T.W. (1999) 'The Foundation of Computer Ethics'. Keynote Address at AICEC99 (The Australian Institute of Computer Ethics Conference 1999), Melbourne, Australia.

Bynum, T.W. and Schubert, P. (1997) 'How to do Computer Ethics – A Case Study: The Electronic Mall Bodensee', in Van den Hoven, J. (ed.) *Proceedings of the Conference on Computer Ethics: Philosophical Enquiry: CEPE 97*. Erasmus University Press, pp. 85–95.

Carpenter, B. (1996) 'rfc1958 Architectural Principles of the Internet'. URL:<http://www.kashpureff.org/nic/rfcs/1900/rfc1958.txt.html>

Cavoukian, A. (1998) *Data Mining: Staking a Claim on Your Privacy*. Information and Privacy Commissioner's Report, Ontario, Canada.

Clarke, R. (1988) 'Information Technology and Dataveillance'. *Communications of the ACM*, **35**(5): 498–512.

Clarke, R. (1999) 'Internet Privacy Concerns Confirm the Case for Intervention'. *Communications of the ACM*, **42**(2): 60–7.

Cohen, J. (1993) 'Freedom of Expression'. *Philosophy and Public Affairs*, **22**.

Collaborative Open Group (COG) on Ethical Issues Final Report, London, 1995. Available from: a.nainby@ccta.gov.uk

Cole, W. (1995) 'The Marquis de Cyberspace'. *Time Australia*, 10 July, p. 53.

Coleman, J. (1990) *Foundations of Social Theory*. Cambridge, MA: Harvard University Press.

Cranor, L.F. (1999) 'Internet Privacy' *Communications of the ACM*, **42**(2): 29–31.

Dahl, R. (1989) *Democracy and Its Critics*. New Haven, CT: Yale University Press.

De Sola Pool, I. (ed.) (1983) *Technologies of Freedom*. Cambridge, MA: Harvard University Press.

DeCew, J.W. (1997) *In Pursuit of Privacy: Law, Ethics, and the Rise of Technology*. Ithaca, NY: Cornell University Press.

Denning, D. (ed) (1998) *Internet Besieged.* New York: ACM Press, pp. 449–73.

Denning, D. (1999) *Information Warfare and Security.* Reading, MA: Addison-Wesley.

DiDio, L. (1998) 'Intranets: Halt Hackers'. *ComputerWorld,* 27 June, pp. 1–7.

Draft International Safe Harbor Privacy Principles (April 19, 1999). URL:<www.ita.doc.gov/ecom/shprin.html>

Dyson, E. (1998) *Release 2.1: A Design for Living in the Digital Age.* Harmondsworth: Penguin.

Ecclesiastes, *The Bible.* King James Version.

Edgar, S.L. (1997) *Morality and Machines*, Sudbury, MA: Jones and Bartlett.

Eisenberg, A. (1996) 'Privacy and Data Collection on the Net'. *Scientific American*, March, p. 120.

Ellul, J. (1964) *The Technological Society.* New York: Knopf.

Enquete-Kommission (1998) Enquete-Kommission Zukunft der Medien in Wirtschaft und Gesellschaft (ed.): Sicherheit und Schutz im Netz. Schriftenreihe Enquete-Kommission Zukunft der Medien, Vol. 7, Bonn: ZV Zeitungs-Verlag Service.

Ess, C. (ed.) (1996) 'The Political Computer: Democracy, CMC, and Habermas', in *Philosophical Perspectives on Computer-Mediated Communication*. Albany, NY: State University of New York Press, pp. 197–230.

Etzioni, A. (1999) *The Limits of Privacy.* New York: Basic Books.

Etzioni, O. (1996) 'The World Wide Web: Quagmire or Gold Mine?' *Communications of the ACM*, **39**(11): 65–8.

Feng, P. (1999) 'If standards affect everyone, should everyone be involved in setting standards, ethical dilemmas in computer standardisation?' Paper at ETHICOMP99, Rome, October.

Fried, C. (1970) *Anatomy of Values*: *Problems of Personal and Social Choice.* Cambridge, MA: Harvard University Press, Ch. IX.

Friedman, B. (ed.) (1997) *Human Values and the Design of Computer Technology*. Cambridge: Cambridge University Press.

Fulda, J. (1998) 'Data Mining and the Web'. *Computers and Society*, **28**(1): 42–3.

Gabber, E., Gibbons, P.B., Kristol, D.M. *et al.* (1999) 'Consistent, yet Anonymous' Web Access with LPWA'. *Communications of the ACM*, **42**(2).

Garfinkel, S.L. (1998) 'The Web's Unelected Government'. *Technology Review,* November/December, pp. 40–5.

Gavison, R. (1980) 'Privacy and the Limits of the Law'. *Yale Law Journal*, **89**. Reprinted in Johnson, D.G. and Nissenbaum, H. (eds) (1995) *Computers, Ethics & Social Values*. Englewood Cliffs, NJ: Prentice Hall, pp. 332–51.

Gert, B. (1998) *Morality: Its Nature and Justification*. Oxford: Oxford University Press.

Gert, B. (1999) 'Common Morality and Computing'. *Journal of Ethics and Information Technology*, **1**(1).

Gert, B. and Moor, J. (1998) 'On Morality and Computer Ethics'. *Proceedings of CEPE 98*, London School of Economics.

Global Internet Liberty Campaign (GILC) (1998) *Privacy and Human Rights: An International Survey of Privacy Laws and Practice*. URL:<http://www.gilc.org/privacy/survey/>

Godwin, M. (1996) 'Libel Law: Let it Die'. *Wired*, March, pp. 116–18.

Goldman, A. (1992) *Liaisons. Philosophy Meets the Cognitive and Social Sciences*. Cambridge, MA: MIT Press.

Goldschlag, D., Reed, M. and Syverson, P. (1999) 'Onion Routing for Anonymous and Private Internet Connections'. *Communications of the ACM*, **42**(2): 39–41.

Goodin, R.E. (1985) *Protecting the Vulnerable*. Chicago: University of Chicago Press.

Goodin, R.E. (1995) *Utilitarianism as a Public Philosophy*. Cambridge: Cambridge University Press.

Gotterbarn, D. (1994) 'Software Engineering Ethics', in Marciniak, J. (ed.) *Encyclopedia of Software Engineering* Vol. II. New York: John Wiley & Sons.

Gotterbarn D. (1997) 'Software Engineering: the New Professionalism' in Myers, C. (ed.) *The Responsible Software Engineer*. London: Springer-Verlag.

Gotterbarn, D. (1999) 'Privacy Lost: the Net Autonomous Agents, and Virtual Information'. *Journal of Ethics and Information Technology,* **1**(2).

Grace, D. and Cohen, S. (1998) *Business Ethics: Australian Problems and Cases*, 2nd edn. Oxford: Oxford University Press.

Grossman, W.M. (1997) *Net Wars*. New York: New York University Press.

Hafner, K. and Lyon, M. (1996) *Where Wizards Stay Up Late*. New York: Simon & Schuster. URL:<http://www.simonsays.com/titles/0684812010/wizards.html>

Hart, H.L.A. (1961) *The Concept of Law*. Oxford: Clarendon Press.

Hauben, M. and Hauben, R. (1997) *Netizens: On the History and Impact of Usenet and the Internet*. IEEE Computer Society.

Heart, F., McKenzie, A., McQuillan, J. and Walden, D. (1978) ARPANET Completion Report, Cambridge, MA: ARPA and BBN.

Hegener, M. (1995) Internet in Africa, November 1995. URL:<http://www.sas.upenn.edu/African_Studies/Acad_Research/it_hagener.html>

IAC (1998) The Project for Information Access and Connectivity – Internet Status at African Universities, 1998. URL:<http://www.piac.org/datad/table5.htm>

Jensen, M. (1996) Bridging the Gaps in Internet Development in Africa, IDRC Study, August 1996. URL:<http://www.idrc.ca/acacia/studies/ir-gaps.htm>

Johnson, D.G. (1994) *Computer Ethics*, 2nd edn. Englewood Cliffs, NJ: Prentice Hall.

Johnson, D.G. (1997a) 'Ethics Online'. *Communications of the ACM*, **40**(1): 60–5.

Johnson, D.G. (1997b) 'Is the GII a Democratic Technology?' *Computers & Society*, **27**(3): 20–6.

Johnson, D.G. and Nissenbaum, H. (eds) (1995) *Computers, Ethics and Social Values*. Englewood Cliffs, NJ: Prentice Hall.

Johnson, D.R. and Post, D.G. (1997) 'The Rise of Law on the Global Network', in Kahin, B. and Nesson, C. (eds) *Borders in Cyberspace*. Cambridge, MA: MIT Press.

Kaplam, Carl S. (1997) 'Big Brother as a Workplace Robot'. *New York Times*, 24 July.

Keen, P.G.W., Mougayar, W. and Torregrossa, T. (1998) *The Business Internet and Intranets: A Manager's Guide to Key Terms and Concepts*. Boston, MA: Harvard Business School Press.

Kernohan, A. (1998) *Liberalism, Equality and Cultural Oppression*. Cambridge: Cambridge University Press.

Khalifa, M.K. and Davison, R.M. (1999) 'Exploring the Telecommuting Paradox'. *Communications of the ACM*, forthcoming.

Klein, H. (1999) 'Tocqueville in Cyberspace: Using the Internet for Citizen Associations'. *The Information Society*, 15(4).

Kotz, D. (1998) 'Technological Implications for Privacy', in Moor, J.H. (ed.) *Proceedings of the Conference on The Tangled Web: Ethical Dilemmas of the Internet*. Dartmouth College.

Krol, E. (1994) *The Whole Internet User's Guide & Catalog*, 2nd edn. O'Reilly & Associates. URL:<http://www.oreilly.com/catalog/twi2/>

Ladd, J. (1998) 'Computers and Moral Responsibility: A Framework for an Ethical Analysis', in Gould C. (ed.) *The Information Web: Ethical and Social Implications of Computer Networking*. London, Boulder, San Francisco, West-view Press.

Langford, D. (1995) *Practical Computer Ethics*. London: McGraw-Hill.

Langford, D. (1996) 'Ethics and the Internet: Appropriate Behavior in Electronic Communication'. *Ethics & Behavior*, **6**(2): 91–106.

Langford, D. (1998) 'Ethical Issues In Business Computing', in Collste, G. (ed.) *Ethics and Information Technology*. Delhi: New Academic Publishers.

Langford, D. (1999) *Business Computer Ethics*. London: Prentice Hall.

Lee, M.K.O. (1993)'Information Privacy Legislation: The Case of Hong Kong'. *Hong Kong Computer Journal*, **9**(11): 23–6.

Long, R.E. (ed.) (1997) *Rights to Privacy*. New York: WH Wilson.

Martin, M.W. *et al.* (1989) *Ethics in Engineering*, 2nd edn. London: McGraw-Hill.

Mason, R. *et al.* (1995) *Ethics of Information Management*. Thousand Oaks, CA: Sage, p. 215.

Moor, J. (1995) 'What is Computer Ethics', in Johnson, D.G. and Nissenbaum, H. (eds) *Computers, Ethics, and Social Values*. Englewood Cliffs, NJ: Prentice Hall.

Moor, J. (1997) 'Towards a Theory of Privacy in the Information Age', in Van den Hoven, M.J. (ed.) *Proceedings of the Conference on Computer Ethics: Philosophical Enquiry: CEPE 97*. Rotterdam: Erasmus University Press, pp. 40–9. Reprinted in *Computers and Society*, **27**(3): 27–32.

Moor, J. (1999) 'Just Consequentialism and Computing'. *Journal of Ethics and Information Technology*, **1**(1).

Mullet, K. and Sano, D. (1995) *Designing Visual Interfaces*. Englewood Cliffs, NJ: Prentice Hall.

Mumford, L. (1964) 'Authoritarian and Democratic Technics'. *Technology and Culture,* **5**: 1–8.

Nagel, T. (1979) 'The Fragmentation of Value', in *Mortal Questions*. Cambridge: Cambridge University Press.

Nissenbaum, H. (1995) 'Should I Copy my Neighbours Software', in Johnson, D. and Nissenbaum, H. (eds) *Computers, Ethics and Social Values*. Englewood Cliffs, NJ: Prentice Hall.

Nissenbaum, H. (1997) 'Can We Protect Privacy in Public?', in Van den Hoven, M.J. (ed.) *Proceedings of the Conference on Computer Ethics: Philosophical Enquiry: CEPE 97*. Rotterdam: Erasmus University Press, pp. 191–204.

Nissenbaum, H. (1998) 'Values in the Designs of Computer Systems'. *Computers and Society*, **28**(1): 38.

Nissenbaum, H. (1999) 'The Puzzle of Priority: Devising New Norms and Conventions in Research for the Context of Electronic Publication'. *Australian Journal of Professional and Applied Ethics*, **1**, July.

Nissenbaum, H. and Introna, L. (1998) 'Notes on the Politics of Search Engines', presented at *Computer Ethics: A Philosophical Enquiry*. London: London School of Economics, 15 December.

Nussbaum, M. (1993) 'Non-relative Virtues: An Aristotelian Approach', in Sen, A. and Nussbaum, M. (eds) *The Quality of Life*. Oxford: Clarendon Press.

Oppliger, R. (1997) 'Internet Security: Firewalls and Beyond'. *Communications of the ACM*, **40**(5): 93–102.

P3P (Platform for Privacy Principles) Guiding Principles, W3C Note 01-May-1998. URL:<http://www.w3.org/TR/198/NOTE-P310-Principles>

Palfreman, J. and Swade, D. (1991) *The Dream Machine: Exploring the Computer Age*. London: BBC Books.

Penenberg, A. (1999) 'Is there a Snoop on your Site'. *Forbes,* 17 May, pp. 322–5.

Privacy Times. URL:<http://www.privacytimes.com>

Python, M. (1973) 'Spam, Spam, Spam... sketch, Monty Python's Flying Circus'. URL:<http://www.pythonline.com/>

Quarterman, J.S. (1996) *The Matrix: Computer Networks and Conferencing Systems Worldwide*. Digital Press: Prentice Hall. URL:<http://www.mids.org/books/matrix/>

Quarterman, J.S. (1999) 'Revisionist Internet History'. *Matrix News* **9**(4). URL: <http://www.mids.org/mn/904/large.html>

Rachels, J. (1975) 'Why is Privacy Important?' *Philosophy and Public Affairs*, **4**(4). Reprinted in Johnson, D.G. and Nissenbaum, H. (eds) *Computers, Ethics and Social Values*. Englewood Cliffs, NJ: Prentice Hall, pp. 351–7.

Raymond, E.S. (1996) *The New Hacker's Dictionary (aka The Jargon File)*. Cambridge, MA: MIT Press. URL:<http://www.tuxedo.org/jargon/>

Raymond, E.S. (1997) *The Cathedral and the Bazaar*. URL:<http://www.tuxedo.org/~esr/writings/cathedral-bazaar/>

Regan, P.M. (1995) *Legislating Privacy: Technology, Social Values, and Public Policy*. Chapel Hill, NC: University of North Carolina Press.

Reiman, J. (1995) 'Driving to the Panopticon: A Philosophical Exploration of the Risks to Privacy Posed by the Highway Technology of the Future'. *Santa Clara Computer and High Technology Law Journal*, **11**(1): 27–44.

Reiter, M.K. and Rubin, A.D. 'Anonymous Web Transactions with Crowds'. *Communications of the ACM*, **42**(2): 32–8.

Reynolds, J. and Postel, J. (1987) *The Origin of RFCs in RFC 1000 – The Request For Comments Reference Guide*. URL:<ftp://ftp.isi.edu/in-notes/rfc1000.txt>

Rheingold, H. (1991) *Virtual Reality*. London: Secker & Warburg.

Rogers, J.D. (1998) 'Internetworking and the Politics of Science: NSNET in Internet History'. *The Information Society*, **14**: 213–28.

SADC (1998) SADC in the Next Millenium – The Opportunities and Challenges of Information Technology, 1999. URL:<http://www.sadc.int/theme.htm>

Salus, P. (1995) *Casting the Net*. Reading, MA: Addison-Wesley.

Satoshi, E. (1999) 'The Unauthorised Access Issue in Japan', read at FINE Workshop, Tokyo, 16 March.

Schmitz, D. and Goodin, R.E. (1998) *Social Welfare and Individual Responsibility*. Cambridge: Cambridge University Press.

Schneider, F.B. (ed.) (1999) *Trust in Cyberspace*, Committee on Information Systems Trustworthiness, Computer Science and Telecommunications Board, Commission on Physical Sciences, Mathematics, and Applications, National Research Council, National Academic Press, Washington, DC.

Sclove, R.E. (1995) *Democracy and Technology*. New York: Guilford Press.

Segev, A., Porra, J. and Roldan, M. (1998) 'Internet Security and the Case of Bank of America'. *Communications of the ACM,* **41**(10): 81–7.

Sen, A. (1985) *Commodities and Capabilities.* Amsterdam: North-Holland.

Shea, V. (1999) *Netiquettes.* URL<http://www.albion.com/netiquette/corerules.html>

Simons, J. (1999) 'Crackdown on Hackers Continues'. *The Wall Street Journal,* 1 June, p. A24.

Spafford, G. and Garfinkel, S. (1997) *Web Security and Commerce.* Cambridge: O'Reilly Publishers, pp. 9–10.

Spafford, E. (1995) 'Are Computer Hacker Break-ins Ethical', in Johnson, D.G. and Nissenbaum, H. (eds) *Computers, Ethics and Social Values.* Englewood Cliffs, NJ: Prentice Hall.

Spinello, R. (1997a) *Case Studies in Information and Computer Ethics.* Englewood Cliffs, NJ: Prentice Hall, p. 7.

Spinello, R. (1997b) 'The End of Privacy', in Long, R.E. (ed.) *Rights to Privacy.* New York: WH Wilson.

Spitz, D. (ed.) (1975) *John Stuart Mill, On Liberty: Annotated Text, Sources and Background Criticism.* New York: WW Norton.

Stallman, P. (1999) 'What is Free Software?, GNU Project / FSF, 1999. URL: <http://www.gnu.org/philosophy/free-sw.html>

Steinhart, E. (1999) 'Emergent Values for Automations: Ethical Problems of Life in the Generalized Internet'. *Journal of Ethics and Information Technology,* **1**(2).

Stone, A.R. (1995) *The War of Desire and Technology at the Close of the Mechanical Age.* Cambridge, MA: MIT Press.

Stubbs, B. and Hoffman, L. (1990) 'Mapping the Virus Battlefield', in Hoffman, L. (ed.) *Rogue Programs: Viruses, Worms and Trojan Horses.* New York: Van Nostrand Reinhold, pp. 143–57.

Tavani, H.T. (1996) 'Computer Matching and Personal Privacy: Can they be Compatible?', in Huff, C. (ed.) *Proceedings of the Symposium on Computers and the Quality of Life: CQL 96.* New York: ACM Press, pp. 97–101.

Tavani, H.T. (1997) 'Internet Search Engines and Personal Privacy', in Van den Hoven, M.J. (ed.) *Proceedings of the Conference on Computer Ethics: Philosophical Enquiry: CEPE 97.* Rotterdam: Erasmus University Press, pp. 214–23.

Tavani, H.T. (1998) 'Data Mining, Personal Privacy, and Public Policy', in Introna, L.D. (ed.) *Proceedings of the Conference on Computer Ethics: Philosophical Enquiry: CEPE 98.* University of London Press, pp. 113–20. Reprinted as 'KDD, Data Mining, and the Challenge to Normative Privacy' *Journal of Ethics and Information Technology,* **1**(4).

Tavani, H.T. (1999) 'Informational Privacy, Data Mining, and the Internet'. *Journal of Ethics and Information Technology,* **1**(2).

Thagard, P. (1999) 'Internet epistemology', unpublished paper. URL:<http://cogsci.uwaterloo.ca/articles/pages/epistemology.html>

Tower, X. (1998) 'Categories of Free and Non-free Software'. GNU Project/FSF, 1999. URL:<http://www.gnu.org/philosophy/categories.html>

Turkle, S. (1997) *Life on the Screen: Identity in the Age of the Internet*. London: Phoenix.

US Department of Commerce (1998) 'Elements of Effective Self Regulation for the Protection of Privacy and Questions Related to Online Privacy' RIN 0660-AA13 AGENCY: National Telecommunications and Information Administration, Department of Commerce. URL:<http://www.ntia.doc.gov/ntiahome/privacy/6_5_98fedreg.htm>

Van den Hoven, J. (1997a) 'Computer Ethics and Moral Methodology'. *Metaphilosophy*, **28**: 234–48.

Van den Hoven, J. (1997b) 'Privacy and the Varieties of Moral Wrong-doing in an Information Age'. *Computers and Society*, **27**(3): 33–7.

Van den Hoven, J. (1998) 'Moral Responsibility, Public Office and Information Technology', in Snellen and Van de Donk (eds) *Public Administration in an Information Age, A Handbook*. Amsterdam: IOS Press.

Van den Hoven, J. (1999) 'Privacy and the Varieties of Information Wrongdoing'. *Australian Journal of Professional and Applied Ethics*, **1**(1).

Van Tassel, D. (1976) *The Compleat Computer*. Chicago: SRA Associates.

Wagner, M. (1999) 'Melissa Puts IT Readiness to Test,' *INTERNETWEEK*, 5 April, p. 1.

Wang, H., Lee, M., and Wang, C. (1998) 'Consumer Privacy Concerns about Internet Marketing'. *Communications of the ACM*, **41**(3): 63–70.

Warren, S. and Brandeis, L. (1980) 'The Right to Privacy'. *Harvard Law Review*, **14**(5).

Weckert, J. (1997) 'Intellectual Property Rights and Computer Software'. *Business Ethics: A European Review*, **6**: 102–9.

Weckert, J. and Adeney, D. (1996) 'Digital Images: Moral Manipulation', in Kizza, J.M. (ed.) *Social and Ethical Effects of the Computer Revolution*. Jefferson, NC: McFarland & Company.

Weckert, J. and Adeney, D. (1997) *Computer and Information Ethics*. Westport, CT: Greenwood Press.

Westin, A.F. (1967) *Privacy and Freedom*. New York: Atheneum Press.

Wiener, N. (1948) *Cybernetics: or Control and Communication in the Animal and the Machine*. New York: John Wiley & Sons; Paris: Hermann et Cie.

Wiener, N. (1950, 1954) *The Human Use of Human Beings*, 2nd rev. edn. Boston: Houghton Mifflin; London: Eyre and Spottiswoode (1950). Doubleday Anchor.

Wingrove N. (1995) 'China Traditions Oppose War on IP Piracy'. *Research-Technology Management,* **38**(3): 6–7.

Winner, L. (1986) *The Whale and the Reactor: A Search for the Limits in an Age of High Technology.* Chicago: University of Chicago Press.

World Bank (1999) Internet Economic Toolkit for African Policy Makers, 1999. URL:<http://www.worldbank.org/infodev/projects/finafcon.htm>

World Population Profile: 1998, accessed 21 April, 1999. Retrieved via Netscape. URL:<http://www.census.gov/ipc/prod/wp98/wp98.pdf>

Wright, M. and Kakalik, J. (1997) 'The Erosion of Privacy'. *Computers and Society,* **27**(4): 22–5.

# Index